FORTS AND SUPPLIES

FORTS AND SUPPLIES

THE ROLE OF THE ARMY
IN THE ECONOMY
OF THE SOUTHWEST, 1846–1861

Robert W. Frazer, 1911–

UNIVERSITY OF NEW MEXICO PRESS
ALBUQUERQUE

Design by Milenda Nan Ok Lee

Library of Congress Cataloging in Publication Data

Frazer, Robert Walter, 1911–
  Forts and supplies.

  Bibliography: p.
  Includes index.
    1. United States. Army—Procurement—Economic aspects—South-
west, New—History. 2. Southwest, New—Economic conditions—His-
tory. I. Title.
UC263.F7 1983   330.9789'04   83-17051
ISBN 0-8263-0630-6

For
Chris, Margaret, and Sandé

Contents

Illustrations

TABLES

Preface

The army defined a military Southwest when it erected Military Department No. 9 and its successor, the Military Department of New Mexico. The department included all of the present state of New Mexico, much of Arizona, and parts of Texas and Colorado. Other military departments embraced portions of the traditional Southwest, but none of them in the pre–Civil War period lay exclusively within its borders.

Between the American occupation of New Mexico in the summer of 1846 and the disruption precipitated by the coming of the Civil War— a span of fifteen years—the army was the single most significant factor in the economic development of the Southwest. In part, this was directly attributable to the army and, in part, resulted from its presence. Insofar as it succeeded in exerting a degree of control over the wild Indians, particularly by establishing military posts in their country, the army encouraged the expansion of settlement, agriculture, ranching, and mining. Military purchases of services and locally produced goods introduced much larger sums of cash than had ever before been available in the area and resulted in a notable increase in production.

I am indebted to many persons for the assistance they have given me in this project. Particularly, I wish to express my appreciation to Myra Ellen Jenkins, James H. Purdy, and J. Richard Salazar of Santa Fe; Stephany Eger of Aztec, New Mexico; and John P. Wilson of Las Cruces, New Mexico. I am especially grateful to my friend and colleague, Nicholas P. Hardeman of California State University, Long Beach, for his aid and encouragement.

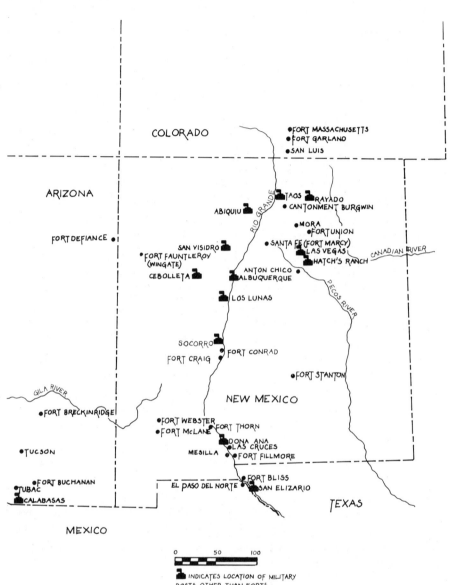

COLORADO

● FORT MASSACHUSETTS
● FORT GARLAND
● SAN LUIS

ARIZONA

■ TAOS ■ RAYADO
ABIQUIU ■   ● CANTONMENT BURGWIN

RIO GRANDE

● MORA
● FORT UNION

FORT DEFIANCE ●

SAN YSIDRO ■   ● SANTA FE (FORT MARCY)
● FORT FAUNTLEROY   ■ LAS VEGAS
(WINGATE)   ■ HATCH'S RANCH
CEBOLLETA ■

CANADIAN RIVER

ANTON CHICO ●
■ ALBUQUERQUE

■ LOS LUNAS

PECOS RIVER

SOCORRO ■
FORT CRAIG ●   ● FORT CONRAD

● FORT STANTON

NEW MEXICO

GILA RIVER

● FORT BRECKINRIDGE

● FORT WEBSTER
● FORT McLANE   ■ FORT THORN
■ DONA ANA
■ LAS CRUCES
MESILLA ■   ● FORT FILLMORE

● TUCSON

● FORT BUCHANAN   ● FORT BLISS
TUBAC ■   EL PASO DEL NORTE ● SAN ELIZARIO
■ CALABASAS

TEXAS

MEXICO

0   50   100

■ INDICATES LOCATION OF MILITARY
POSTS OTHER THAN FORTS

– – – – PRESENT-DAY STATE BOUNDARIES

DRAWN BY SHARIFA-ELLY GORDON

X

1

⚜ ⚜ ⚜

The Occupation of New Mexico

New Mexico, established in 1598 on the northern frontier of New Spain, existed for two and a quarter centuries in comparative isolation. The population remained small, and economic development was limited. Surrounded on all sides by often hostile Indians and separated by distance and difficult terrain from the rest of New Spain, the inhabitants, perforce, attained a considerable degree of self-sufficiency. Once Mexico achieved its independence from Spain and foreigners were no longer rigidly excluded from New Mexico, the fur trade and the Santa Fe trade had their impact upon the economy. In both activities, however, New Mexico functioned as something of a middleman: most of the products taken back to the States did not have their origin in New Mexico, and many of the goods imported over the Santa Fe Trail simply moved through New Mexico to other markets.

On the eve of the Mexican War New Mexico's own production was still essentially for local consumption. Donaciano Vigil remarked with considerable justification that there was "but little attention given to agriculture and manufacturing, in fact this last is not yet known."[1] The population of New Mexico was too small to absorb large quantities of imported goods,[2] and its undeveloped economy further weakened its position as a market. What was needed to stimulate New Mexico's internal economy was a lucrative outlet for the goods New Mexico could produce.

The occupation of New Mexico by Brigadier General Stephen Watts Kearny[3] and the Army of the West in August 1846 provided an economic impetus previously lacking. The army constituted an essentially nonproductive element for which goods, services, and facilities of many kinds were required. In addition, it injected comparatively large sums of money into what had been primarily a barter economy. The money was widely, if unevenly, distributed, reaching all segments of the population, including the Pueblo Indians. Not only did the army provide a market for some of New Mexico's traditional products; it created a demand for products that either had not been available at all or had been produced in very limited quantities.

The original occupying force consisted of 1,658 officers and men. A scant three hundred were regulars, five companies of the First Regiment of Dragoons; and the rest were units of Missouri volunteers, most of them mounted.[4] Five weeks after he entered Santa Fe, General Kearny took up his march to California, taking two of the dragoon companies with him. Two undermanned dragoon companies remained in New Mexico, and the fifth was broken up and its men distributed among the companies departing with Kearny.[5] A short time later Colonel Alexander Doniphan[6] and most of the Missouri volunteers undertook a token campaign against the Navajo Indians, and then they embarked upon the invasion of northern Mexico.

The troops leaving New Mexico were replaced by the Second Regiment of Missouri Mounted Volunteers, more than twelve hundred strong, under Colonel Sterling Price,[7] who would be in command in New Mexico until the volunteers were withdrawn in August 1848. Accompanying Price to New Mexico was the Mormon Battalion, some five hundred men, under instructions to follow Kearny to California. For a brief period, while all of the various units were still within its borders, the total number of troops in New Mexico exceeded three thousand. With the departure of the several expeditionary forces it declined to fewer than fifteen hundred, but in the summer of 1847 it was again built up to about three thousand men and remained at that level until the close of the occupation period.

Initially, virtually all commissary and quartermaster's supplies were freighted (or driven) to New Mexico. When the Army of the West marched from Fort Leavenworth it was preceded, accompanied, and followed by mule-drawn wagon trains loaded with stores and equipment of all kinds deemed necessary to maintain the troops. Behind the army came herds of beef cattle, perhaps as many as a thousand head, none of which were to be slaughtered until the army had passed beyond the buffalo country. When Colonel Sterling Price and his command reached Santa Fe toward the end of September more wagon trains and more beef cattle came with them. In addition to the military trains there were the caravans of traders, intent upon carrying on their commerce in Santa Fe and Chihuahua as if no war existed. Traffic on the Santa Fe Trail was more congested than ever before in its brief history, and there would be little change as long as the volunteers occupied New Mexico.

The army had no choice but to import because New Mexico afforded so few of the goods that it required. Such items as military clothing, ordnance stores, and medical supplies were completely unavailable. Of the many and varied stores for which the quartermaster's department was responsible, it was expected that New Mexico would furnish fuel and a large part of the forage for public animals, but even some feed grains were hauled from Fort Leavenworth. Accommodations such as quarters, barracks, stables, and storehouses were obtained locally. The army occupied either existing structures or erected new buildings, making use of materials available in the vicinity. The commissary department assumed that for some time to come New Mexico would offer very little for the subsistence of the troops. New Mexico was depended on for none of the components of the regularly constituted ration; all would be brought over the trail from Fort Leavenworth.

The army ration of the day was both uninviting and dietetically impoverished, designed to fill the stomach at minimum cost. The prescribed daily ration consisted of the following items and amounts:

salt pork or bacon, 12 ounces; or fresh or salt beef, 1 pound 4 ounces
flour, 1 pound 2 ounces; or hard bread, 12 ounces
beans, .064 gill; or rice, 1.6 ounces
coffee, .16 ounce; or tea, .24 ounce
sugar, 2.4 ounces
salt, .16 gill
vinegar, .32 gill

In addition, each rank and file was allowed .16 ounce of sperm candles and .64 ounce of soap daily. Officers received more than a single ration, ranging from four rations for lieutenants and captains to forty for a lieutenant general. It was not that they were expected to eat more; this was, rather, an augmentation of pay in the form of commutation of rations, with a ration being valued for the purpose at thirty cents.[8] Another advantage made available to officers was the privilege of buying hams and some other delicacies, imported by the commissary department, at cost with no charge for transportation.

Very few modifications were allowed in the prescribed ration. The only substitution authorized by regulation was 1 pound 4 ounces of corn meal for the flour or bread. Significant to New Mexico was the absence of any provision for the issue of mutton or other meat in lieu of pork or beef.

3

Specifically, fresh vegetables, pickles, sauerkraut, and dried fruits could "only be purchased and paid for out of the hospital fund and issued to the sick." However, dried apples were sometimes substituted for other items of the ration because they were considered an efficacious anti-scorbutic. Other special foods—such as fresh fruits, butter, eggs, chickens, and milk—might be issued in hospitals with the approval of the Secretary of War.[9]

Of the items making up the regular ration only salt, beans, and insufficient quantities of flour and fresh beef were available in New Mexico during the first years after the United States occupation began. In the older parts of the United States the army normally procured subsistence stores under contract, but purchases on the open market were permitted under certain circumstances, notably when a deficiency made speedy action desirable or when the quantities bought were small. Because so little was available, very few subsistence stores were acquired by contract in New Mexico prior to 1849.

The supply of flour and meat, other than beef on the hoof, was critical as both were costly to transport and subject to much wastage and spoilage. Flour, hard bread, bacon, and salt meat were packed in barrels. The bacon, cut in squares, and the hard bread did not completely fill the round barrels and further space was lost in packing the barrels in the wagons. Colonel George A. McCall of the Inspector General's Department stated in 1850 that the "whiskey barrels" in which bread was packed weighed half as much as their contents. Under the contract in force at the time McCall made his report, it cost more than thirteen dollars to transport the barrel itself from Fort Leavenworth to Santa Fe. He recommended the use of square boxes as a means of saving weight and space.[10] The barrels containing salt meat and flour often sprang leaks during their transit across the plains. The meat, in particular, suffered as the brine drained away and, as a result, large quantities were condemned as unfit for issue.

The army soon adopted the practice of putting up bacon in canvas sacks. Both weight and space were saved, but the combination of mid-summer heat and the pressure exerted on the bottom layers of piled bacon led to much loss of the fat part of the bacon. Colonel Joseph K. F. Mansfield, Inspector General's Department, pointed out that in the almost complete absence of butter and lard in New Mexico, "it is this grease that is mixed with the soldiers flour, and enables him to make biscuit on the road."[11] Eventually, as McCall had suggested, the army did pack the bacon in boxes, which were neither light nor inexpensive but did afford greater protection to the contents.[12] Even with this improvement the commissary still condemned large amounts of bacon and salt pork. However, these provisions were not an entire loss to the army, for the condemned meat, even when it was blamed for illness among the troops, was sold at public auction.

Fresh beef was a partial solution to the problem of cost, but it would be years before enough cattle were available in New Mexico to satisfy army demands. As long as the animals were driven to the department, beef was comparatively expensive and the supply uncertain. Army regulations provided that when fresh beef could be purchased it should be issued as often as the commanding officer ordered, but at least twice a week; and when the cost of fresh beef did not exceed that of salt pork, beef should be issued five times a week. Furthermore, wherever feasible, the commissary department was expected to maintain herds of beef cattle at each post and to slaughter the animals as needed.[13] At some of the smaller posts this was not always possible. When he inspected the post of Abiquiu in 1850, McCall commented that fresh beef could only be issued in the winter, when it would spoil less quickly, because there was "no market for beef beyond the consumption of the troops."[14]

The regular ration did not provide in itself a diet particularly conducive to the health of the troops. There was speculation that the high consumption of salt pork contributed to the prevalence of scurvy and vinegar was a part of the ration primarily for its value as an antiscorbutic. One medical director of the department claimed that fresh beef of good quality would aid in the prevention of scurvy. However, another officer held that many of his men had ulcerated gums because of "long continued use of fresh beef."[15]

The Army of the West was not well supplied during its march to New Mexico, particularly after it crossed the Arkansas River and left the comparative abundance of Bent's Fort. This was, in part, because the supply trains lagged behind the troops. As one volunteer recorded, the men "had to feast or famish by turns."[16] When the army left Bent's Fort it took only enough rations to last, "by uninterrupted and most rapid marches," until it arrived at Santa Fe.[17] Long before the troops reached their goal they were reduced to half rations of flour and coffee. On August 10, 1846, near the Vermejo River, there occurred what was probably the first transaction between the military and a resident of New Mexico. Charles Town of Taos sold eight hundred pounds of coarse wheat flour at 12 cents per pound to Colonel Doniphan's men.[18]

Better documented sales took place on August 13 when the army approached the Mora River where it came upon a scattering of ranches, at least one of them the property of an American citizen. A good many horses and cattle were grazing nearby, and one of the ranchers drove his herd of cattle into the camp and presented the "largest and fattest" animal to the troops. From another rancher First Lieutenant William H. Emory, Topographical Engineers, purchased butter for 50 cents per pound. Some of the soldiers bought a pig and others secured bread, cheese, and milk.[19]

At Las Vegas, where the army encamped the following evening, trade was brisk. Green corn, chickens, and cheese found willing purchasers, as did milk, bread, butter, and cream. Marcellus Ball Edwards, a private in one of the Missouri volunteer companies, remarked that those who had anything to sell "took care to demand a very high price."[20] Also at Las Vegas the army encountered a problem of a continuing nature: the destruction, inadvertent or otherwise, of crops. At this time General Kearny assured the New Mexicans that "not a pepper, not an onion, shall be disturbed or taken by my troops, without pay, or by the consent of the owner."[21] The men would not always be so concerned with the niceties of acquiring food, and, as the New Mexicans rarely fenced either field or garden, the control of public animals was virtually impossible. Sentinels were posted to protect Las Vegas corn fields from hungry army horses. Nevertheless, some damage was done, for all of which Kearny promised to pay. Private Edwards believed that not "an ear of corn [was] pulled by any of our men unless the Mexican owner received a liberal compensation for it."[22] From the outset an exchange of one kind or another developed between the New Mexicans and the invading army. Though on a small scale, trade was mutually beneficial, and the Spanish Americans gained some idea of what their conquerors wanted and how they might profit therefrom.

When the army arrived in Santa Fe on August 18, it was immediately obvious that the New Mexicans desired to engage in trade and equally clear that the Americans were ready to purchase their products. Whatever the attitude of the two presumably opposed parties may have been, here was a point of common interest that soon expanded beyond mere trade to a degree of interdependence. The first night spent in Santa Fe was miserable, for few of the supply wagons came in before the next day. Not only did most of the men go to bed without supper, but without tents and blankets as well. Yet, even on the first evening some of the townspeople, although they were "shy," brought a few things into camp to sell, but far too little to satisfy the hunger of the occupying army.[23]

The situation began to improve as wagons loaded with government stores rolled into Santa Fe in increasing numbers, but weeks would elapse before order emerged in the chaotic supply system. Despite the grumbling, only half rations were issued to the troops until September 2.[24] Captain Philip St. George Cooke, First Dragoons, reported that "the territory seems quite unequal to feed its seventeen hundred conquerors; they have received for weeks but nine ounces of ground wheat per day and no sugar or coffee."[25] When the ration was increased to a pound of Taos flour and three-quarters of a pound of salt pork, Edwards complained that the flour was very coarse and filled with bran, and the pork was "salt, fat, and often tainted."[26] Another Missouri volunteer was equally critical of the flour. "When we first came here," he wrote, "the commissary issued to the companies flour made here, called Taos flour which is half bran, dirt and sand and not fit for a white man to eat." He also noted that the "principal food" issued to the troops was "coffee, bacon or pork, sides of beef or mutton, only one at a time, and bread."[27]

The rank and file were expected to "preserve, distribute, and cook their own subsistence." The only exception to individual responsibility for preparing food was the baking of bread. The commissary department was authorized to build ovens (but not bake houses), and the expense of baking bread—such as the cost of purchasing hops, yeast, and the necessary equipment, and the pay of a baker (usually an enlisted man who received 15 cents extra duty pay per day)—was drawn from the post fund.[28]

To his limited and monotonous ration the soldier could add fresh and preserved vegetables and fruits, or whatever else his restricted purchasing power would permit, and company funds were sometimes expended to enliven the ration. The selection of foodstuffs available in Santa Fe was limited and, most believed, the prices were high, especially for men who had yet to receive their first pay.[29] Fruits and melons (peaches, grapes, nectarines, apricots, plums, apples, pears, muskmelons, watermelons, and cataloupes) were in greater variety than other products. The grapes were uniformly praised, but the melons and other fruits were accorded a mixed reaction. Lieutenant Emory went so far as to say that, except for the apricots and grapes, "the fruit of this place . . . would scarcely be eaten in the States."[30] Apricots were the only fruit raised in any quantity in Santa Fe. The grapes came from the Rio Abajo country, and the melons and much of the other fruit were brought to Santa Fe by the Indians of Santo Domingo Pueblo.[31] Green corn, onions (some "of a mild and pleasant flavor"), pumpkins, and peas were a welcome addition to the diet. Even the unfamiliar chili was sampled. Beans too were available, but the soldiers had little need of beans.

The Americans enjoyed the novelty of the piñon nut and virtually exhausted the town's supply of eggs and chickens. Wheat bread, various meats and cheeses, and locally produced corn sugar and molasses were sold in the market. Butter was rare, but goat and cow's milk was available in some quantity. Second Lieutenant George R. Gibson, Missouri volunteer infantry, recorded that all of the milk was dirty. In mid-October, when commissary stores had been built up considerably, he wrote, "Santa Fé is completely eaten out—scarcely a red pepper is to be found in market." However, even by the end of the month, melons and piñon nuts were plentiful.[32]

While the individual soldier could purchase whatever took his fancy and lay within the limits of his funds, the army per se provided a selective market for New Mexico's products. Because the army demanded certain things only, but demanded them in comparatively large quantities, it had a greater impact on production than did the individual purchaser. In the early months of the occupation the commissary department sought primarily to acquire meat and flour. Some wheat was grown throughout New Mexico, including El Paso del Norte district, but especially in the Taos Valley.[33] Small gristmills produced wheat flour, corn meal, or both. Either was quite expensive by Missouri standards. In Santa Fe, in October 1846, corn meal, which was scarce, cost $5 per *fanega*.[34] Wheat flour brought $4.50 per bushel, although in Taos it sold for only $2.50 per fanega.[35] Neither was available in sufficient quantity to meet the army's needs. Because the flour was unbolted the bread made from it was coarse and dark, but it was necessary to augment the army's supply of imported flour. Of more lasting importance, the demand for wheat flour was impressed on the New Mexicans and, as a result, both wheat production and the milling industry underwent something of a revolution.

The commissary department had far more difficulty in securing an adequate supply of meat. Salt pork and bacon constituted the principal meat items in the ration, but pork products of any kind were practically unavailable in New Mexico. Cattle were more common than swine but were not numerous. Governor Antonio Narbona's census of 1827 estimated that there were only five thousand cattle in the province, and slightly more than half of them were in the Rio Abajo country.[36] By 1846 there were a few small herds east of the Sangre de Cristo Mountains, but cattle continued to be more plentiful in the Rio Abajo than elsewhere. The cattle were chiefly work animals, for the New Mexican people consumed little beef, and even the minor output of dairy products depended more on goats than on cattle. New Mexico could provide only a small part of the beef the army wanted.

New Mexico had long nourished vast numbers of sheep, numbers far in excess of any conceivable need. Though nowhere in army regulations was mutton mentioned, it afforded an obvious and indeed a necessary solution to the problem of securing fresh meat locally. Shortly after the occupation of Santa Fe began, public notices were posted, calling for proposals to furnish the troops stationed there with beef and mutton to be issued alternately, twice a week, until the following June. Two contracts were drawn up, at least one as a result of the notices. No one in New Mexico could provide beef on a regular basis, but a contract was made to purchase eighty head of cattle at 16.87^{1/2}$ each on the hoof. It is probable that the cattle thus acquired were work animals that had been recently engaged in pulling wagons over the Santa Fe Trail. The request for mutton was easily met. A contract was concluded for the delivery of fresh mutton at 6 cents per pound for a seven-month period.[37]

Throughout New Mexico sheep were generally available for $1 per head, which was roughly the same value placed on sheep for decades past.[38] According to Gibson, the commissary could purchase mutton in any quantity "at $1.50 a carcass, butchered and dressed."[39] The dressed carcasses of three-year-old sheep weighed, on the average, only seventeen pounds and sometimes as little as twelve.[40] Mutton was regularly issued in Santa Fe, and flocks of sheep often accompanied troops on expeditions into Indian country. Sheep were so numerous that army purchases had no effect on price. As in the case of flour, the army's need for meat opened a market for a product which New Mexico could, in time, supply. Sheep were already present in abundance and there was now the inducement to build up herds of beef cattle. Although pork was also in demand, there was no appreciable increase in the number of swine in pre–Civil War years, and an army experiment in raising hogs at Fort Union proved too expensive and was abandoned.[41]

Several years would pass before New Mexico began to provide a significant part of the army's subsistence, and shortages were a major concern, particularly during the early months of the occupation. All of the expeditionary forces, when they marched from New Mexico, were hard put to obtain the supplies necessary to get them to their destinations. Kearny, who left first, had the least difficulty. His command was small, but, even more, as an experienced campaigner he had a better idea of his needs and as commander of the army in New Mexico he was in a better position to fill them. There is also reason to believe that the regular army was somewhat more efficient than the volunteers. When the Mormon Battalion left Santa Fe less than a month after Kearny's departure it had rations for only sixty days—full rations of flour, salt, sugar, and coffee; half rations of salt pork; and only enough soap for twenty days—and this for a march that would require more than ninety days.[42]

Doniphan's command fared no better, except that it had a shorter and less difficult stretch of unsettled country to traverse. Between Santa Fe and El Paso del Norte his troops got along as best they could, sometimes resorting to commandeering both food and forage. El Paso del Norte, with its irrigated fields, orchards, and vineyards, proved a veritable garden spot. Of the ration, flour, beans, salt, vinegar, and soap were available, but meat animals were few. Even though it was winter, the markets were amply stocked with fresh quinces, apples, pears, and oranges as well as a variety of dried fruits. For the weary animals the supply of corn and fodder was more than adequate.[43] Doniphan occupied El Paso for a month, and during that time the army purchased some forty thousand dollars worth of stores from the people of the district, leading James L. Collins,[44] Doniphan's interpreter, to remark, "I expect [this] presents the only instance in history where the people of an invaded country have benefited."[45]

The acquisition of quartermaster's stores presented the army with sim-ilar problems. The principal items obtained in New Mexico were feed and fuel, and for the latter the army had to rely entirely on local supplies because of the complete impracticability of importing it. Grain and long forage were required by regulation to feed public animals—army mounts, work animals, and even beef cattle where grazing was insufficient. Some feed grain was brought from Fort Leavenworth, and wheat was occa-sionally purchased for feed, but the chief reliance was on corn. Corn was the principal grain, and was, in fact, the major field crop grown in New Mexico. For both the Spanish Americans and the Pueblo Indians it was a staple item of diet, but they were not accustomed to feeding it to animals. The Spanish Americans raised little more than enough to meet their immediate wants, while the Pueblo Indians, with their long experience with pillage and drought, sought to store up a surplus against future need. Thus the Spanish Americans had limited quantities of corn to sell and the Pueblo Indians were reluctant to sell what they had. For a number of years the army found corn expensive to buy and an adequate supply impossible to obtain.

The Army of the West arrived in Santa Fe before the new crop of grain had been harvested, and the little that was available sold for as much as $6 per fanega, declining to $4 as the new crop came in.[46] Lack of pasturage near Santa Fe made it necessary to send most of the army mounts to grazing camps almost immediately. Cooke, while he was in charge of the dragoon camp near Galisteo, purchased entire patches of corn. The farmers cut the stalks at ground level and hauled them to the camp where they were "fed at night to the horses, ear, blade, and stalk," thus compensating to some extent for the shortage of native grasses.[47] By the end of October it was impossible to buy feed for cattle within fifty miles of Santa Fe, "the whole country being literally eaten up."[48] The difficulty of procuring feed plagued the army for years, and there was no particular improvement in the situation as long as the troops were stationed in towns.

The quartermaster's department purchased lumber for construction and firewood locally. Firewood was not a problem. Most of it was cut by Spanish Americans in the foothills and mountains behind Santa Fe, transported by burro for a distance of five or six miles, and sold for 25 cents per load. The quartermaster reckoned two burro loads the equivalent of a cord. The troops were soon put to work cutting and bringing in part of the firewood, which was not an easy task, as the ox teams provided to pull the wood wagons were weak from lack of forage. The wood obtained by the soldiers was frequently green. Between the quality of the wood and the uncertain arrival of the teams, Gibson lamented that the meals for his company were most irregular, and he prophesied a hard winter unless the situation improved.[49]

Lumber was almost impossible to acquire. There had never been a sawmill in operation in New Mexico, and all lumber was sawed and shaped by hand.[50] The *vigas* used in roof construction and the uprights supporting *portales* often were nothing more than peeled logs. Floors, even in the Palace of the Governors and in the churches, were earthen. There was only one plank floor in Santa Fe, the floor in the store of Juan Sena,[51] located on the southeast corner of the plaza.[52] Before he departed for California, Kearny sent to Fort Leavenworth for the necessary parts to construct a sawmill. Soldiers were sent into the mountains to get out timber so that no time would be lost once the parts arrived. On September 5 "a set of saw mill irons nearly complete" was discovered in Manuel Alvarez's store. Apparently it was not complete enough, and not until the summer of 1847 did the army's sawmill go into operation. In the interim, lumber continued to be in very short supply. The quartermaster offered to pay $80 per thousand feet but could obtain none at that price. In fact, lumber was so scarce that it was necessary to break up wagon boxes to secure wood to make coffins.[53] Other than Fort Marcy,[54] an earthwork and log blockhouse overlooking the Santa Fe plaza from the northeast, little new construction was undertaken by the army during the occupation period.

The quartermaster's department also sought to fill part of its need for cavalry mounts and work animals in New Mexico. Mexican horses, descendants of animals brought from Spain, were smaller than the American horses normally employed by the army to mount troops. Often referred to as "Mexican ponies," they were considered inferior in both strength and stamina and were rarely purchased for army use. Conversely, Mexican mules had long been highly regarded in the States, and there was no prejudice against the available work oxen, many of which had their origin in Missouri. The army purchased large numbers of mules and used them widely in place of horses. Some companies were mounted on mules exclusively. Insofar as records are available, the price paid for mules during the early months of the occupation ranged from $50 to, in one instance, $150 per head.[55]

It is difficult to determine the immediate effect of the unusual demand on prices in New Mexico. The local barter trade of the past provides little basis for comparison for most commodities. In any case, few Americans bothered to record the prices paid for casually purchased items, and it is evident that in many transactions the price was open to negotiation. Emory reported that coffee and sugar, both imported, sold for 75 and 35 cents per pound, respectively, while Cooke recorded prices of 50 and 40 cents for the same items. Eggs cost 25 cents per dozen and a single egg could be bought for 3 cents. Cheese sold for 12$\frac{1}{2}$ cents per pound and milk for 6 cents a pint; chickens, which were soon difficult to obtain, brought 12$\frac{1}{2}$ cents each; bacon, an imported item, cost 40 cents per pound; and the local but scarce fresh pork was 18$\frac{3}{4}$ cents per pound.

Good brandy commanded $10 per gallon. Whether it was imported or "Pass" brandy was not stated, but if it was the latter the price represented an enormous increase. John D. Lee,[56] who came to Santa Fe with the Mormon Battalion, paid $1 for a pint of whiskey. Unlike most persons who bothered to voice an opinion, he believed that "goods are sold remarkably cheap in this city on account of competition running so high among the Sutlers & Traders."[57] On the other hand, Susan Magoffin, who with her husband, Samuel Magoffin, arrived in Santa Fe on August 30, thought that the New Mexicans were inclined to overcharge and to give short weight but that they were amenable to bargaining. She expressed dismay when she was asked to pay 5 cents for four squashes and 7½ cents for six ears of green corn. The regular price for a melon, she wrote, was 5 cents.[58] Albert G. Wilson, a sutler in Santa Fe, charged $1.00 per pound for both coffee and sugar, $3.00 for peach jelly (quantity not stated), $1.75 per quart for brandy and whiskey, and 25 cents for a "tot," of what not specified.[59]

When the army itself was the purchaser and thus created a demand that tended to exhaust the available supply of a product, the effect was inflationary. This was true of the price of corn, flour, and mules, but the price of the ubiquitous sheep remained relatively stable. The first few months of the occupation disclosed clearly that it would be expensive to maintain a military force in New Mexico, far more so than for a similar force in the older sections of the United States. A major factor in this expense was the cost of freighting the great bulk of quartermaster's and commissary stores to New Mexico. During the Mexican War the army hired civilian teamsters and wagon masters but provided the necessary equipment, including wagons and draft animals, and supervised the operation. For the army this meant planning and for the troops, at times, deficiencies, even to the point of hardship. It also meant, as Philip St. George Cooke commented, that "the greatest expense of this invasion, possibly, will be found in the matter of transportation."[60]

Despite the comparatively large army purchases, one of the immediate results of the war was a shortage of specie in New Mexico. Most of the coin and bullion involved in the Santa Fe trade came from Old Mexico, principally Chihuahua. When the Mexican War interrupted the trade to the south it cut off the major source of coin. For the army this was an inconvenience not easily overcome. The Army of the West brought little money with it, and the individual soldier soon spent the money he had. As early as mid-September Gibson could state with only slight exaggeration, "there is no such thing as money in the army." The arrival of a paymaster was awaited with understandable anticipation.

Major Dunham Spaulding, additional paymaster, volunteers, reached Santa Fe on September 23, but he brought only about twenty thousand dollars in gold, plus some treasury drafts, Bank of Missouri notes, and a little small coin.[61] The drafts and notes were virtually useless. The average New Mexican, if he was familiar with money in any of its various forms, was accustomed to silver. He was unwilling to accept paper, and even gold coin was viewed with suspicion by many individuals.[62] The pay department had expected to exchange its treasury drafts with the traders, but they would have little coin until commerce with Chihuahua resumed a more normal pattern. Major Spaulding paid the officers with the small amount of gold, but he lacked the specie to pay the men.

Two weeks later Major Benjamin Walker, paymaster for the Army of the West, came in from Fort Leavenworth, but he brought no specie with him. By this time the volunteers had been in service for more than four months without pay, even though regulations required that they be paid at two-month intervals. Their own funds were exhausted, and with no pay forthcoming they were forced to get by as best they could. Some of them learned that brass buttons, pins, or tobacco were ready mediums of exchange. Private Edwards wrote that "a Mexican will give as much for a common brass button as they will for a dime." He also noted that he "frequently got a melon for a pin, a worthless piece of wire, or anything of the kind, but they will ask a picayune or a bit for one." He added that "some of our men have supplied the place of buttons on their clothes with wooden pins." Another private recorded, "I traded off *two needles* . . . for six ears of corn and some onions."[63] It is fairly obvious from the expressed glee over these sharp transactions that most of the volunteers were unaware of the value placed on the baser metals by the people of New Mexico. However, still another private, one of somewhat more perspicacity, wrote that "articles of metal are very scarce. I do not believe that there are two doors in all Santa Fé hung on metal hinges."[64]

Doubtless the men were inconvenienced but they were also commendably ingenuous. For the army, however, brass buttons and pins offered no solution. Often the owners of goods refused to sell except for specie, or if they could be induced to accept a draft or note they did so at a discount. Cooke, faced with the frustration of equipping the Mormon Battalion, noted, "I find the quarter-master department without funds; and with much allowance for dissatisfaction, and private ignorance, it is strange to add, with little credit."[65] Those few traders who had specie, most of them Americans, cashed quartermaster's drafts only at discounts ranging as high as 25 percent, transactions unprofitable to the army. When Captain William S. Murphey of the Missouri volunteer infantry brought some $120,000 in gold to Santa Fe in mid-January of 1847, the short supply of coin was temporarily eased, but it would recur periodically for the next several years.[66]

The provision of facilities for housing and storage was another source from which New Mexico would eventually derive financial benefit. Santa Fe, with a population usually estimated between five and six thousand, was hard pressed to accommodate an influx of about one-half that number. The city was compact only in the vicinity of the public plaza. Elsewhere the houses were interspersed with small fields in which corn, wheat, and some vegetables were raised. Hence, existing structures were scattered over a more extensive area than the population might suggest.[67]

On August 19 General Kearny appointed a board of officers to examine and report on the "Public Buildings, Arms, and other property pertaining to the Government of New Mexico" in Santa Fe and its environs.[68] The public buildings were few in number. Most impressive was the venerable Palace of the Governors, occupying the entire northern length of the plaza and joined at its western end by the *calabozo,* or jail. On the eastern side of the plaza, at the northern corner, was the customs house and associated storerooms. Midway on the east side, probably next to the customs house, was the *ayuntamiento* of Santa Fe, which housed the offices of the prefecture. Near the center of the west side of the plaza was the post office, "where mail sometimes arrived from the south," which also was the outlet for the government tobacco monopoly. Most of the other structures on the plaza were private homes, in many of which the front rooms were rented to serve as stores during at least part of the year. All of these buildings, public and private, fronted immediately on the plaza with no yard before them nor space between. On the north and south sides of the plaza ran small *acequias* lined by rows of cottonwood trees. In front of the palace and the buildings on two other sides of the plaza were portales that also served as a market place where local products, notably foodstuffs, were offered for sale.[69]

Pertaining specifically to the military were the *cuarteles* (barracks), storehouses, and stables, all in various stages of disrepair and occupying an extensive area north and west of the palace. Much of the space assigned to the Mexican garrison had been devoted to gardens cultivated by the troops, with most of the parade serving as a cornfield. There was also a small powder magazine and, on the south side of the plaza, the military chapel or *castrense,* the property of the Catholic church dedicated to Nuestra Señora de la Luz. Aside from these buildings, the only military structures in what was soon to be designated Military Department No. 9 were those constituting the Presidio of San Elizario, located some twenty miles below El Paso del Norte at the southern end of an island in the Rio Grande.[70] The presidio had not been regularly garrisoned for many years and was in an extremely dilapidated condition. There were, then, few public facilities available for the use of the army, far too few to accommodate the number of troops in New Mexico.

General Kearny made his headquarters in the Palace of the Governors, which also served as the seat of civil government, as it had for more than two centuries past. The plaza became a military park. The dragoon companies occupied the buildings east of the palace along the present Palace Avenue, the volunteer cavalry and artillery encamped south of the town, and the volunteer infantry was quartered in buildings close to the plaza.[71] On September 15, two volunteer companies were sent to Abiquiu, and three to Cebolleta, to provide protection for those outposts of settlement on the western Indian frontier. In both places, already existing structures were taken over for the use of the troops. When Kearny marched from New Mexico the dragoon companies left behind took station at Albuquerque, where they occupied property belonging to former governor Manuel Armijo, who had fled from New Mexico upon the approach of the Army of the West.

Colonel Sterling Price, who assumed command in Santa Fe in October 1846, found the capital "literally alive with artillery, baggage wagons, commissary teams, beef-cattle and a promiscuous throng of American soldiers, traders, visitors, stragglers, trappers, amateurs, mountaineers, Mexicans, Pueblo Indians, women and children." It was estimated that some fourteen thousand people were crowded into the town.[72] Over the next several months Price distributed the troops more widely. Detachments, some as large as two companies, were stationed for varying periods of time at Taos, Las Vegas, El Paso del Norte, Cebolleta, Galisteo, San Miguel, Socorro, and in the Mora Valley and as far away as Bent's Fort. In the New Mexican towns privately owned facilities were occupied, and there is nothing to indicate that rent was paid for any of them.

As long as the Mexican War continued cost was a secondary consideration, nor is there much to suggest that the experience helped the army to cope with the problem of expense after the war ended and the military force stationed in New Mexico was drastically reduced. On the other hand, the New Mexicans soon recognized the opportunity presented to them and sought to increase production of those things for which there was a certain demand. This would eventually lead to the introduction of improved methods, the investment of considerable amounts of capital, and, finally, the emergence of new industries. In the process some additional jobs were created for civilians and a small entrepreneurial class emerged, whereas in the past there had been a few merchants operating on a comparatively large scale and a large number of vendors operating on a very small scale, but little in between. It must be noted that most of those who derived the major advantage as purveyors to the army were Anglo-Americans, often middlemen who purchased the products of the Spanish Americans for resale to the military. With the passage of time, however, native New Mexicans assumed a more important role in supplying the army directly.

2

⟨≈≈≈≈≈≈≈≈⟩

The Occupation Period

All of the volunteers who came to New Mexico in the summer of 1846 had enlisted for a one-year period. As their term of service approached expiration the men who so desired were discharged in Santa Fe. The others left New Mexico during the summer of 1847, in detachments of one or two companies to be mustered out at Fort Leavenworth. From those who chose to stay, plus a few teamsters who volunteered to serve, three cavalry companies and one company of light artillery were formed. Called the Santa Fe Battalion, they were under the command of Major Robert Walker, recently a lieutenant in the Second Missouri Volunteers.[1] The dragoon company that had been broken up in 1846 was reconstituted at this time, made up largely of volunteers discharged in Santa Fe who reenlisted "for the duration." These companies, together with the two dragoon companies already in the department, provided New Mexico with a total strength of about six hundred men. The departed troops were soon replaced by Missouri and Illinois volunteers who arrived in Santa Fe during the late summer and fall, bringing the force in the department to some three thousand officers and men.

The number of Anglo-Americans, other than military personnel, residing in New Mexico with some degree of permanence increased markedly. Some were discharged soldiers, and some were traders who chose to establish residence in New Mexico; but others were men, or, in a few cases, women, who were attracted by the opportunities, either real or imagined, that they hoped to find. The growth of the nonmilitary Anglo population is not surprising. The army provided some jobs for both skilled and unskilled workers, and the expansion of private enterprise created additional employment. The professions were soon represented by a growing number of practitioners and other individuals who engaged in commerce, farming, and ranching; provided a variety of services; or, in a few cases, developed industries. Rather clearly, from the beginning of the occupation it was anticipated that New Mexico would remain a part of the United States. Credence was given to this belief when, on November 3, 1846, Military Department No. 9 was created "to embrace so much of the Mexican province of New Mexico as has been or may be subjected to the arms or the authority of the United States."[2]

Santa Fe, from the beginning of the occupation until July 1861, held a position of primary importance for the army. Not only was it the seat of government (which was under military control until March 1851); it was also the headquarters for the military department and the general depot for all military stores. Army funds were concentrated in Santa Fe, in the hands of the disbursing officers (not in banks, which did not yet exist), and there the decisions regarding significant expenditures were made. Usually there were more troops stationed in Santa Fe than at any other post, and by far the most civilians employed by the army were in Santa Fe. All of these things combined to encourage commercial activity and to attract new business enterprises. Although Santa Fe drew the largest number of newcomers, there was a sprinkling of Americans in many of the other towns, particularly in those where troops were stationed.

It is possible to get a better picture of Santa Fe than of any other New Mexican town because of the *Santa Fe Republican*, the only newspaper published in New Mexico during the occupation period. The first issue came from the press on September 10, 1847, and the masthead announced that it would be "devoted to science, literature, and the earliest news from the United States and the general movements of the army." Appended was the somewhat extraneous sentiment, "we die but we never surrender." The newspaper itself was a product of the occupation and owed its existence to the army. Its proprietors, Oliver P. Hovey and Edward T. Davies, arrived as members of the occupying force, Hovey in Doniphan's regiment and Davies with Price's command. Hovey, a native of Vermont, was twenty-two years of age in 1847. He remained in New Mexico following his discharge, married a daughter of James Conklin,[3] and engaged in a variety of business enterprises. Davies ended his association with the *Republican* to return to Missouri in the spring of 1848, but he resumed the editorship some time in 1849 and was one of the publishers of the Santa Fe *New Mexican* when it first appeared in November 1849. Apparently he left New Mexico before the census was taken in 1850. The press on which the *Republican* was printed was brought by the army from St. Louis in the spring of 1847. Hovey and Davies arranged to use the press to launch their newspaper.[4] It was intended to be a weekly, printed in English and Spanish, but it did not always appear that regularly. Government and military printing was given priority and was often the excuse for the late appearance of the paper.

The *Republican,* which was inclined to boast of the improvements resulting from the American occupation (or, less frequently, to voice criticism of the lack of them), informed its readers that "when Genl. Kearny entered Santa Fe . . . there was but one Public House in the place, and it was so badly kept and supplied that but few paid it a second visit."[5] Now there were four hotels and a number of boarding houses, reflecting clearly both the increase in transient visitors and the change in customs brought about by the occupation. In the Mexican period, persons who came to Santa Fe commonly stayed with friends or acquaintances and even at the Palace of the Governors if they were of sufficient prominence. The traders who came over the trail from Missouri rented rooms in private houses, which were to serve both as living quarters and as salesrooms.

Tradition has it that an inn, located on the site occupied today by La Fonda, marked the end of the Santa Fe Trail,[6] yet this inn is strangely absent from the accounts of visitors to Santa Fe during the Mexican period. Matt Field, who made his trip over the trail as a journalist-tourist in 1827 and wrote his amusing descriptive sketches for the New Orleans *Picayune,* made no mention of an inn.[7] Neither Josiah Gregg nor James J. Webb said anything about it,[8] and the list of those who ignored the inn would include almost everyone who wrote about Santa Fe in these years. One visitor, probably in 1842, stated categorically, "there was no such thing" as a hotel in the town.[9]

The initial issue of the *Republican* carried advertisements for two hotels, appropriately named the Missouri House and the Santa Fe House. The Missouri House, located on Main Street (now San Francisco Street) at the southeast corner of the plaza, offered the "rarest and best served dishes of the season," a well-stocked bar, two billiard tables, and an almost completed ballroom which the proprietors, John N. Abell and Nicolás Pino,[10] promised would be the equal of any in the city. The Santa Fe House, located on the "east corner" of the plaza, provided for its guests the best of liquors; "a table supplied with every thing which the market and country affords"; an apartment suitable for a clubroom, with servants in attendance; and, as a final inducement, the owner, W. W. Amos, guaranteed "Oysters, Sardines, &c., always on hand, and cooked if desired."[11] The German and the Beck and Redman hotels presumably were of lesser quality,[12] as they did not advertise and received bare mention in the *Republican*. Only one boarding house solicited patronage through the press: a "private boarding house, located a few doors above the Missouri House." The proprietress, Mrs. Gabriel de Habiles, recently arrived from New Orleans, undertook to please her clientele "in the future as in the past."

Beyond much question, Santa Fe's early bonifaces encountered many vicissitudes in their calling. The German and the Beck and Redman hotels seemingly were short-lived. However, by December a new hostelry, the United States Hotel, had opened its doors. It soon gained the reputation of serving the best meals in town, dinner for a relatively expensive 50 cents and board for $1 per day.[13] In March 1848, the Independence House, conveniently located next door to the United States Hotel, announced that it was ready for business. In the meantime the Missouri House had been sold, and then reacquired by Abell in partnership with Alex Duval.[14] The Independence House soon passed from the hands of its proprietor, John G. Moody,[15] who briefly operated the former Santa Fe House as the Missouri Bar and Boarding House, providing room and board for $5 per week. A few weeks after these services were first announced the *Republican* carried the information that Moody had sold his establishment to the Independence House, which planned to maintain it in conjunction with the hotel. The Independence House again underwent a change of ownership in the spring of 1849. In July 1848, the newly opened Taos Hotel became the first hotel outside of Santa Fe to seek patronage through the press.

During the summer of 1848 the *Republican* frequently listed the weekly arrivals at the United States Hotel and at the Independence House. They usually exceeded one hundred persons, many of whom were army officers. The hotel was something new as far as New Mexico was concerned: a public convenience, commercial and competitive. It offered opportunity for a social life completely disassociated from the home and one which was class-conscious, if only because of its cost. Something else is clear from the listings of new arrivals: those who made use of the residential accommodations were almost exclusively Anglo-Americans. After the issue of November 25, 1848, only scattered numbers of the *Republican* were known to exist, making it impossible to follow in detail the changing hotel scene.

All of the hotels of the period were former private houses, adapted to their new function with a minimum of remodeling. Only the Santa Fe House existed throughout the entire short life of the *Republican*: it began as a hotel, was turned into a boarding house, and ended as an appendage to the Independence House. None of the hotels survived, at least under the same name and management, until 1852, when reasonably complete files of the *Santa Fe Weekly Gazette* become available. In that year a new Santa Fe House, the first hotel built specifically for the purpose, opened under the proprietorship of Louis Dorrence.[16] Also in 1852 the Exchange Hotel, soon popularly referred to as the Fonda, began operation on the southeast corner of the plaza, apparently occupying the refurbished structure first called the Missouri House.[17] Although it underwent various changes of ownership, the Exchange was the first hotel to have an extended period of existence.

Another notable change in the commercial life of the town was the growing number and variety of business establishments. In the Mexican period only a few stores had functioned on a year-round basis. Merchants offered their wares beneath the portales of the plaza or in the plaza itself. Wood, brought into town on the backs of diminutive burros, was sold in what is now Burro Alley. Most of the Missouri traders' stores were rented rooms, serving their purpose for a few weeks or months until the stock was disposed of or until the traders moved on to the south. This changed with the occupation as new methods of doing business augmented the old. Goods, particularly foodstuffs, were still displayed in the shade of the portales, and traders from Missouri still brought wagons loaded with merchandise to be sold as quickly as possible. Merchandising, in fact, ran the gamut from peddlers, who moved from community to community, to stores that assumed considerable permanence, particularly in towns where troops were stationed. The number of licenses issued to merchants grew from year to year, leveling off in the later 1850s. During the occupation, and for some time thereafter, very few licenses were taken out by Spanish Americans, but in the final years of the 1850s they accounted for about 40 percent of the total.[18]

A comparison of the goods offered for sale by the purveyors of general merchandise and the goods which entered into the prewar Spanish trade discloses both similarities and differences.[19] Cloth, especially the less expensive kinds, continued to be of major significance, as was hardware, including a choice of laborsaving devices such as iron pumps, plows, small scales, and coffee and corn mills. More groceries were imported, both staples and such relative luxuries as butter, candies, spices, condiments, syrups, sardines, jellies, and canned fruits. Wines and liquors from the United States and Europe were available in variety and quantity. Imported articles of clothing—hats, caps, shirts, neckties, trousers, overcoats, boots, shoes, and complete suits—were frequently advertised. Fancy dry goods, dishes and glassware, books in both English and Spanish, and an extensive selection of drugs and medicines were available. Even imported toys, jewelry, and perfumes were offered to the public.

Merchants also stocked an assortment of goods intended specifically for sale to army sutlers or to compete with them. Merchandise from Old Mexico seemed to be plentiful, even while the war was still in progress. Hartley and Powers (the firm became Hartley and Cuniff in January 1848) carried wines and dried fruits from El Paso del Norte.[20] Mexican blankets, rebozos from the fairs of San Juan de los Lagos and Guadalajara, and a variety of Mexican horse and mule furnishings was always in good supply.[21] Taos again made the news when Robert Carey and James H. Quinn placed an advertisement asserting that they had in their store the best and lowest priced selection of goods in the Taos Valley.[22]

Aside from the general merchants a few more specialized enterprises advertised their wares and services. While not an advertisement, one of the very few references to a business owned by a Spanish American was a brief notice informing the public that Don Francisco Ortiz y Delgado, prefect of Santa Fe County, had for sale in his store a large stock of schoolbooks. That there was a need for schoolbooks became more apparent in August 1848, when the opening of the first term of John W. Dunn's "Classical and English High School" was announced. The tuition, though not unreasonable, would exclude most New Mexicans—primary English branches cost $20 for six months; languages and mathematics cost $30 for the same period.[23]

The entertainment encountered in Santa Fe, or elsewhere in New Mexico, had been of a simple nature. Almost everyone who visited during the Mexican period, and who left an account of his impressions, commented on the fandango, the gambling, and the local wines and brandy. Billiard tables joined the repertoire of amusements, probably in the early 1840s. Any room, from the poorest home to the Palace of the Governors, could serve as setting for a fandango, although if it were sufficiently elegant it was called a *baile*. The monte table was accommodated even in the open air. The most fashionable gambling salon, that maintained by Gertrudis Barceló (La Tules),[24] was located on the corner of Burro Alley and Main Street. It was a room of about fifty by twenty feet, comfortably furnished for its purpose and adjoined by several smaller rooms for private games.

American commentators of the Mexican period were prone to dwell on what they considered to be the lax morals of New Mexican women.

The opinion often was based on nothing more than a casualness of dress, the habit of smoking *cigarillos*, or a flirtatious glance from a dark eye. Even though the temporary *ménage* was not uncommon, it would seem that the oldest profession was not practiced on an organized basis before the American occupation. One observer noted that young women who permitted themselves to be escorted home from fandangos expected their companions to stay the night. This felicitous practice was blamed for much of the venereal disease prevalent in Santa Fe.[25]

The Americans elaborated on the entertainment that they found in New Mexico, although they added few new pastimes. Some of the hotels had ballrooms and all had barrooms. Numerous dramshops continued to cater to the thirsty as they had before the occupation, and the variety of potables offered to potential customers was more comprehensive than before. In October 1847, Oliver P. Hovey and Company opened what must have been New Mexico's most elaborate pleasure resort, containing a bar, ballroom, billiard saloon, and tenpin alley. Aside from the tenpin alley, the only innovation announced in the press came nine months later in the form of a lending library. The proprietor of a billiard parlor announced that he had a "large collection of late and popular novels" that he offered "to loan at reasonable prices."

Santa Fe's first advertised theatrical performance occurred in November 1848, when the Thespian Association presented "How to Pay the Rent," followed by a comic song and the one-act farce, "Perfection," admission $1.[26] In the years after the regular army replaced the volunteers, public plays were occasionally put on by the soldiers, and military band concerts in the plaza entertained Santa Feans with some regularity. The bawdy house, though not advertised in the press, soon became a fixture in many of the towns where troops were stationed. Doctor James D. Robinson,[27] who took the census in San Miguel County in 1850, listed occupations more frankly than did his colleagues. Las Vegas supported a surprising number of "courtezans," ranging in age from as young as eleven years.

For the army, gambling, drunkenness, and even the fandango were never ending sources of trouble. Every commander of the department during the occupation period sought to regulate games of chance, dramshops, and public dances, but with very little success. Kearny imposed comparatively low license fees on all of these activities. His successors increased the fees and took various measures to stop or limit the participation of enlisted men in most forms of public entertainment. Yet a private described Santa Fe in September 1847 as "a great 'gambling mart.'" There were, he wrote, over one hundred monte tables in operation, the dealers being mostly Spanish men and women, the betters American soldiers. The sums lost on this game are immense, and many a poor volunteer has been left penniless by betting on monte. The scenes of drunkenness daily and nightly enacted, filling the guardhouse with soldiers, demand a reform in the dramshops.[28]

Early in 1848 the tax on gambling houses in Santa Fe was raised to $500 per quarter. Moreover, any proprietor who permitted a person under twenty-one years of age or an enlisted man to gamble was subject to a fine of $100 and the loss of his license.[29] The large number of licenses issued under these restrictions is an indication of the profits that could be made from operating games of chance.

Efforts to control vice were largely futile. For the volunteers there was too little to occupy their time, with consequent boredom and resultant misconduct clearly reflected in the records of courts-martial. Once the regular army took over there was some improvement, but only because there were fewer troops involved. Court-martial records were still replete with cases involving drunkenness, brawling, and occasional killings. Officers as well as men were found guilty of these charges, although there was a tendency to treat the officers with greater lenience. Gambling and women were often at the root of the more violent crimes, and the fandango provided a frequent setting for fisticuffs and knifings.

Illness plagued the troops and sometimes infected the general population. The military hospital in Santa Fe was crowded, and deaths were numerous, notably from measles and scurvy. With the coming of spring in 1847 a surprising number of men were discharged because of physical inability to serve. Common among the listed causes were incipient phthisis, chronic hepatitis, scurvy, and general debility. John T. Hughes stated that Price had lost more than four hundred men from his original command as a result of battle and disease,[30] which meant disease primarily, as battle losses were comparatively few. George R. Gibson, who visited the post cemetery in Santa Fe in May 1847, less than nine months after the occupation began, was astonished at its extent:

300 new made graves attest the mortality which existed amongst the troops and teamsters. . . . Various causes brought the men to an untimely end. Some from dissipation. Some from Exposure. Some the want of attention. Some broken down constitutions. Some from fever and some from the affects of colds. The health of the army here though I found good at this

time, the weak and sickly having pretty much all died off. Measles was also a fruitful disease in filling up the ground.[31]

Health continued to be a problem throughout the second year of the occupation. In the autumn of 1847 Assistant Surgeon Horace R. Wirtz reported that the army hospital was crowded. Most of the patients were suffering from "remitant fever in its low stages," which he diagnosed as typhoid. Once again a few cases of scurvy had appeared. Conditions were not as bad as they had been in the previous autumn, but deaths in the hospital averaged four a week, counting both soldiers and teamsters. The *Republican* charged that there were many factors responsible for the sickness and pointed

to the filth and dirt about town—to the putrid carcasses of animals which were permitted to rot all over it—to the decayed and decaying matter in all the streets and corrals, and private places, which if permitted to go on must necessarily affect the town, and probably corrupt the water. The whole soil is nothing but an amalgam of putrid matter, which in warm weather will give forth an effluvia both disagreeable and sickly.

The editor called on both the civil and military authorities to do something to correct the conditions while the weather was still cold, and thus protect the health and comfort of the inhabitants.[32]

Santa Fe, if the *Republican* can be believed, was in an ebullient mood, confident and progressive, in the spring of 1848. The press painted a glowing picture of the changes already made and of those the future promised. Merchants were preparing light and commodious salesrooms in place of the cramped quarters of the past. The ruinous houses scattered throughout the town were being replaced by new and better structures as fast as workers could be secured. "Not a street in the place presents the appearance it did this time two years ago, and if things continue, in one year more the whole appearance of the city will be changed." Many young soldiers, according to the editor, expressed a desire to settle in New Mexico and he saw no reason why there was "not as strong an inducement to settle here as in California or Oregon." With the coming of spring business was improving, and everything pointed to an excellent season. The citizens of the town were planting large fields with crops. "Americans and capitalists" were purchasing land, both to build on and to cultivate. The trains from Missouri would soon be arriving over the trail with their loads of goods, and "we believe that Santa Fe never saw the same spirit manifested, nor the same hum of every kind of business it does at present."[33]

The expanding business activity was dependent, in part, on the patronage of military personnel. Through the press many of the merchants invited the army to examine their wares and to make use of their facilities. Some of the hotels and bars gave evidence of an awareness of rank when they stated that officers were welcome. This was almost amusing, considering that most of the troops in New Mexico were citizen volunteers and that today's private might tomorrow hold officer's rank through the process of democratic election. Perhaps no more overt solicitation of military patronage was made than that by James M. White and his brother,[34] who, billing themselves as "cheap merchants," claimed that "officers and soldiers about returning to the States can purchase suits here as cheap as at Home."

The business of Santa Fe or of any other town in which troops were stationed profited from their presence, but this was only one of the ways in which the army spurred New Mexico's economy. The full impact of military purchases during the occupation period cannot be determined precisely because the army made few contracts and the records of casual transactions are scant. Two notices in an early issue of the *Republican* give some idea of the extremes of military needs. Captain William D. McKissack, assistant quartermaster, called for bids for five thousand bushels of corn to be delivered in Santa Fe. Eli Webb, hospital steward, advertised for one dozen or more hens and for one or two roosters. Whether either request produced results is not known.

In September 1847, the *Republican* reported that the commissary department was well supplied as a result of the stores hauled from Fort Leavenworth during the summer. Boding well for the future comfort of the troops, "large trains" of government stores arrived "every day or two." The *Republican* also noted that grass and forage were ample and the corn and wheat crops good; hence, it predicted, the high prices previously charged for corn and flour could not be maintained. The army, of course, imported almost all of its flour from the States. Money was no longer in short supply, and drafts could be exchanged "on very favorable terms." The men continued to spend their frugal pay for goods and entertainment and in the year 1846–48 they were paid with some regularity.

There is nothing to suggest that gardens were planted at any of the posts in New Mexico, even though some vegetable seeds were sent from Fort Leavenworth to the commissary depot in Santa Fe.[35] Seemingly, the troops depended entirely on locally grown fresh produce, and, from the prevalence of scurvy, it was not always enough. The *Republican* from time to time emphasized the opportunity provided by the presence of the army:

> Marketing of all kinds has greatly increased in volume since this country was occupied by the American troops. At no period within the history of the country have vegetables paid so well for cultivation. We recommend that persons with suitable land plant vegetables to sell to the army. Irish potatoes are the first, then cabbage, beets, radishes, lettuce, sweet potatoes, turnips, cucumbers, etc. All will find ready market at the military posts. Many of the native population lay aside their native dishes and begin to eat vegetables which are finding their way to market, thus creating a further outlet.[36]

On the front page of its first issue the *Republican* carried the request, "will some person inform us whether a satisfactory experiment has been made to cultivate the Irish Potato or not in N. Mexico." The potato was sorely missed, with both army men and civilians regretting its absence. Even though the demand was present, the first success in growing potatoes in New Mexico was not reported until the summer of 1854, and this by a private citizen in his kitchen garden.[37] Imported potatoes were comparatively expensive for many years to come. They were usually available in the market by the middle of the fifties, but they were not produced in New Mexico in any quantity until the eve of the Civil War. In 1860 more than one thousand bushels of Irish potatoes were raised in northern Taos County, most in the vicinity of Culebra (in what is now part of Colorado); and some seven hundred bushels were harvested at Rio Bonito near Fort Stanton, in what was then Socorro County.[38]

At no time during the occupation was rent paid for the facilities occupied by the army. In Santa Fe some of the old presidial barracks were repaired and made rudely comfortable. They were capable of housing a regiment, so, except when an unusual number of troops were stationed in the town, the public buildings were adequate to accommodate the rank and file.[39] During the occupation of El Paso del Norte the presidio there quartered some of the troops; but other buildings were pressed into use, and most officers took rooms in private homes, with no record of compensation to the owners. In Albuquerque the extensive property of former Governor Manuel Armijo continued to be used as barracks for the dragoon companies until 1851. No information has been found in regard to the particular structures occupied by the army in Taos, Las

Vegas, Socorro, and in the other towns where volunteers were stationed at one time or another.

The army hired some local labor, though here again records are too few to give an accurate indication of the extent. Many years later a prominent New Mexican recalled that anyone who wanted work could find employment for which he was regularly paid.[40] One of the few extant quartermaster contracts of the occupation period provided for two Anglo-Americans to herd government cattle anywhere between Santa Fe and Las Vegas for $1 per head per month.[41] At about the same time the *Republican* carried an offer to graze stock for $1.50 per head per month. The enterprising advertiser agreed to be "responsible for all stock . . . (death and accident excepted) unless it should be run off by Indians"![42] Some use was made of Spanish Americans and Pueblo Indians as spies and guides; but what they were paid, or if they were paid, was not stated.

By August 1848, when it was known that the volunteer troops would soon be pulled out of New Mexico, the appeal of many advertisers shifted from an emphasis on quality to the inexpensive prices of their goods. The optimism of a few months earlier gave way to a feeling of apprehension that the merchants might be in for a period of hard times. As large numbers of troops began to assemble in Santa Fe, prior to leaving for the East, the *Republican* informed its readers that they might expect the town to be busier than ever before and, by implication, busier than it would be again for some time. Two weeks later, the troops gone, it commented that "notwithstanding the many departures during the past week, our city continues to wear a lively and businesslike appearance, instead of decreasing, it seems to be increasing." Despite this hopeful assessment, the space devoted to advertising had already fallen off by more than half.

On August 27, 1848, when Price and his staff left Santa Fe, almost two full years during which New Mexico had been commanded and largely garrisoned by volunteers came to an end. In the issue of September 6, the best the editor of the *Republican* could do was to "feel proud" of the quiet past weeks in Santa Fe. "We have not the boistrous [sic] and loud cries of the drunkard, whose abode was that of the grog shop,—no loud and shrill voice of the sergeant of the Guard, or that of a file of men escorting some poor wretch to the guard house." Expressing a cautious optimism, the *Republican* predicted that "instead of the [a]dobe, we hope soon to see fine three and four story brick dwellings erected, so in a few years more, we may be proud to record the name of Santa Fe, among the most beautiful and flourishing cities in the west."

The *Republican* continued to appear regularly until June 9, 1849, when it was forced to suspend publication because it had completely exhausted its supply of newsprint. The last known extant issue is an extra dated August 8, 1849.[43] The demise of the *Republican* left New Mexico briefly without a newspaper, a void filled temporarily when the Santa Fe *New Mexican* published its first issue on November 28, 1849. The editors were Edward T. Davies and William S. Jones, the latter a twenty-four-year-old native of Virginia. The *New Mexican* was intended to be a weekly, but how long it was published is not known.[44] It was printed on the same press that had produced the *Republican;* that is, the press belonging to the army. On February 14, 1850, the press was sold at public auction by the quartermaster's department in Santa Fe. That, incidentally, may be a clue to the length of time the *New Mexican* was published.

The press was purchased for $180, presumably by Hugh N. Smith,[45] Thomas S. J. Johnson,[46] and James L. Collins, all of whom had been associated with the army or military government. All were fully involved in the factional struggle, revolving around the question of statehood versus territorial status for New Mexico. Dr. James D. Robinson, who had political ambitions of his own, took the lead in challenging the sale of the press, claiming that many irregularities were involved. At the request of Captain Alexander D. Reynolds,[47] assistant quartermaster, a court of inquiry was assembled in Santa Fe in March. Richard H. Weightman,[48] who was leader of the faction favoring territorial status, told the court that he and his associates had been prepared to bid as much as $1,000 for the press. Although some of the charges were found to be substantially correct, the court decided that the army had received for the press "all that anyone at the time appeared disposed to pay for it." Sometime thereafter the Santa Fe *Weekly Gazette* commenced publication, with the old army press carrying on its tradition of printing the news for New Mexico.[49]

3

~~~~~~~~~~~~~~~~~~~~~~~~~~~~~~~~

The Regular Army Takes Over

With the departure of General Price and the volunteers, command of the department devolved on Major and Brevet Lieutenant Colonel Benjamin L. Beall. Under him were three companies of First Dragoons, two of them undermanned and the third a mere skeleton soon to be broken up. For the moment the military force in New Mexico numbered less than two hundred officers and men. A recruiting office was opened in Santa Fe, only to be closed two weeks later for lack of business.[1] Additional troops were en route to New Mexico. A company of First Dragoons from Fort Gibson in Indian Territory arrived in Santa Fe on September 25. Two weeks later Major and Brevet Lieutenant Colonel John Macrae Washington, Third Artillery, reached the city with one company of his own regiment and one of Second Dragoons,[2] having marched across northern Mexico from Monterrey. On October 11, 1848, Washington took command of the department and assumed the governorship of New Mexico.[3] Even with the additional troops, there were fewer than five hundred soldiers in New Mexico, and no more could be expected until the following summer. The little force was divided between six towns; two companies in Santa Fe, one in Taos, and the other two distributed between Albuquerque, Socorro, Tome, and Doña Ana. The widespread dispersion of troops was intended, in part, to assure the availability of sufficient forage for public animals.[4]

One result of the great reduction in military strength was a drastic curtailment of purchasing power, both that of the army per se and that of army personnel. Moreover, far fewer supplies were required, which meant not only a substantial decrease in expenditures in New Mexico but fewer wagons coming over the trail from Fort Leavenworth and fewer animals and teamsters to be provided for. Equally important, the army became cost-conscious once the war ended and it was possible to engage in more accurate planning and careful purchasing.

Business was dull in Santa Fe as the summer of 1849 began. A visitor to the town in June reported that the market was glutted, and between the overabundance of goods and the competition provided by a superfluity of merchants there was a "stagnation in trade." The *Missouri Republican* noted pessimistically that there was already a two-year supply of merchandise in Santa Fe and that dry goods there sold at St. Louis prices. William S. Messervy, for years a leading figure in the Santa Fe trade, asserted that anyone who introduced new goods would inevitably lose money. One of the reasons given for the excess of merchandise in Santa Fe was the virtual disappearance of the market in Chihuahua.[5]

The impact on New Mexico's economy was cushioned by events occurring outside of the area but affecting both New Mexico and the army. The discovery of gold in California and the subsequent rush to the mining districts brought a stream of gold seekers across New Mexico and created a demand for New Mexican products, particularly for feed and food. The emigrants came by almost every conceivable route. Some entered the settled areas as far to the north as Taos, but more came over the Santa Fe Trail or the roads opened to the south. Whatever the route—and all of the principal areas of production were involved—there was a drain on resources, causing some increase in prices and reducing the availability of some items to the army. Captain Thomas L. Brent, chief quartermaster for the department, reported in 1850:

> Add to all causes the large number of emigrants which entered the Territory at different points, nearly all requiring a complete change of outfit for the continuance of their long overland journey to California by the route of the Gila, and it will sufficiently explain the difficulty of obtaining supplies of every description in New Mexico—a country which heretofore has produced barely sufficient for its own population.[6]

Emigrants complained about the high prices asked for almost everything in New Mexico. Mules sold for as much as $150, yet the worn-down American horses they replaced could scarcely be given away. The price charged the emigrants for corn varied considerably but was usually in the range of $6 to $9 per fanega, much more than the army paid for most of the corn it purchased in the year 1849–50. However, some goods were high only in comparison to Missouri prices, and some recorded purchases were actual bargains. At Galisteo a California-bound party bought five hundred sheep for $250, half the price that the army normally paid for live sheep. Flour was available for $7.50 per one hundred pounds and in a few cases was even cheaper, which was less than the price paid by the army for New Mexican flour and much less than the price of imported flour sold in Santa Fe. One man reported that he paid the "most exorbitant rate" of 20 cents for a pound of bacon at San Miguel. Others paid as little as 25 cents per pound for sugar and coffee.[7]

Emigrants could not always obtain what they wanted and sometimes found it easier to barter than to buy. One traveler traded an old sword for 350 onions near El Paso del Norte. He had earlier described the large white onions as the finest he had ever seen, "except at fairs." Fresh fruit was abundant and cheap, "and a little powder, caps, or almost anything will purchase considerable," He bought wheat at $5 and local flour at $7, each per fanega. Beef was scarce, and pigs could "hardly be bought for any price," but goats and sheep, "not very fat," were common at $2 to $3 per head. At Doña Ana the post commissary offered to sell the emigrants salt pork, brown sugar, and rice at 25 cents per pound and "fine sifted flour" at 15 cents per pound.[8] These items were all part of the ration and all were imported, so the price charged was little if any above the army's cost. Even so, one migrant complained that the prices charged for government stores at the post were "exorbitant."[9]

The opening of new roads was another development of significance to New Mexico and the army. Until 1846 New Mexico had only only two principal connections with the outside world. The centuries old *camino real* stretched from Santa Fe down the Rio Grande Valley to El Paso del Norte and then south into Old Mexico. Much more recent in origin was the Santa Fe Trail, the great commercial route between New Mexico and Missouri. To the west, by a roundabout course, the so-called Old Spanish Trail provided a tenuous contact with southern California, one not traversable by wheeled vehicles. In 1846 Colonel Philip St. George Cooke laid out a wagon road to the coast when he led the Mormon Battalion to California. Cooke's route was shortened and improved over the next few years and, with its variations, became a major highway during the California gold rush.

The only route used by the army for troop movements and freighting during the occupation years was the Santa Fe Trail, but in 1849 new approaches were opened, most of them by military exploration. Captain Randolph B. Marcy of the Fifth Infantry laid out a road from Fort Smith to Santa Fe along the south side of the Canadian River. He escorted a large number of California-bound emigrants over the route, which, it was hoped, would prove superior to the already existing trails.[10] Called both the Canadian route and the Fort Smith road, it became more important in the later 1850s. Marcy returned to Fort Smith by dropping down the Rio Grande Valley to Doña Ana, striking northeast across New Mexico and Texas, crossing the Red River below the mouth of the False Washita, and then going on to his destination. This offered a more direct approach for travelers taking the southern route to California, and Marcy considered it better than either the Santa Fe Trail or the Canadian route, but it did not become popular.[11]

More important was the opening of wagon roads from San Antonio to El Paso del Norte in 1849. The upper road, as it came to be known, was laid out, under the auspices of the army, by a party led by Major Robert S. Neighbors of the Texas Rangers; and the lower road was made by second lieutenants William H. C. Whiting, Corps of Engineers, and William Smith, Topographical Engineers. The lower road, which would be the more useful of the two, was modified and improved later in the year as a result of further reconnaissance conducted by Captain and Brevet Lieutenant Colonel Joseph E. Johnston of the Topographical Engineers. It soon became a significant route for supplying the southern posts in New Mexico as well as for mail and civilian travel. Both roads directed their quota of emigrants through the oasis-like El Paso district.[12]

New Mexico's most important internal line of communications and travel was the north-south camino real, which branched to either side to serve the areas of settlement not touched by the main highway. New Mexico's roads were generally poor, although they had been adequate for the slow-moving *carretas* of the past. Once New Mexico was erected into a territory, the territorial legislature clamored consistently for better roads. In its first session, it made the charge that "owing to the poverty or carelessness of the late Mexican Government the improvement of roads was entirely neglected . . . they are mere bridal paths, resembling more the trail of the Indian, than the highways of a civilised people." Particularly, it urged the appropriation of $50,000 to open a wagon road between Santa Fe and the Taos Valley, "a region rich in the most fertile valleys, admirably adapted to agricultural pursuits," but largely cut off from potential markets.[13] Improvement in New Mexico's internal roads, when it came, was largely the work of the army.

In February 1848, Sterling Price, who by that time had been promoted to the rank of brigadier general of the volunteers, provided for the revenue of New Mexico by decreeing a 6 percent *ad valorem* tax on all merchandise imported into the territory. Exempted from the impost were certain specified items imported by post sutlers. Charles Blumner,[14] treasurer in the civil government, was named ex officio collector, and subcollectors were stationed at Taos, San Miguel, and Valencia. Price, who placed the value of imports in 1848 at $300,000, estimated that the tax would produce $18,000 a year, sufficient to meet the administrative expenses and to pay the salaries of the civil officials appointed under the military government.[15] As soon as the Mexican War ended, the merchants of Santa Fe sent a petition to Price, contending that as New Mexico was now part of the United States it was "unjust and unconstitutional" to collect customs duties on goods imported from the United States. Price refused to rescind the tax on the ground that it was properly a matter for the president to decide.[16]

When he assumed command Colonel Beall cancelled the tax, but without it revenue was inadequate to pay the comparatively small expenses of the civil authorities. Within a month of his arrival, Colonel Washington found that the government had already incurred a deficit of $15,000. He suggested to Secretary of War William L. Marcy that either the tariff be collected or that Congress be asked to appropriate funds to pay the necessary expenses. Unwilling to permit the debt to mount while he awaited a reply that probably would not reach Santa Fe for months, he reimposed the tariff on November 30. However, in his annual message delivered on December 5, 1848, President Polk stated that it would be necessary, "at an early period," to extend the revenue laws of the United States to the newly acquired territories. When Polk's views were known in Santa Fe, Colonel Washington reversed himself and did away entirely with all import duties.[17]

Undoubtedly the merchants approved, but if they expected a windfall in the form of a substantial refund they were disappointed. The 6 percent tax had yielded a little less than Price had estimated, only $16,638.48 during the twelve months in which it was actually imposed. This would indicate a value of $277,308 for the goods imported, although it may be assumed that there was some evasion of the payment of duties, as there had been in the Mexican period. In four and one-third months—from November 30, 1848, to April 10, 1849—a 20 percent tax on goods imported from Mexico had returned $3,461.49. Of the total amount collected, $2,244.94 had gone for salaries and other expenses of the collector's office, and $16,073.32 had been disbursed by the treasurer. Only $1,671.71 was refunded to the merchants.[18]

The health of the troops continued to be a matter of concern as illness seriously depleted the small force in the department. There were too few medical officers in New Mexico, and when a detachment of dragoons was sent to establish a post at Las Vegas in November 1848, Colonel Washington found it necessary to hire a civilian doctor, paying him $20 per month for his services, and "deducting the time the detachment may be absent from the post."[19] In the spring of 1849 scurvy struck again, particularly at Taos, where it was so prevalent that consideration was given to relocating the post. Assistant Surgeon Lewis A. Edwards, then the senior medical officer in the department, insisted that scurvy was not, as was so often supposed, the result of "contagion, impure air, cold weather, or even the continued use of salt provisions." Rather, it was "especially due to the long *privation* of *fresh succulent vegetables.*" As both preventative and remedy he recommended the Irish potato, which he pronounced almost as valuable as lime juice, followed in efficacy by onions and cabbages.[20] Instructions were given to the post commanders to issue all procurable fresh vegetables, but it would be weeks before any of New Mexico's crops were ready to harvest.[21]

Antiscorbutics were often in short supply during the early years of the department. First Lieutenant Francis J. Thomas, Third Artillery, who became chief commissary officer in October 1848, noted that extra issues of onions were made to the troops; except in the vicinity of El Paso, however, neither onions nor any other fresh vegetables were available in adequate quantities. He requested that increased supplies of "Pickles, Molasses, Vinegar and other antiscorbutics" be sent to the department.[22] When they were available, green onions were issued at the rate of three bushels per one hundred rations. Also, when available, ten gallons of molasses and five to ten gallons of pickles were issued to each company per month, and twenty pounds of dried fruit per hundred rations were issued once a week.[23] Vinegar, of course, was part of the regular daily ration. Of these items, only onions and vinegar were procured in New Mexico, and all were often in short supply and sometimes entirely depleted. In 1850 Surgeon Charles McDougall, medical director for the department, recommended that citric acid be requisitioned for issue as an antiscorbutic, but his advice was not followed.[24]

Scurvy was not the most common ailment. Diarrhea, dysentery, various fevers, rheumatism, and venereal diseases were consistently more prevalent, and other diseases were occasionally so.[25] Yet scurvy received more attention, perhaps because methods for dealing with it were so well known. Thomas found a small quantity of garden seeds in the depot and distributed them to the posts. He also asked that additional seeds be sent before the spring of 1849.[26] Garden seeds were again furnished to all of the posts in 1850, yet there is no record that gardens were planted by the troops prior to 1852.[27] After visiting the post hospitals in the northern part of the department Assistant Surgeon Edwards pointed out that at all of them land suitable for cultivation was available; but, even though the therapeutic value of fresh vegetables was recognized, gardens were not planted.

Doctor Edwards was critical of a number of things. The efforts of the medical department were hampered, he claimed, because the comfort of the sick was neglected, with attention being given to everything else at a post before the hospital was considered. Most of the hospitals in the department were built of adobe, and were either converted houses or, in Santa Fe, a newly constructed building. Edwards had low regard for adobe as a building material:

> These ground [earthen] floors are unsuitable for persons in health, much less for a room for the sick. Indeed, all Mexican-built houses are calculated to impair health. The earthy surface, if not cold & damp, must affect by exhalations, the constitution of the atmosphere of the rooms, which are always illy ventilated. And even were this not the case, they must ever be dusty and dirty.

He also condemned the "filthy unhealthy & unsightly condition of the public streets & alleys" and branded the generally unhygienic condition of Santa Fe a potential threat to the health of civilian and soldier alike.[28] Apparently the earlier pleas of the *Republican* in the same cause had gone unheeded.

The department was greatly strengthened in the summer of 1849 by the arrival of long awaited reinforcements. A company of Second Dragoons reached Santa Fe on July 12, followed a few days later by four companies of Third Infantry and two of Second Artillery, all from Fort Leavenworth. The other six companies of the infantry regiment marched from San Antonio and, early in September, four took post at the ranch of Benjamin F. Coons,[29] on the left bank of the Rio Grande immediately opposite El Paso del Norte; the remaining two companies were sent back to occupy the Presidio of San Elizario. They came by the newly laid out lower road and spent considerable time making it passable for the wagon train that accompanied them.[30] Finally, in October, Major and Brevet Colonel John Munroe, Second Artillery, arrived to assume command of the department and the military governorship.[31] Coming with him were two more companies of Second Dragoons and a detachment of Third

Infantry recruits.[32] There were now nineteen regular army companies in New Mexico, but because they were undermanned the total force was only about one thousand.[33] The augmentation, however, made it possible to distribute the troops more widely.

By the summer of 1850 garrisons were stationed at Santa Fe, Abiquiu, Taos, Las Vegas, Albuquerque, Cebolleta, Socorro, Doña Ana, Coons' Ranch, the Presidio of San Elizario, and at Lucien B. Maxwell's nascent settlement on the Rayado Creek,[34] all of which were, for the moment, considered permanent. Seven of the posts were in the Rio Grande Valley, on or not many miles away from the river. They were intended to pro-tect—and police if necessary—the principal areas and the vital north-south highway. The Post of Las Vegas had a similar function. It was roughly centered among the little villages nestled against the eastern base of the Rockies and was in the first New Mexican town touched by the Santa Fe Trail. The other three posts were different in purpose and more in keeping with the pattern soon to emerge. Cebolleta was within the borders of the country viewed by the Navajos as their own, and Abiquiu was in an area subject to Ute, Jicarilla Apache, and Navajo incursions. Both towns were in need of protection, and the posts served also as convenient points of departure into Indian country. The Post of Rayado, the only post not immediately associated with a town, was partly intended to encourage the growth of settlement in a region of Ute and Jicarilla depredations.

The cost of maintaining troops in the Ninth Military Department was proportionately higher than in any other department in the United States, and surprisingly high considering the small number of troops in New Mexico and their relative lack of success in controlling the Indians. The War Department was fully conversant with the expenses of its operations in the far western territories. Even before the occupation period ended Captain Langdon C. Easton, the quartermaster at Fort Leavenworth, estimated that the government was paying 14³/₄ cents per pound to move stores from Fort Leavenworth to Santa Fe.[35] The same rate applied, of course, to the boxes, barrels, and other containers as to their contents. The cost of transporting some supplies, notably most commissary stores, exceeded the cost of the supplies several times over.

Transportation was the first area in which an attempt was made to reduce expenses. In May 1848, a series of contracts was signed with James Brown of Independence, Missouri, to transport stores from Fort Leav-enworth to Santa Fe for 11³/₄ cents per pound, delivery to be made within sixty-five days from the time the goods were received. Brown also agreed to purchase from the government up to 120 ox wagons and other equipment at cost. When the volunteers left New Mexico later in the year, a contract was made to haul the equipment of the Missouri mounted troops from Las Vegas to Independence, Missouri, for 8 cents per pound or for 6 cents from Point of Rocks.[36] This reflected the fact that the wagon trains which came fully loaded to New Mexico normally went back over the trail to Missouri nearly empty, but not until 1851 did the army again negotiate such a favorable contract.

Private contractors were required to provide surety bonds to guarantee satisfactory performance. The resultant service was an improvement, although it was expensive. Stores were delivered to the general depot in Santa Fe and to some of the posts; however, much of the distribution within the department was handled by the quartermaster's department, which hired civilian teamsters and made use of military personnel. New contracts were drawn up in 1849 and 1850, each providing for a small reduction in cost. Three contracts signed in 1851 for transportation from Fort Leavenworth during the fiscal year 1851–52 were on the most favorable terms yet obtained.

Table 1
Freight Rates, 1851–52[37]

Destination	Cost per 100 pounds
Las Vegas, Mora, Rayado	$ 7.87½
Santa Fe	8.39
Taos	8.83
Albuquerque	9.50
Doña Ana	12.50
El Paso	12.84

Most military freight had its origin at Fort Leavenworth; beginning in 1849, however, part of the supplies for the southern posts came from the army depot in San Antonio. In the first year of operation over the southern route stores were carried by quartermaster's trains, but in 1850 Benjamin F. Coons was given the freight contract. The terms were $13.50 per hundred pounds from the port of Indianola, Texas, to El Paso, or $12.00 from San Antonio, which was considerably more per mile than for stores hauled over the Santa Fe Trail. Between drought, unruly teamsters, and mismanagement, Coons was bankrupt by the enterprise.[38] In

1851 the government resumed handling its own transportation between San Antonio and El Paso.

Because the cost of transportation was so great the army sought to purchase more supplies locally and to encourage the New Mexican people to increase their production. Even though the price for almost everything normally bought by the army was appreciably higher in New Mexico than at Fort Leavenworth, the saving in freighting costs more than compensated for the difference. New Mexico, at the level of development it had achieved, could expand the quantity of its production but could do little to diversify its output of army requirements. However, the military constituted a lucrative and dependable market for the limited number of things that New Mexico could furnish, a market much greater than any heretofore available for New Mexican products.

Corn and wheat were grown throughout New Mexico wherever Spanish American or Pueblo Indian settlements existed. The means for manufacturing flour and corn meal were primitive, the *mano* and *metate* and gristmills capable of grinding very small quantities and completely unable to meet army needs. The commissary department purchased some New Mexican flour in casual transactions, but not until the war ended was an effort made to promote the development of a local milling industry. Instead, flour and hard bread were imported from Fort Leavenworth. In the years 1846–49 the cost of flour at Fort Leavenworth varied from a little more than 2 cents to almost 3^1/$_2$ cents per pound. During the same years, the cost of transporting the flour to Santa Fe was as much as six times the value of the flour, and even after freight contracts were made in 1848 the cost was five times its value.

When Lieutenant Thomas took over the administration of the commissary department he found a large quantity of imported flour on hand, some dating from the early months of the occupation and part of it already deteriorated. He was reluctant to ask for a board of survey to pass judgment on the flour, because if it was condemned before it was offered for sale "it would not bring the original cost but if sold without submitting it to a board, the proceeds will be at least double." Thomas asked Commissary General George Gibson for permission to sell some eighteen hundred barrels of flour, which would still leave in the depot more than a year's supply for twelve hundred men.[39] Some of the flour, as well as other subsistence stores, was sold at prices above the original cost; however, as a result, Thomas considered it necessary to ask that additional stores be sent from Fort Leavenworth.[40]

The army itself experimented in manufacturing some of its own flour.

In September 1849, Thomas received from the East "a large and handsome Portable Grist Mill calculated to grind and bolt from twelve to fourteen Barrels of Flour per day." He arranged with Elias P. West[41] to set up the mill on West's property on the Rio Grande in Albuquerque.[42] Although Thomas optimistically expected to have the mill in operation within three weeks, it did not begin to grind wheat until May 1850, and even then its output was restricted by the inability to secure enough grain to keep it working at full capacity.[43] The experiment was short-lived and could hardly be termed a success. The mill produced 1,096 pounds of flour in May and June, and an additional 1,592 pounds were purchased from West, who operated a small mill of his own. Combined, this was sufficient flour to provide a month's ration for the one company then stationed in Albuquerque, but it was only a minor part of the total required for the department. How long the mill operated is uncertain, but toward the end of 1851 Henry Winslow,[44] army agent in Albuquerque, was instructed to take charge of it until it could be removed to Fort Union.[45] The subsequent history of the mill is not known, but it was probably converted into a sawmill.

When Captain and Brevet Major Jefferson Van Horne, Third Infantry marched from San Antonio in the summer of 1849 to establish a post at Coons' Ranch he took with him the parts for two small gristmills, one to be set up at his post and the other at a proposed post near the Gila River.[46] Neither mill was put to use in the intended area, but it is possible that one of them was the mill installed by the army in Santa Fe. It was erected on the Santa Fe River above the town in the building originally built in the year 1846–47 to house a sawmill. There is no record of flour production by this mill while it belonged to the army. Indeed, most of the information pertaining to it concerns litigation and the sale of the property where the mill was located. The property was still in the possession of the government as late as February 1854, but it underwent various changes of ownership in the next few years, and the structure which housed the gristmill and sawmill eventually became a private residence.[47] There is no information about the second mill brought by Captain Van Horne. The military efforts to grind flour were of scant significance other than as an indication of the government's desire to reduce expenses. Actually, these efforts came at a time when private enterprise was about to fill the demand for flour in the department.

In the summer of 1849 Thomas advertised for bids to furnish the department with locally milled flour.[48] A contract was signed on December 3, 1849, with Ceran St. Vrain and Isaac McCarty,[49] calling for 1 million pounds of "good merchantable superfine flour" per year for three years, subject to an increase or decrease of 350,000 pounds for the third year. Deliveries were to commence on July 1, 1850, and to be made quarterly at the various military posts from Doña Ana to the north. For the first year the army agreed to pay 8$^{1}/_{2}$ cents per pound, for the second year 8 cents, and for the third year 7 cents.[50] This was expensive flour, but the cost still represented an appreciable saving. The price paid for flour at Fort Leavenworth in 1850 averaged about 2$^{8}/_{10}$ cents per pound, but transportation to Santa Fe added 8$^{7}/_{8}$ cents, and the cost of distribution from the general depot to the other posts was a further expense.

St. Vrain constructed two gristmills: the first large, "modern" gristmills in New Mexico. One was located on the Rio Grande de los Rancho near the little settlement of Talpa at the southern edge of the Taos Valley. It was also close to the roundabout wagon road that provided the only reasonable freighting route between the valley and the rest of New Mexico. The second mill was erected at Mora and was powered by a ditch leading from the Mora River. St. Vrain went to Westport, Missouri, in the spring of 1850 to hire a number of experienced millers and to purchase the parts for five mills.[51] The Talpa mill drew grain from the principal wheat growing area in New Mexico, the Taos Valley, which had an estimated fifteen thousand acres of land under cultivation, devoted largely to growing wheat and corn.[52] There was no such concentration of grain to serve the Mora mill, but potentially a much larger supply could be obtained from the scattered settlements east of the mountains. Once the mills were in operation and a market was assured the expansion of wheat planting was immediate.

Simeon Hart, who initiated the transaction, received a flour contract on March 28, 1850, without being required to submit a bid. Hart first came to New Mexico in 1847 as adjutant of the Third Regiment of Missouri Mounted Volunteers. During the war he met and later married Jesusita Sequieros, whose father, Don Leonardo, owned a large gristmill in Santa Cruz de Rosales, Chihuahua. In 1849 he settled with his bride on the Rio Grande, where El Paso, Texas, now stands. He erected a small gristmill, soon called Hart's Mill or El Molino; then he added a sawmill in 1850, and built a larger gristmill in 1854. Much of the flour supplied by Hart to the army, probably a major portion of it, was not manufactured at his mill on the Rio Grande but came from the Santa Cruz mill, which he operated with his father-in-law. Hence, the purchase of flour from Hart had less impact on the local economy than would otherwise have been the case.[53]

Hart's first contract did not specify a quantity but called for him to furnish flour for 11 cents per pound, as required, to the posts of El Paso, San Elizario, and Doña Ana. In December 1850 he was given a new contract to run to March 1, 1853, again with no quantity specified, to supply the same posts and, if required, the United States–Mexico boundary commission escort for 16 cents per pound.[54] Hart's flour always brought a higher price than was paid any other contractor in the department, in part because of the added cost of transportation from Santa Cruz. Although it was not a factor in the price, his flour was considered superior in quality to any other produced locally. Between them, St. Vrain and Hart provided the bulk of the flour consumed by the army in the years 1850–53.

To provide for both military and civilian personnel, one year's supply of subsistence stores (excepting flour) for fifteen hundred men was freighted from Fort Leavenworth to Santa Fe in 1850. Although the contracts with St. Vrain and Hart provided more flour than was necessary for the number of men to be subsisted, an additional six-month supply of flour was included in the shipment. Further, a full year's supply of subsistence stores for the three southern posts (including flour) was sent from San Antonio to the Post of El Paso, and a further full year's supply was readied for shipment. When the Post of El Paso was broken up in the fall of 1851 there was a two-year supply of flour on hand, in addition to the flour to be delivered under Hart's contract. All other commissary stores were described as "more than abundant," and some supplies had been on hand so long that they were unfit for issue.[55] Even when taking into account wastage and spoilage, it was evident that the cost of transportation did not deter the army from amassing a superabundance of flour and other stores in New Mexico. However, the last recorded importation of flour, a mere 1,600 pounds, was in 1852.[56]

In September 1850 a board of survey was assembled in Santa Fe to report on the quality of the flour delivered under St. Vrain's contract. In order to make a proper comparison, bread was baked using equal quantities of imported and New Mexican flour. A loaf of bread made from St. Vrain's flour was slightly lighter in weight and contained a small amount of "sand grit, disseminated of course, but still perceptible to the touch and taste." It was also less porous, "consequently not as digestible." The board labeled the flour "not bad" but advised Colonel Munroe that 102 pounds of New Mexican flour were required to equal 100 of American flour.[57] Throughout the decade of the fifties the quality of the flour milled

45

in New Mexico was considered inferior to that manufactured in the United States.

For the army the local availability of flour meant a considerable saving. Colonel Joseph K. F. Mansfield, when he inspected the department in 1853, reported that the army filled all of its needs for flour at a saving "of from 10 to 14 dollars the barrel."[58] More important to New Mexico, army demands led to the development of what amounted to a new industry in the Southwest, new at least in modern form. Flour soon became one of the principal items purchased by the army in the department. Undoubtedly, the contractors derived the greatest but certainly not the sole profit. They purchased the wheat from which they ground the flour wherever it was available, some of it from small farmers in quantities of only a few fanegas, and some from merchants who accepted it from customers in lieu of cash. The milling industry also employed civilian employment in the mills and to deliver the flour to the various posts.[59]

One of the results of the commercial milling industry, one not anticipated by the army, was a temporary reduction in the quantity of corn planted in New Mexico as land was diverted to grow wheat, particularly in the Taos Valley.[60] Barley and oats, common feed grains in the East, were not raised in New Mexico in significant quantities, and later attempts by the army to introduce them met with little success. Corn was the only grain available to feed public animals, and cornstalks constituted the principal long fodder, although wheat straw was occasionally used. Hay was obtained exclusively by cutting native grasses, and efforts to grow timothy and clover ended in failure. Available feed was limited in variety and often in quantity, yet the cost of transportation made it mandatory that the army obtain what it needed in the department.

Once the volunteer troops were pulled out of New Mexico the problem of securing feed theoretically became more manageable. Because the regulars were dispersed in comparatively small numbers at relatively permanent posts it was expected that sufficient feed could be obtained, but this was not always possible. In the autumn of 1848 corn was purchased from the farmers in small quantities for no more than $4 per fanega, but by the summer of 1849, some months before the new crop was ready to harvest, all of the corn between Santa Fe and Las Vegas as well as in the Pecos Valley had been consumed. The Post of Las Vegas, garrisoned at the time by one company of Third Infantry and one of New Mexico volunteers, had on hand only a twenty-day supply, if half rations were issued, and no more could be obtained "for any price." At Albuquerque, toward the end of March 1849, there was not enough fodder to be had within a twelve-mile radius to supply the post for more than one month. Prices had already increased and no improvement was expected before July.[61]

In late autumn of 1849, after the crops had been harvested and when prices were at their most favorable level, Captain Brent visited many of the posts. At all of them he found an ample supply of corn and fodder on hand. The corn had been acquired at prices ranging from $3 to $5 per fanega, the price increasing from north to south. Fodder, mostly cornstalks, had cost from $1.00 to $1.50 per hundred pounds. The Post of El Paso, from which San Elizario also drew its supplies, was an exception to the general picture. There, corn was obtained under contract in Chihuahua for $8.50 per fanega, shelled, sacked, and delivered. No long forage was available, but grass could be bought in sufficient quantity at $1.50 per hundred pounds.[62]

Prices for corn, wheat, and fodder increased further in the district around El Paso in 1850, and for an unusual reason. After the conclusion of peace with the United States, the Mexican government sought to induce Mexicans who resided in the newly ceded territory to migrate to Mexico. Mesilla was established in 1850 in what continued to be part of Chihuahua until the Gadsden Purchase of 1853. It was located west of the Rio Grande, a few miles south of Doña Ana, in an excellent agricultural region. Intended to attract Mexicans from the United States, it was reasonably successful in attaining an estimated population of nineteen hundred by 1852.[63]

The island below El Paso del Norte was one of the areas from which persons were persuaded to move. The drain was so great that if many more people moved all would go because there would be too few left to maintain the acequias that made agriculture possible. As a result of the migration crop production of all kinds declined. Locally grown cob corn sold for $6.50 per fanega and was relatively scarce. Adding to the problem, crop failure in Chihuahua reduced the amount of surplus corn, and the price rose to $10.50 and $11.00 per fanega and would go even higher. Captain William B. Johns of the Third Infantry, who commanded at San Èlizario, believed that if the quartermasters at the posts south of the Jornada del Muerto would estimate their corn needs for 1851 and offer a guaranteed price, the residents of the island would be encouraged to stay where they were and an adequate supply of corn would be assured.[64]

Prior to the summer of 1851 the army bought much of its corn from individuals who brought it to the posts. Often these transactions were quite small, involving only a few fanegas, and it may be assumed that in most cases the sellers were also the producers. The quartermaster's department also made use of agents, particularly when corn was scarce, to visit the towns and agricultural villages and purchase all that was available. This method of acquiring corn left the posts inadequately supplied. In 1850 Captain Brent estimated that the army would be able to buy only 78,435 bushels (31,370 fanegas) of corn in the entire department. In his opinion, the least expensive way to purchase corn was to buy it in small quantities directly from the farmers. When bids were called for in 1849 the lowest submitted was $4.75 per fanega, but by dealing directly with the farmer corn was obtained for a price ranging from $3.12 to $4.00 per fanega. Brent believed that unless a better system of supply was devised, it would never be possible to buy enough corn to feed more than one thousand public animals for less than $4 per fanega.[65]

The price of corn rose at all posts in 1850, ranging from a low of $3.50 per fanega at Taos to as much as $6.50 at Santa Fe and even higher at the Post of El Paso. Colonel McCall concluded that as a result of the reduced acreage planted in corn, "the amount saved in the Commissary Department by purchase (by contract) of New Mexican flour, if any, is perhaps doubly lost by the Quarter Master Department through the advanced price of corn." Another factor reducing the supply of corn available to the army was the purchases made by emigrants on their way to California. Finally, both 1850 and 1851 were drought years, limiting the yield of all field crops and greatly inhibiting the growth of native grasses.[66] John Greiner, recently appointed Indian agent, who arrived in New Mexico via the Santa Fe Trail in July 1851, noted that there had been "no rain scarcely in New Mexico for nearly a year, and the whole face of the country is dried up." Over a large area no grass had come up, the wheat crop was ruined, and, he predicted, the corn crop would be scant. By early summer of 1851 the price of corn had skyrocketed to between $5 and $15 per fanega.[67]

Cebolleta was the most difficult post to supply at this time. The inadequate spring rains of 1850, followed by a plague of grasshoppers in the summer, adversely affected all crops, and grain and grass were so scarce that it was necessary to send public animals miles away from the post to graze. The post quartermaster hauled 150 sacks of corn all the way from Socorro, the closest post that had any to spare. Captain and Brevet Lieutenant Colonel Daniel T. Chandler, Third Infantry, when he became post commander in September, turned to the western Indian pueblos. From Ácoma and Laguna he purchased for $3.50 per fanega all the corn the Indians were willing to sell. He noted that the quantity was small and that it was necessary to pay in silver on delivery.[68]

Henry L. Dodge,[69] who owned property and kept a store in Cebolleta and also acted as agent for the commissary and quartermaster's departments, went to Zuñi Pueblo in April 1851 and arranged to buy one thousand bags of corn. The corn was to be shelled by the Indians before the army sent a train to transport it to the post. An additional thousand bags were obtained later from the same pueblo. The corn acquired at Zuñi was paid for, at least in part, by an assortment of goods, the value of which was not stated. Still another thousand bags were hauled from the Rio Grande Valley, and Chandler hoped to get fifty bags at Cubero, apparently all the corn that could be purchased close to the post.[70]

Too little corn and forage were available in the department to meet requirements from one crop to the next. Once grass was up in the spring the army depended primarily on grazing, and that kept neither mounts nor work animals in fit condition for hard duty. Grazing camps were established at the very outset of the occupation. They were maintained almost continuously in the Galisteo Valley and less frequently in the vicinity of San Miguel and Las Vegas. In the spring of 1849 a grazing camp for beef cattle was established on Thomas Biggs's ranch, some fifteen miles south of Socorro.[71] Later in the year a separate camp for worn-down and surplus horses and mules was opened just outside Socorro, employing civilian herders under the supervision of a foragemaster.[72] During its short existence, the Post of Rayado was also a station for wintering surplus stock because of the superior grazing in the vicinity.

During the winter of 1849–50 the public animals in the camps near Socorro suffered considerably because insufficient forage was grown in the region to feed them adequately, and the little that was available was exorbitant in price.[73] Major and Brevet Lieutenant Colonel Thomas Swords, Quartermaster General's Department, obviously skeptical of the usefulness of the camps, wrote in 1851 that "although as high as two dollars and fifty cents per bushel was paid for corn, and some of it had to be hauled a distance of forty miles, this had been considered an advantageous place for keeping surplus stock." He also questioned the continued use of Rayado as a grazing camp because he believed it was too expensive. The corn needed to supplement grazing was brought across the mountains from Taos at a delivered cost of $6.25 per fanega.[74]

The first recorded contracts for any kind of feed produced in New Mexico were made in 1851. In March, Philip Shoaff was given a contract for four hundred tons of hay at $39.85 per ton for the Post of Socorro.[75]

The hay was native grass, cut, dried, and delivered by the contractor. A month later Edward Ownby was awarded a contract to deliver four hundred tons of hay at Cebolleta at $45 per ton for all hauled less than twenty-five miles and $50 for all hauled a greater distance.[76] Ownby established a camp near Ojo del Gallo and began putting up hay. On the night of July 12, 1851, the camp was attacked by a large party of Navajos who killed three of Ownby's employees, wounded eight others, and destroyed everything in the camp except the scythes and, strangely, the hay. Ownby appealed for protection, and a dragoon detachment was sent with all the horses from Cebolleta for the dual purpose of grazing the horses and protecting the hay cutting operation.[77]

Robert Nesbitt and Hiram R. Parker received a contract to furnish hay at Santa Fe and Abiquiu.[78] They established their camp in the Valle Grande, where, on the night of July 2, they were attacked by Navajos who drove off forty-three mules and six horses. Only one casualty was inflicted by the Indians, a camp guard wounded by an arrow. A detachment of dragoons left the Post of Abiquiu on the morning of July 3 but failed to overtake the Indians. However, a small party of Jemez Pueblo Indians was more successful. They caught up with the Navajos, killed two of them, and recovered five mules.[79] As the hay camp was only some thirty miles from Abiquiu, the army considered it unnecessary to provide closer protection.

Still another contract was made with Tomás Ortiz of Santa Fe County and Domingo Baca of Santa Ana County—one of the few feed contracts made with Spanish Americans—to deliver twenty thousand arrobas of grass and fodder in equal parts at four different locations along the road between Albuquerque and Santa Fe, for 50 cents per arroba.[80] Lieutenant Colonel and Brevet Colonel Edwin Vose Sumner, First Dragoons,[81] who assumed command of the department in the summer of 1851, branded the Ortiz and Baca contract, which he referred to as a contract for cornstalks, "the worst transaction in New Mexico." Less than half the quantity called for had been delivered and he was reluctant to pay even for that.[82] Other contracts were made to supply hay for the posts of Albuquerque and Rayado. Most of the contracts, none of them more than half-filled, were cancelled shortly after Sumner took command, with some compensation given to the contractors.[83]

It is not surprising that meat, long New Mexico's chief export, occupied only a distant third position in military purchases of local products. The army's demand for pork and beef could not be met. Mutton was purchased occasionally under contract, sometimes because nothing else was available and sometimes for the convenience of moving sheep on the hoof. The only record of pork acquired in New Mexico was of imported bacon purchased from local merchants to fill temporary shortages. Some bacon was available in Old Mexico, but it was considered too poor in quality for issue to the troops. The problem of providing pork for the army could not be solved locally; hence, the cost of pork remained high.

The reduction of troop strength at the war's end temporarily relieved the difficulty of obtaining fresh meat. In June 1848 a contract was given to Benjamin F. Read[84] to furnish mutton for nine months at 6^1/$_2$ cents per pound. When the contract expired it was replaced by one with James H. Quinn and Lucien B. Maxwell to provide fresh beef for nine months at 8 cents per pound. Very probably the beef came from the Rayado Valley. In 1851 Alex Duvall received a one-year contract for beef at 14 cents per pound.[85] This was the last long-term contract made for meat or meat animals in the department until 1860, although the army continued to buy cattle and sheep, as it always had, in individual transactions. Cattle were sometimes available in surprising numbers, as in January 1850, when a total of more than a thousand head were acquired from four suppliers.[86] After Forts Defiance and Webster were established in 1851 sheep bought in the Rio Grande Valley were regularly driven to both posts, usually in flocks of about five hundred head.[87]

Although some beef cattle were always available in New Mexico, Thomas insisted that none of them were fit for issue to the troops and urged that all beef cattle be driven from Missouri. Not only would this assure an improved quality of meat but, he said, it would reduce the cost by half.[88] His recommendations were apparently heeded because most of the beef cattle were driven from the East. These cattle, once delivered, were turned over, under contract, to private individuals to be herded, grazed, and eventually slaughtered. In both 1852 and 1853 contracts were made at Fort Leavenworth for beef cattle to be delivered at Fort Union. The price in 1852 was a reasonable 4^{84}/$_{100}$ cents per pound on the hoof, but in 1853 it jumped to 8^{89}/$_{100}$ cents.[89] Even at that price beef was cheaper than salt meat, but it was expensive enough to make a local supply desirable.

It had long been known that the country east of the Rocky Mountains was excellent for nourishing horses and cattle if they could be protected from Indian depredations. As soon as the United States placed garrisons at Las Vegas and on the Rayado cattle ranching expanded along the eastward and southeastward flowing streams from the Cimarron in the north to the Pecos and Gallinas in the south. Although the growth of the area was not spectacular it was substantial. In 1854, sometime after the troops had been withdrawn from the Rayado, a group of Taos citizens petitioned to have military protection restored to the Rayado Valley because they had there "more than one hundred thousand dollars worth of stock of different kinds," which were entirely at the mercy of the Indians.[90] By that date the region had become the principal local source of beef for the commissary department. A company of dragoons was sent to the Rayado, where Maxwell provided all the necessary facilities free of charge in return for the protection afforded, but the troops remained for only a month.[91]

The southern posts always obtained part of their beef from other sources. In 1849 a contract was made with Frank White of Frontera, Texas, to furnish the newly founded Post of El Paso with beef at 9 cents per pound.[92] The following year bids were solicited, but there were no takers. The drought then affecting the Southwest had greatly curtailed grazing and with it the availability of beef. White offered to continue supplying beef without a contract at 12 1/2 cents per pound, but he could not guarantee a specific quantity.[93] As a result, arrangements were made with the commissary department at San Antonio to furnish some beef, with the cattle driven from San Antonio and sometimes arriving in the department with very little advance notice.[94] Even though Texas cattle helped to feed the southern posts, cattle also came from the government herd in New Mexico.

Despite the relatively high cost of fresh beef and the shortages which sometimes occurred, no long-term contracts were made for mutton after 1848, probably because sheep were always available. In 1850, when the drought made it difficult to keep cattle in fit shape to be slaughtered, instructions were issued to substitute mutton for beef in the ration.[95] It is impossible to determine the number of sheep purchased by the army, but it was not enough to replace the market lost by the disruption of trade with Chihuahua, and it had little if any effect on price. The value of New Mexican sheep did increase sharply as a result of the opening of a new market in California, where the gold rush rapidly depleted California's own supply of meat animals. The demand for meat and the premium price paid for it attracted herds and flocks from as far away as Ohio and provided the New Mexican sheep raisers with the first genuinely lucrative market for their animals. In 1849 sheep brought as much as $25 per head in California and, in 1850, from $12 to $16 in the vicinity of the gold fields and $8 in southern California. The price declined further in 1852, and by 1854 $5 per head was an average offer.[96] As a result of the demand in California the value of a sheep in New Mexico was about $2.50 by the mid-fifties.

Aside from flour and fresh meat, there was comparatively little that New Mexico had to offer that formed part of the prescribed ration, and those items that were available were largely ignored in the early years. In the fall of 1848 a contract was made to deliver to the general depot in Santa Fe 500 bushels of salt at $2.00 per bushel and 2,500 gallons of vinegar at $1.25 per gallon.[97] The following year bids were requested for 3,000 bushels of salt, 3,000 bushels of white field beans, 20,000 pounds of candles, and 1,500 gallons of cider vinegar.[98]

White field beans and cider vinegar were not available in New Mexico, at least not in the quantities desired. A contract was made with William C. Skinner of Peralta to provide 5,000 pounds of tallow candles, increased almost immediately to 15,000 pounds, at 30 cents per pound. As soon as a supply of better-quality candles was received from Fort Leavenworth, the tallow candles were turned over to the quartermaster's department to be used not as candles but as rather expensive tallow.[99] Several contracts were made in 1849 and 1850 for salt, and some beans were acquired under contract, but additional quantities of all of the items sought in New Mexico were shipped from Fort Leavenworth.[100]

The salt purchased by the army came from the salt beds east of the Manzano Mountains in the present Torrance County. It was described as too coarse, but the New Mexican vinegar, which was wine rather than cider, was considered excellent. Beans were grown throughout New Mexico, but like wheat and corn, there had been little surplus production. In the spring of 1852 a contract was drawn up with Samuel Ellison and William J. Davy[101] of Santa Fe for 1,000 bushels of "beans or frijoles," half to be delivered at Santa Fe and the rest at Albuquerque and Socorro. The army agreed to pay $3 per bushel but, before the contractors could plant, the subsistence department had to provide them with 12 bushels of beans to use as seed. The saving in the cost of beans was excellent because "new white field beans" delivered at Fort Leavenworth cost $1.75 per bushel in 1851, which meant that, with transportation added, the army paid $6.00 or more for the beans freighted to Santa Fe. On the other hand, some local beans were purchased on the open market in 1850 at $1.50 and $2.00 per bushel, but not in sufficient quantities to fill army needs.[102] Although the army found no fault with New Mexican beans, no beans were again purchased by contract until 1857.

The savings resulting from purchasing New Mexican products were more than offset by the growing number of troops stationed in the department, by the increase in civilian employees for whom rations were provided, and by special demands. First Lieutenant John C. McFerran, who succeeded Thomas as chief commissary for the department, originally submitted an estimate for the fiscal year 1851–52 that called for 927,860 rations.[103] Of the required components only the larger part of the flour and some of the fresh meat were to be acquired in New Mexico. In addition to the items making up the regular ration, McFerran requisitioned molasses, authorized for occasional issue; whiskey, which could be issued under special conditions, such as excessive fatigue and exposure; hams, sperm candles, lard, dried peaches, and buckwheat (these for "sales to officers only"); and pickles, dried apples, and sauerkraut, which, by regulation, could only be issued to the sick in hospitals but in New Mexico were issued as antiscorbutics. The requisitions allowed for a 10 percent "probable wasteage" for most items. Despite the existing flour contracts, McFerran called for the importation of 700,000 pounds of flour, some for the use of officers and some to cover possible deficiencies in delivery by the contractors. He also provided for an unspecified number of beef cattle to be driven from the States.[104]

By 1851 the saving achieved by purchasing in New Mexico had been negligible, and the effect was more important to New Mexico's economy than to the military budget. Transportation costs remained high, and there was the growing belief that everything available in New Mexico, not only supplies but rentals and civilian labor, was more expensive than it should be; hence, all expenditures were considered subject to appreciable reduction. The rising cost of rented facilities soon became one of the principal arguments advanced for removing garrisons from the towns and putting them in government-owned posts.

At all of the posts in the department there were rental costs, although they varied greatly from one to another. Quarters, storehouses, corrals, hospitals, rooms for laundresses, guardhouses, and everything else required by the military were rented. Even in Santa Fe and San Elizario, where government-owned buildings were adequate for most purposes, rooms were rented as quarters for officers. Elsewhere entire houses were leased to serve as barracks; in Albuquerque, for example, one house of six rooms and another of seven accommodated a company each. In Santa Fe a slaughterhouse and cattle pens were set up on property leased by the commissary department. A group of citizens promptly petitioned to have the slaughterhouse removed from "the heart of the city," stating that it was "offensive" and was "thought to be dangerous to the health of the city."[105] When New Mexico was erected into a territory and James

S. Calhoun became territorial governor,[106] Colonel Munroe and his adjutant moved out of the Palace of the Governors into quarters rented from Gertrudis Barceló, for which the government paid $60 per month.

At the posts of El Paso and Rayado facilities were rented exclusively from Anglo-Americans. In 1851 at Santa Fe the cost of rentals from Anglos came to $526 per month, and that from Spanish Americans amounted to $233. Some of the Anglos had long resided in Santa Fe, and some were naturalized Mexican citizens; most, however, were newcomers. The quarters rented for Surgeon Charles McDougall were owned by the ambitious Captain Alexander W. Reynolds, who had engaged in real estate speculation from the time he was transferred to the department.[107] At other posts (where information is available), the rented property was largely, and in some cases exclusively, owned by Spanish Americans. In most of its arrangements with property owners the army agreed to make repairs and additions at its own expense, with these to revert without cost to the owner when the army moved out. Critics of military expenditures were quick to note that the cost of restoring a building to useable condition frequently exceeded its original value.

Table 2
Facilities Rented in Department, 1849–1851[108]

Post	1849	1850	1851
Santa Fe	—	$180 per month	$759 per month
Abiquiu	—	183	280
Taos	—	120	135
Las Vegas	—	260	439
Rayado	—	200	283.33
Albuquerque	$337 per month	165	275 and 391
Socorro	212	—	290
Doña Ana	170	260	362
El Paso	250	350	410
San Elizario	75	45	($5 per room)

Records of rent paid at Cebolleta have not been located.

Another area in which expenses constantly rose was the employment of civilian personnel, and this too became a target for economy. Civilians were hired to fill a variety of jobs. The largest category of employees was teamsters, who in 1851 were paid $22 per month each. Among the others were common laborers, cooks (for civilian employees), masons, carpenters, blacksmiths, wheelwrights, saddlers, and expressmen. Highest paid were a clerk and a foragemaster, $100 per month and a ration each. Because Santa Fe was the general depot for the department many more civilians were employed there than elsewhere, particularly by the quartermaster's department. The 1850 census listed more than 160 individuals employed by the army in Santa Fe. For most of them the place of birth was not recorded, but not one had a Spanish surname. In July 1851, 134 civilians worked for the quartermaster's department in Santa Fe, 19 of them located at points away from the post.[109] At that time the only positions held by Spanish Americans were as herdsmen, while one or two were hired as common laborers.

Agents constituted a small but important class of quartermaster's department employees. They were entrusted with purchasing corn, fodder, and other commodities, and with renting facilities, supervising storage, and a variety of other tasks. Some of the agents were stationed in settlements where there were no posts, such as Peñasco, Algodones, La Joya, and San Miguel, where they were employed primarily to buy and to store feed. Agents were also hired at some posts where their duties tended to be somewhat broader. The commissary department hired a few agents but more commonly made use of the same individuals who served as quartermaster's agents. Where separate commissary agents were employed they were paid $30 per month.[110]

The number of civilian employees, particularly teamsters, laborers, and herders, varied almost from day to day. Complete records for the fiscal year 1850–51 have not been found, but in Santa Fe alone more than $50,000 was paid in salaries to civilians, and in the rest of the department the cost was probably between $10,000 and $20,000. Also entering into the civilian economy were the payments made to spies, guides, and, when called into service, volunteer troops. The spies and guides were paid regularly (their pay was a responsibility of the quartermaster's department), but the volunteers had to await congressional appropriations, which were sometimes delayed for years.

The death of President Zachary Taylor on July 9, 1850, had a considerable impact on New Mexico and even more on the policies which were to prevail in the Ninth Military Department. Whether it kept New Mexico from becoming a state in 1850, as many advocates of statehood chose to assume, is doubtful. Certainly Millard Fillmore had less personal involvement with the territory acquired from Mexico than had his predecessor. Taylor, a career army man, had played a prominent part in securing the Mexican cession for the United States and had been elected president as a result. As president he retained his interest in the well-being of the army, with whose problems he was so familiar. Fillmore, by contrast, was a civilian who had never served in the armed forces. His accession to the presidency was followed by a number of cabinet changes. Replacing Taylor's Secretary of War was Charles M. Conrad, who, like Fillmore, was without military experience. It was only natural that the new administration adopted a different attitude toward the army, one considered by many military men as lacking in understanding of their needs and best interests.

The Fillmore administration was devoted to economy, and it viewed the military establishment as a logical place where economy could be applied. In his efforts to reduce expenditures, Conrad issued General Orders No. 1 for the year 1851, a document much criticized as an attempt to turn soldiers into farmers. The orders contained two main clauses. First, "to promote the health of the troops, and to reduce the expense of subsisting the army," post gardens were to be planted at all permanent posts where land was available or could be leased on reasonable terms. Hopefully, enough vegetables would be raised to supply the troops and the post hospitals throughout the year. Second, in the western departments, at all posts "as may be designated by department commanders," post farms were to be cultivated by the troops to raise grains for bread, forage, and long forage.

The orders authorized "all necessary expenditures for the farm cultivation" and provided that commanders of posts where farms were undertaken would "adopt all necessary measures to carry it on successfully." Each July they were to report the condition of their crops and each October the quantity of their harvests. The products of farm and garden which were part of the ration, or which were used as feed, would be purchased by the commissary and quartermaster's departments of the posts. In New Mexico they would be paid for at prevailing St. Louis prices. From the amount received all costs would be deducted; then the rest, the profit, would be distributed among the enlisted men at the post. The post commander would be held responsible "for any improper management, or loss not strictly unavoidable."[111] Farming, then, was not something to be carried out when military duties permitted but was itself a military duty. Conrad hoped that the result would be an appreciable reduction in army expenses and that the profit-sharing plan would make the program popular with the men.

There was some reason to expect that post farms would save money for the army. For many years a successful farm had been cultivated at

Fort Leavenworth. In 1850 it showed a profit of $6,300 and produced, among other crops, 18,000 bushels of wheat and 1,200 bushels of Irish potatoes.[112] Both Commissary General George Gibson and Quartermaster General Thomas S. Jesup had advocated agriculture at all posts as early as December 1847, even before the Mexican War ended. They also recommended that civilians be encouraged to settle near the posts and that they be granted land on condition that they "cultivate such grain & grasses as may be suitable for the subsistence of troops & the support of horses and other animals in the public service."[113] Hence, Conrad had both precedent and support for his farming program.

When Colonel John Munroe received the orders toward the end of February 1851, he apparently assumed that his department would not be expected to participate in the farm program and addressed himself only to the matter of kitchen gardens. Even in these he saw no great urgency because he anticipated difficulties for which he did not feel empowered to seek a solution without proper authorization. Virtually all of the troops were stationed in towns where, he believed, they were not within convenient distance of land available to them for cultivation. Munroe offered a deceptively simple solution: Move the troops to locations where land was available and establish new posts. He noted that "the rent already paid for quarters since our Troops have occupied the Territory would nearly have accomplished these ends." The government, he said, paid in rent each year from 25 to 50 percent of the value of the buildings it occupied; yet wood and adobe, the principal building materials necessary to erect its own facilities, could be obtained almost anywhere at little cost other than the labor of troops. Once the army was in its own posts there would still remain two problems not encountered in the East. Irrigation systems would have to be provided, and most of the garden seeds would have to be imported. The solution thus outlined seemed to pose no insuperable difficulties and implied a saving in expense, an appealing thought to an economy-minded War Department.

Analyzing the existing distribution of troops from a military-agricultural point of view, Munroe believed that ten of the eleven posts were properly positioned and that if the government decided to replace them the new posts should be in the same general areas. Taos was an exception in one respect. The post was not required for defense against the Indians as long as Abiquiu and Rayado were garrisoned, but it should be kept up for "civil considerations." Munroe suggested that the eleventh post, that at Socorro, be replaced by a post at Valverde. He was certain that new locations embracing as much arable land as was desired could be found for all of the proposed posts. Even more important as an economy measure, he recommended that the general depot be moved from Santa Fe to the vicinity of Las Vegas or Barclay's Fort,[114] thus appreciably reducing the cost of transportation to the department.[115]

Having expressed his opinion of the feasibility of the agricultural program, Munroe did nothing to implement it at any of the existing posts. He did take some steps to further his own recommendations. He ordered a survey of the area east of the Sangre de Cristo Mountains to select a suitable site for a depot and to determine whether the Post of Rayado was properly located. In both cases the proximity of cultivable land was to be a consideration. The officers entrusted with the examination selected a position on the west bank of the Gallinas River, "about one mile above Upper Vegas Town," as the best location for a depot because it was central to the grain-growing areas; the Gallinas was deemed superior for powering mills, and an abundance of building material was close at hand. Admittedly, there was no land available for a post farm, but an extensive post garden could be planted. The report ended with the gratuitous opinion that "a worse position than Santa Fé could not be selected in the whole 9th Military Department for a General Depôt."[116]

The gardening and farming program applied to the entire West, but nowhere would it be attempted as extensively as in New Mexico. Colonel Munroe's failure to carry out Conrad's orders had the effect of delaying their application in the department for a full year. His belief that farming was not feasible at the existing posts had much to justify it, but land suitable for gardens was available near most of them, particularly because Conrad had authorized the leasing of land for the purpose. Munroe failed to act, but his successor would pursue all aspects of the economy program with the utmost vigor.

4

꒰ᔆᕕᨳ꒱ ꒰ᔆᕕᨳ꒱ ꒰ᔆᕕᨳ꒱

The Economy Years

On April 1, 1851, Secretary of War Conrad issued instructions to Colonel Edwin Vose Sumner, newly designated commander of the Ninth Military Department. The instructions indicated the concern of the War Department with the cost of maintaining troops in New Mexico and with the relative lack of success in establishing control over the Indians. Sumner was enjoined to carry out changes intended to provide more efficient protection at less cost. When he reached the department he was to "revise the whole system of defence," determining particularly whether the existing posts were satisfactory, which Conrad obviously doubted. "The [War] Department is induced to believe, that both economy and efficiency of the service would be promoted by removing the troops out of the towns where they are now stationed, and stationing them more towards the frontier and nearer to the Indians."

If new posts were established the locations were to be determined with three things in mind: the treaty obligations to prevent Indians from crossing from the United States to commit depredations in Mexico; the protection of New Mexico; and "economy and facility in supporting the troops, particularly in regard to forage, fuel, and adaptation of the surrounding country to cultivation." Finally, Sumner was directed to make "every effort to reduce the enormous expenditures of the army in New Mexico, particularly in the quartermaster's and subsistence departments." He was ordered to scrutinize the administration of these departments and to "rigidly enforce all regulations having reference to the economy of the service."[1] As a further measure to reduce expenses, Colonel Thomas Swords accompanied Sumner to New Mexico to inspect and to bring about reforms in the quartermaster's department.

Colonel Sumner left Fort Leavenworth on May 26, escorted by a detachment of dragoons and infantry recruits. In his party were four young civilians, three farmers and a machinist, each employed at $65 a month plus a ration. Sumner justified the somewhat unusual outlay on the ground that he had a number of large farms to establish and operate "by a system of cultivation altogether new" to New Mexico; that is, by the farming methods of the well-watered East. The three farmers, with their practical knowledge, would provide the troops with an example of proper agricultural practices. The machinist was necessary, Sumner explained without further elaboration, to set up and run "the Mills, and other machinery."[2]

Sumner sought the reduction of expenses with a vigor that made a virtual fetish of economy. Expenditures in some categories were temporarily reduced; but it was a questionable economy that hampered efficiency, led to shoddy results, and, in the long run, increased costs. Sumner had been with General Kearny in New Mexico in 1846, and apprently he determined the broad aspects of departmental reorganization before he reached Santa Fe on July 19. He did not conduct an examination to select the most suitable locations for posts, nor did he await the recommendations which might result from Colonel Swords's inspection. On the very day that he arrived in Santa Fe Sumner transferred the headquarters and general depot to the Mora River and ordered all military stores then in Santa Fe moved to the new location at once. At the new site the public property was placed under canvas and was soon damaged by the weather.[3] Sumner's own often quoted explanation for the precipitate action was that "my first step was to break up the post of Santa Fé, that sink of vice and extravagance."[4] Actually, the post was not broken up, for one company of artillery remained behind. Even so, the removal of headquarters and the depot had a dulling effect on business activity in Santa Fe.

Before the close of 1851 Sumner ordered the abandonment of the posts of Las Vegas, Rayado, Abiquiu, Socorro, Cebolleta,[5] Albuquerque, Doña Ana, San Elizario, and El Paso. The citizens of the towns involved objected strongly to the execution of the order. There is no question that most of them welcomed the protection afforded by the presence of the troops, but even more, they recognized the economic advantages. In most cases, when the garrisons were withdrawn small detachments remained behind temporarily to protect public property. To replace the abandoned posts Sumner established nine new posts, six of them considered to be permanent. The sites were chosen, according to Sumner, "with a view to cultivation as well as the defence of the frontier." All of the posts were built by the troops, and their cost was held to a minimum.[6]

Alexander Barclay, an Englishman by birth and at one time chief factor at Bent's Fort, purchased rights to the John Scolly (La Junta) Grant in March 1848. Later in the year he began constructing his imposing adobe trading post, "under the expectation of selling it to the government as a military post."[7] Barclay engaged in extensive agricultural activities on the land adjacent to his fort, planting a wide variety of vegetables and grains, including some not previously raised in New Mexico. He also set out an orchard and vineyard and erected a small gristmill.[8] Barclay later sold a half interest in the property to Joseph B. Doyle, a Virginian who was married to a daughter of Barclay's common-law wife.[9] The establishment of Fort Union destroyed Barclay's hope of selling his establishment to the army, but his successful operation may have influenced Sumner's choice of a site for the post and the army's largest farming operation.

Sumner intended Fort Union to be the most important post in the department. It was located on Coyote (Wolf) Creek, an affluent of the Mora River, near the point where the two branches of the Santa Fe Trail came together and in country frequently traversed by the Jicarilla Apaches and less commonly by Utes and Comanches. The surrounding area was watered by a number of streams, afforded excellent grazing, and appeared to be suited to farming. The Scolly Grant overlaid the Mora Grant in the vicinity of Fort Union. Both grants had been confirmed by the United States Congress, but neither had been surveyed; and Sumner mistakenly, though understandably, decided that the post was on Scolly land. Hence, it was from the claimants of the Scolly Grant that he obtained a twenty-year lease of one square mile for five dollars.[10] A dispute developed at once between the army, on one hand, and Barclay and Doyle, on the other, over water usage and the size of the reserve, which Sumner unilaterally and without additional compensation enlarged to eight miles square.[11] After a number of incidents that reflected little credit on either side, Barclay and Doyle instituted a series of suits for trespass and ejectment.[12] The army lost all of the cases and, as a result, signed a new lease with Barclay and Doyle, agreeing to pay what it considered the exorbitant sum of twelve hundred dollars per year for as long as it made use of the property.[13] The outcome was ironical, considering that the Fort Union reserve, even after it was expanded, was located entirely on the Mora Grant and not on land belonging to Barclay and Doyle. However, the specific location of the Scolly Grant was not finally determined until 1893, two years after Fort Union was deactivated.[14]

Three new forts were established in September 1851. Fort Conrad was built on the west bank of the Rio Grande, about twenty-five miles below Socorro and ten miles above the northern end of the Jornada del Muerto. Grazing was reasonably good in the area; and the cottonwood trees, useable though not particularly suitable for fuel and construction, grew in considerable numbers in the river bottom. As soon as an acequia was dug to bring water from the river it was expected that a satisfactory farm and garden could be developed. Here again, the reserve was on privately claimed land, the Pedro Armendáriz Grant; more specifically, it was on that portion of the grant claimed by Hugh N. Smith and Thomas Biggs. Neither the grant, dating from the close of the Spanish period, nor the Smith-Biggs claim had been surveyed, and Sumner did not arrange with the claimants to use the land set aside for a reservation.[15]

Fort Fillmore was erected on the east bank of the Rio Grande, some six miles below Mesilla and facing what was still Mexican territory. The site was in the area known as the "Cotton Wood." Sumner, perhaps rendered cautious by the presence of a name, instructed Major Gouverneur Morris, Third Infantry, who established the post, to learn if there was a claimant to the land, and, if there was, to secure written permission for the army to occupy one square mile for twenty years without paying rent. If suitable timber was available, the troops were to erect log buildings, "as they were quicker built, and much cheaper."[16]

Major Morris was reluctant to move his command from Coons' Ranch, possibly because the thought of engaging in agriculture was distasteful to him. He sent Sumner a most attractive proposal made by Benjamin Coons, who offered to let the army have the quarters already occupied free of rent for one year and to provide additional land on which to construct additional buildings; he would also provide two hundred acres suitable for a farm "free of all charges and rents" for twenty years, with the privilege of purchase at the expiration of that time.[17] Moreover, Morris had learned that the entire valley south of Doña Ana was subject to overflow, thus rendering the land useless for agriculture and probably making the site unhealthful. "And lastly every portion and parcel of the soil is so perfectly saturated with saline matter called by the Mexicans 'Tequesquite' and salitre that I doubt whether it can be rendered suitable for cultivation."[18]

Sumner was unmoved, probably influenced by the report of Major Electus Backus, Third Infantry, Morris's predecessor as commander of the Post of El Paso. Backus had described Coons' Ranch as neither defensible nor comfortable, excessively expensive, and lacking in land for farming.[19] Morris obtained from Hugh Stephenson and his wife, the claimants to the land, a twenty-year lease of one square mile for ten cents a year, "together with the protection of being thus occupied by a military post." All improvements made by the army were to revert to the lessors when the post was abandoned.[20] Sumner did leave a detachment of twenty men and an officer when the Post of El Paso was broken up. They were quartered at Magoffinsville, the establishment of James W. Magoffin, where, at Sumner's stipulation, no rent was paid.[21] The detachment was decimated by constant desertions and was withdrawn to Fort Fillmore early in September 1852.[22]

Finally, in September 1851, during the course of his expedition into Navajo country, Sumner established Fort Defiance. It was located in Cañoncito Bonito, deep in Navajo territory and isolated from areas of settlement and sources of supply. There was good grazing within reasonable distance for a limited number of animals but no land suitable for extensive farming. Springs provided an adequate water supply for the post and limited water for irrigation. Fort Defiance's closest neighbor was the pueblo of Zuñi, 50 miles to the south, while the nearest Spanish American settlements were Cubero and Cebolleta, 100 miles to the east but almost 150 miles by the existing road. The post had one purpose, to curb Navajo depredations, which for generations had ravaged both the European and the Pueblo Indian in the settled portions of New Mexico. Sumner realized that Fort Defiance would be difficult and expensive to maintain, but if it achieved its purpose the saving in lives and property would more than justify the cost.

The final post established in 1851 was inherited rather than erected. Early in the century the Santa Rita copper deposits were discovered; and a private fortification, triangular in shape with towers at the three corners, was built to protect the miners from the Apache Indians. The mines were worked intermittently, as the Apaches permitted; and the fort, strongly constructed of stone and adobe, remained in a reasonable state of preservation.[23] The United States–Mexico boundary commission, with its escort of one undermanned company of Third Infantry, occupied the old post throughout much of 1851. When the commission moved on Major Morris was ordered to occupy the position. Toward the end of 1851, one company of infantry and one of dragoons took post at what was soon designated Fort Webster, in honor of Secretary of State Daniel Webster.[24]

Morris was no more interested in farming at Fort Webster than he had been at Fort Fillmore. As the spring of 1852 approached, he informed Sumner there was so little water available that the results would probably be negligible. "Still," he wrote, "I will plant, and trust to the genial influence of the earth for a crop." Looking to the future, he predicted that as soon as the nearer towns in Chihuahua and Sonora learned of the establishment of the fort they would bring their surplus produce to sell and that the post would be provided with all the supplies it required "at a moderate cost, much less than at any place on the Rio Abajo."[25] A month later Morris entered into a contract with a civilian to open up a farm on the Rio Mimbres, which, he said, would cause the "country to become improved, cultivated and settled."[26]

Sumner rejected the contract; but at the end of May 1852, Morris proposed that the post be moved to the Mimbres Valley, where water was ample, the land better for cultivation and settlement, and the country so open that there was less danger that Indians would run off government stock. He also claimed, with some exaggeration, that the move would greatly reduce the distance to Fort Fillmore and would avoid the worst portion of the road.[27] This was important because the cost of transporting army stores from Fort Fillmore to Fort Webster topped $5,500 in the first half of 1852.[28] Sumner acquiesced, and toward the beginning of September 1852 the post was relocated on the Rio Mimbres about fourteen miles northeast of the original site.

If he had achieved nothing else, Morris had avoided farming for the entire season. In November he was transferred to the command of Fort Union and was replaced at Fort Webster by Captain and Brevet Major Enoch Steen, Second Dragoons.[29] Steen, who was no more enamored with farming than Morris had been, proposed that the farm be worked by contract labor; for, he informed Sumner, "as you are well aware, soldiers are but bad farmers at best, even in countries better adapted to cultivation than New Mexico." He also asked for a sawmill and a gristmill, the latter to grind corn meal to be issued in lieu of flour.[30]

Sumner had become disenchanted with the continued objections raised by his officers. He informed Steen:

> the cultivation of a good farm by your command, [is] next in importance after the preservation of discipline at your post, and quiet among the Indians. If, in addition to the above important duties, you may have time to devote to the improvement of your quarters, no objection, of course, will be urged to your doing so; but the Col. Commdg. cannot authorize such improvements or even permit them, if they are to interfere in any degree with your farming operations.

Sumner did not send a sawmill to Fort Webster; but he recommended that Steen "get along by pit sawing," the method employed at all of the posts in the department except Fort Union.[31] He did not deign to mention the gristmill. Sumner was not inclined to pamper his men. If pit sawing increased the appetite the ration was fixed so no additional expense was incurred.

Sumner had intended to establish a fort in the San Luis Valley (in what was then Ute country) before the end of 1851, but the approach of winter delayed him until the following spring. It must be said that in establishing five forts in fewer than six months, in supplying them, and in making them habitable, at least by loose definition, he displayed commendable zeal. His final fort, Fort Massachusetts, was established in June 1852 by Major George A. H. Blake, First Dragoons, with one company of dragoons and one of infantry. It was located in a sheltered valley on Ute Creek near the southeastern base of Blanca Peak in the present Colorado, about eighty-five miles north of Taos but separated from it by rugged terrain. The closest settlements were Costilla, on the present New Mexico line, and the beginnings of a little agricultural community near the later San Luis, Colorado. A ten-mile square reserve was set aside for the post.[32] Both Fort Massachusetts and its successor, Fort Garland, were on the extensive Sangre de Cristo Grant, later rejected *in toto,* and no arrangements were made with the claimants for the use of the land.

Fort Massachusetts was in most regards a difficult post. It was situated at an altitude of more than eight thousand feet in a region where the growing season was very short and the winters intensely cold. The trail— it could scarcely be called a road—from Taos to the San Luis Valley was extremely poor. So little grass grew along much of the route that Blake recommended that pack mules rather than ox trains be used for transportation. Near the post, there were large stands of pine timber and abundant water, but only restricted grazing and not enough grass to cut for hay. Blake did not like the site but considered it the best in the general area.[33] Both farming and gardening were to prove all but impossible because of the limited growing season. Nevertheless, Sumner instructed Blake to obtain agricultural implements from Fort Union, sending his own transportation to pick them up if necessary. Blake was expected to raise most of the grain required by the post.[34] In addition to its other drawbacks, Fort Massachusetts proved to be unhealthful.

Aside from the "permanent" forts, Sumner established three posts which were as permanent as the other six. The Taos Valley—with its agricultural importance, its ostensible vulnerability to Indian depredations, and the army's mistrust of its people since the uprising of 1847—inevitably became the site for a garrison. Colonel Sumner visited Fort Massachusetts in August 1852, and on his return he stopped at Taos long enough to instruct Second Lieutenant Robert Ransom, First Dragoons, to establish Cantonment Burgwin.[35] The site selected by Sumner was in the foothills of the Sangre de Cristos, on the Rio Grande del Rancho about three miles upstream from St. Vrain's gristmill, and on the highly important wagon road connecting Santa Fe and Taos.

Because it was not intended to be permanent Cantonment Burgwin did not participate in the farming program. Other than wood and native grass, cut and stacked by the men, the garrison had no part in providing its own supplies.[36] Like so many of Sumner's posts Cantonment Burgwin was on private land, the Rancho del Rio Grande Grant, which dated from 1795.[37] The citizens of Ranchos de Taos, who claimed the land, petitioned the territorial legislature to restore it to them, offering documentary proof of their ownership. However, Lieutenant Ransom insisted that he had examined all official papers at Ranchos de Taos and had found no evidence that the land had ever been granted to anyone.[38] Nothing further was done by the claimants to recover the land during the life of the post.

Although Sumner had transferred department headquarters to Fort Union even before the post was actually established, he spent much of his time elsewhere. On New Year's Day of 1852, he announced that it was "indispensably necessary" to move his headquarters to Albuquerque "in order to be nearer the new posts in the indian country."[39] He had already asked Henry Winslow to examine all available properties to determine whether suitable facilities could be obtained at "reasonable rates." Sumner was most interested in the Thomas Ranch, where the land had been broken the previous fall, undoubtedly an asset in view of the current interest in agriculture.[40]

On December 28, 1851, Sumner leased the Thomas Ranch for one year for $400.[41] With the coming of spring he planted a farm and garden on thirty acres of land. To supervise the project he employed a civilian farmer, who also served as his interpreter, paying him $30 per month and a ration. In addition, he hired an unspecified number of laborers as temporary help. Sumner appeared to take great pride in his small agricultural enterprise, viewing it, perhaps, as a model for his subordinates to emulate. When he went to Santa Fe in May 1852, he left strict instructions regarding the vegetables: "do not allow anything to be gathered by any one but the gardner."[42]

Sumner's final post came about almost by chance. In October 1851, two companies of dragoons were detached from Fort Union to take post in the Galisteo Valley, where Sumner set up a grazing station for mounted troops engaged in escorting trains to and from Fort Defiance. However, when the pasturage proved insufficient for two companies he instructed Captain Richard S. Ewell, First Dragoons, to move his company either to Los Lunas or Sabinal. Ewell was to choose between the two on the basis of "good winter quarters and sufficient forage at reasonable prices." Sumner originally intended to occupy the station only until the following spring. Ewell took post at Los Lunas in January 1852, renting quarters for the men, a corral, and storehouses for $25 per month and quarters for the officers at $10 per month per officer. At the time corn was available in the district for $3 per fanega and forage for 75 cents per hundred pounds.[43]

Los Lunas was not involved in the farming program, but Ewell planted an extensive garden on rented land in the spring of 1852. When his company was ordered temporarily to Albuquerque he asked permission to leave at least one man behind because he had "a large quantity of onions, beets & cabbages sown there," as well as some other vegetables. He hoped, if nothing else, to recover seed to plant the next year. As it was, many of his men were suffering from scurvy because of a lack of fresh vegetables.[44]

Ewell was back at Los Lunas in June, and a month later he wrote to his brother that the garden was "coming on finely." He was "delightfully fixed just now, cows, chickens, etc., and I make my own butter and all that sort of thing, as comfortably as any farmer." In the same letter he remarked, "I am only afraid Colonel Sumner will find out how luxuriously I am living and will move me away before I reap the full benefit of my garden and grapes, for I have hired a vineyard which promises to yield finely." Ewell probably had a more genuine interest in agriculture than did Sumner. He continued to experiment with gardening as long as he was stationed in the Southwest.[45]

Once reoccupied, Los Lunas was garrisoned until 1860. It was in a good agricultural region, and the availability of grazing and forage made it a satisfactory post for mounted troops. Much of the time it was a one-company post, always accommodated in rented facilities. Other positions were similarly occupied for a few weeks or months, but none achieved the relative permanence of Los Lunas.

Sumner's reorganization of the department had been carried out in less than a year. Most of the troops had been withdrawn from towns and placed in posts constructed largely by their own labor and at minimum cost. Only the dragoon companies in Albuquerque and Los Lunas occupied rented quarters. At all of the permanent posts the garrisons were expected to cultivate gardens that, hopefully, would furnish all needed fresh vegetables; and, at all posts except Santa Fe, they were under orders to engage in farming. The effectiveness of the new posts in reducing military expenses and in checking Indian depredations had yet to be determined.

In retrospect it is fairly obvious that Colonel Sumner's sometimes questionable efforts to achieve economy ended in virtual failure. In part Sumner was to blame, but his superiors must bear some of the onus. The objectives of the farming program were laudable, but it was instituted too hastily and without adequate knowledge of the problems and conditions encountered in the arid Southwest. It was assumed that crops raised in the East would grow successfully by employing essentially the same practices for their cultivation in the West. Sumner had a low opinion of the New Mexicans' farming methods, which he made clear when he issued instructions not to permit persons hired to work on government farms to use "their miserable method of cultivation except in irrigating, about which they know more than we do."[46] At the same time, his commitment to the program was emphasized when he stated that "no officer will be entrusted in command of a post in this Department who does not manifest zeal and ability in carrying out the orders of the government, relating to agriculture and the reduction of army expenses."[47]

The results of the farming program varied from one post to another, but nowhere were the desired goals achieved.[48] Farms were planted at Forts Union, Defiance, and Fillmore in 1852 and at those same posts as well as Forts Massachusetts, Conrad, and Webster in 1853. The farm at Fort Union was most nearly successful, at least in the quantity it produced. It was located on Ocate Creek, some twenty-three miles north of the post, on land rented from Manuel Alvarez[49] but, even though the land was fertile and the crops did well, not enough was grown to feed the public animals at the post and general depot through the winter. At the other extreme was Fort Massachusetts, where frost might occur even in midsummer. In October 1853 Major Blake reported "that in consequence of the shortness of the season, the farming operations cannot be successfully continued at this post."[50]

The achievements at Fort Defiance were not much greater, although a genuine effort was made. Major Backus, then in command, planted a farm and garden under the supervision of one of Sumner's civilian farmers,

Jonathan F. Wyatt. The procedure astonished the observant Navajos, who expressed the wish to obtain ox-drawn plows so that they might plant larger fields for themselves. They were probably less impressed by the results. Major Backus concluded, as early as July 1852, that he could not raise enough grain "to pay for the seed and the expense of plowing the land."[51]

Captain and Brevet Major Henry L. Kendrick, Second Artillery, who succeeded Backus as post commander in August 1852, had to report the farm (in which oats, barley, and corn had been planted) a failure. In his opinion, and Wyatt concurred, the failure of the field crops was due, in part, to poor soil and lack of water and, in part, to the field mice that ate much of the planted grain before it sprouted. He was more optimistic than Backus, however, believing that with the proper use of the fertilizer from the post stables and with careful irrigation satisfactory crops might be grown.[52] When Colonel Mansfield inspected the post in September 1853 he concluded that farming had "been tried and proved a failure."[53]

Field crops in the post farms included corn, barley, buckwheat, oats, timothy, and clover. Also planted were wheat and pumpkins, useable as either food or feed, and beans intended for food. Some of the crops had been staples in New Mexico for many years, and they were generally more successful than the crops that were innovations. By-products of the farms, cornstalks and grain straw, provided an important source of long fodder, and native grasses cut by the troops for hay were considered part of the yield of the farms.

Sumner relinquished command of the department in June 1853, and he left New Mexico before the results of the second year's farming were known. His personal opinion of the program must remain conjectural, but officially he made every effort to carry out Conrad's instructions relating to agriculture. Conrad, the initiator of the program, was replaced as Secretary of War by Jefferson Davis, a graduate of the Military Academy and a career army man, in March 1853, when President Franklin Pierce, himself a veteran of the Mexican War, was inaugurated. The chief advocates of military farming were no longer in a position to press for its continuation.

Winfield Scott, General-in-Chief of the Army, had consistently opposed farming on the grounds that it infringed on the duties of the troops, hampered military discipline, and discouraged civilian settlement.[54] At the close of his inspection tour of the department Colonel Mansfield branded the farming program "a failure generally," and added that the methods required for farming in the Southwest differed so greatly from those employed in the East that the failure was inevitable. Like Scott, Mansfield considered military farming highly injurious to discipline and an encroachment on the true duties of the army.[55] Any idea that post farms would result in economy was dispelled when Colonel Cooke, in command of Fort Union, announced that the corn raised on the post farm in 1853 had cost the government more than four times as much as if it had been purchased on the open market.[56]

Colonel Samuel Cooper, Adjutant General of the Army, reported at the end of the third quarter of 1853 that the farm program for the West as a whole was more than $18,000 in debt. By far the largest part of the sum was the deficit of $16,701.12 incurred by the Ninth Military Department (exclusive of Fort Webster), of which it was noted: "the Commanding Officer reports the farm a complete failure." The only post to show a profit was Fort Defiance—a profit of $682.88, achieved by the "sale" of hay to the quartermaster. The hay, of course, was native grass rather than the product of the farm. Fort Union, with the largest farm, had the largest loss, more than $13,000.00; and Albuquerque, so much a source of pride for Sumner, had amassed an indebtedness of $480.17. Captain Isaac Bowen, chief of the subsistence department in New Mexico, provided more favorable figures, showing a loss of only $10,168.29 at the close of 1853. Cooper recommended that the program be discontinued and that the farming equipment, work animals, and other items purchased for the experiment be sold. Jefferson Davis concurred, and an order was issued terminating the farming program.[57]

In contrast to the farms, the post gardens were for the most part a success. They had long been an aspect of garrison life in many parts of the country and were considered essential to improve the health of the troops. As anticipated, the regular availability of vegetables brought about a drastic reduction in scurvy, which ceased to be a serious problem in the department.[58] Gardens were planted at all posts except Cantonment Burgwin. They did reasonably well everywhere, except at Fort Massachusetts where "little or no benefit" resulted because most of the plants were killed by early frosts long before they were sufficiently mature to produce anything to be eaten.[59] At Fort Defiance the garden "yielded all that could have been expected" and added "much to the comfort of the troops."[60]

Interest in raising Irish potatoes continued over the years, and they were attempted at all of the posts but nowhere produced a crop. Even wild potatoes (Solanum jamesii Dunn), described as about the size of a wren's egg, were planted, but the hope that they would improve in quality

as a result of cultivation was not realized. At Fort Defiance, Major Kendrick gave the Navajo Indians a few seed potatoes in 1855 and 1856.
He did not report the outcome, but potatoes planted in the post garden
failed. Seeds of various kinds were regularly given to the Navajos, as
well as instruction in their culture. Some were much too exotic to interest
the Indians, and they rejected such things as cresses, mushroom spores,
sweet vernal grass, Italian crimson clover, mignonette, spinach, and
celery.[61]

A complete list of the vegetables planted in post gardens cannot be
compiled; unlike the post farms, a report on production was not required.
In preparation for the 1853 planting season Colonel Sumner simply asked
that an assortment of fresh garden seeds sufficient for ten companies be
sent to the department.[62] William Carr Lane,[63] newly appointed territorial
governor of New Mexico, paused for several days at Fort Union on his
way to Santa Fe in September 1852. He recorded in his diary the crops
growing in the post garden, and his is the most complete listing that has
been found. Crops unrecorded in New Mexico before the American
occupation were turnips, parsnips, okra, and asparagus. Crops already
grown in New Mexico were peas, cabbages, cucumbers, beets, radishes,
onions, carrots, pumpkins, chilis, and wild potatoes. Tomatoes had been
planted, but Lane did not expect them to bear fruit; and Irish potatoes,
sweet potatoes, and melons had been planted but had failed. Lane also
noted that various berries were growing in the garden, but he did not
identify them.[64] At Fort Defiance corn, beans, peas, cabbages, potatoes,
radishes, turnips, beets, onions, and "some other small vegetables" were
planted.[65] For none of the crops were varieties stated, but it is probably
that some were new to New Mexico.

The military farm experiment had little noticeable affect on the New
Mexican economy. At none of the posts was enough feed raised to fill
the needs of the post itself; hence, the army continued to provide a
market for civilian production without any significant reduction in prices.
A few jobs were created for civilians as farm supervisors and laborers,
but under Sumner's parsimonious administration they were held to a
minimum. At the seven posts where farms were attempted, five of the
farms were supervised by Anglo-Americans, most of whom had no previous experience in farming in the Southwest. They were paid from $30
to $65 per month, plus one or more rations. Almost all of the farm
laborers were Spanish Americans, and they varied in number literally
from one day to the next. They were employed for only about half the
year and received 25 to 50 cents per day.

The impact of post gardens was undoubtedly greater. They reduced army dependence on local production; but army purchases of foodstuffs, other than flour, beans, and meat, had been limited. Although the military introduced a few new vegetables, there was no immediate diversification of civilian crops, which continued to be grown primarily for the consumption of the producers. As late as 1856 the *Santa Fe Weekly Gazette* reported:

> We ought to have all the seeds our soil is adapted to producing, but instead of this our only productions are wheat, corn, and beans, with perhaps a few others, including potatoes, which, however, is but a very moderate addition to the list; and even these staples are not of as good a quality as they might be made by the proper attention to their culture. Our fruits too, are very limited in kind and of inferior quality with the single exception of the grape.[66]

The reorganization of the department and the agricultural program had been carried out under instructions. The other economy measures applied or proposed by Sumner were his own, or partly so. Some were intended to achieve appreciable savings, some were ill-conceived, and a few can only be characterized as petty. Because transportation was a continuing expense it became a major object of the attempt to economize. Convinced as he was that soldiers could do anything, or at least could be made to do anything, Sumner urged that contractors' trains be eliminated and that the responsibility for freighting to the department be assumed by the quartermaster's department.[67] The cheapest transportation, in his opinion, would be by ox train under the supervision of a competent quartermaster. The trains should come out in the spring and return to Fort Leavenworth in the fall, "where the animals could be cheaply wintered on [Captain and Brevet Major Edmund A.] Ogden's farm,"[68] and where necessary repairs could be made. Because the returning wagons would be empty, half the oxen would be turned over to the commissary in New Mexico, thus providing the department with a large supply of beef at Missouri prices. If his recommendations were accepted, Sumner believed that transportation would be no more than $4 per hundred pounds.

This was not Sumner's decision to make, but he did have jurisdiction over the movement of military freight within the department. He fully intended that all internal transportation be handled by his quartermasters, using soldiers as teamsters insofar as that would be possible. He proposed to do this despite the dispersal of the troops and the difficulty of supplying Forts Webster and Defiance, not to mention Fort Massachusetts after it was established. That being his intent, his decision to send 71 wagons and 475 mules back to Fort Leavenworth in the fall of 1851 is almost incomprehensible; yet Sumner had his reason and that reason was economy. The animals could be fed there at less cost (and, although Sumner did not say so, the cost would not be charged to his department), and they would be on hand to bring out trains in the spring.[69]

In assuming responsibility for internal transportation, Sumner deliberately embraced a policy of scarcity. According to his estimates, some quartermaster's stores would be required in 1852, but a two-year supply of subsistence stores was already on hand and no more would be needed prior to August 1, 1853. The only items which Sumner admitted were in less than a two-year supply were beef, beans, and vinegar (all available to some extent in the department), and soap.[70] The supplies in the department were in the Fort Union depot; and the difficulty of distributing them to the posts where they were needed, using only the quartermaster's limited transportation, was immediately obvious. As early as November 1851, Sumner authorized the employment of private trains to freight government stores from the abandoned Post of El Paso to Fort Fillmore and Albuquerque. Before the winter was over, he not only made occasional use of private trains but permitted the hiring of civilian teamsters and the purchase of additional oxen. Even so, as spring approached he was forced to admit that the department was "very much pressed for transportation."[71]

The winter took its toll of both wagons and draft animals. In February 1852, Captain and Brevet Major Ebenezer Sprote Sibley, Sumner's chief quartermaster, had difficulty in finding thirty government oxen in fit condition to haul stores from the depot to Fort Defiance. The situation was saved when Lucien Maxwell offered to sell as many as two hundred oxen that he had intended for use in the Santa Fe trade. Some unbroken mules were purchased in Santa Fe at $40 per head, and more were available at the same price. Sibley advised buying additional "gentle, well broken Mexican mules" to aid in training the "wild" mules to harness. This was accomplished a short time later when William F. Moore and Burton F. Rees of Tecolote sold him 129 mules broken to harness for $51.50 each.[72] When the government train arrived with stores from Fort Leavenworth in the summer of 1852, rather than resting the animals for the return trip, Sumner put them to work hauling flour from Taos to

Fort Union and bringing corn from Anton Chico and Questa (the present Villanueva). He did have the grace to say that he did not want the animals overworked.[73]

Despite these measures, the difficulty of supplying the more distant posts continued. Trains were constantly on the road, and as a result the draft animals, particularly the oxen, were in uniformly poor condition. The train hauling supplies to Fort Defiance in May 1852 could travel only three or four miles a day because the oxen gave out and there were no replacements. The animals were so worn-down that it was necessary to double the teams on each wagon to get over "every piece of sand or little hill."[74] Fort Massachusetts posed its own problems. In addition to the very poor road linking it to Taos, the long period of cold weather and frequent heavy snowfalls made freighting arduous and at times impossible. Nevertheless, Major Blake was expected to haul his own corn and flour from the Taos Valley, even though his draft animals were poorly fed and constantly in bad shape.[75]

Fort Webster was supplied from Fort Fillmore, which obtained its flour under Hart's contract and the rest of its stores from the general depot. Because neither Fort Fillmore nor Fort Webster had sufficient transportation facilities, privately owned trains, often provided by James Magoffin, were occasionally employed. Both posts, but particularly Fort Webster, were faced with frequent shortages of commissary and quartermaster's stores, and at times the lack of transportation made it impossible for Fort Fillmore to fill requisitions from Fort Webster.[76] Because of the danger posed by the Apaches, escorts had to be provided in both directions. Colonel Miles estimated that it cost $4 to freight a fanega of corn from Fort Fillmore to Fort Webster.[77] When the water in the Rio Grande was high there was the further problem of moving wagons and teams across the river; the closest boat sufficiently large to serve as a ferry was at El Paso.[78]

As long as Sumner remained in command, transportation within the department was handled largely by government trains. Sumner conceded that it was a "heavy task" to supply the more distant posts over uniformly poor roads, but he insisted that he was reducing expenses thereby. He consistently demanded economy and efficiency in the use of transportation within the department. At the same time, he accepted advice if it seemed probable that it would promote his objective. When Sibley recommended that oxen were unsuitable for use in New Mexico and that "mule power" was less expensive and more reliable, oxen were eliminated entirely for internal transportation, and the quality of service improved as a result. Also at Sibley's suggestion, Sumner hired a wagon master to supervise transportation at the general depot.[79]

Despite Sumner's economies the cost of transportation within the department remained high. The loss of draft animals was always excessive, often occurring as a result of overwork but also because of inadequate feed. Wagons were usually in bad repair and in short supply. It is difficult to evaluate the effect of Sumner's efforts to reduce the cost of transportation because the wider dispersion of posts injected expenses that previously had not been incurred. Sumner also deliberately failed to provide an adequate quantity of supplies at both the general depot and the individual posts. There were frequent deficiencies and even complete depletion of various items, including elements of the ration. Sumner's successor found it necessary to make unusually large requisitions of virtually all stores, a direct legacy of his predecessor's policy.

One of the continuing expenses involved in transportation and in the maintenance of all public animals was the cost of feed. With the failure of the farm program the army could do little to reduce the expense of feed other than to require the troops to put up native grasses for hay, which they did at all posts except Santa Fe. Sumner tried to hold down the price that the army had to pay for corn and long forage, but with limited success. He also reduced the number of public animals to be fed. Not only did he send most of his draft animals back to Fort Leavenworth in 1851, but he made the astounding proposal that four of the nine dragoon companies be withdrawn from the department and replaced by unmounted troops.

> In all protracted military operations [he wrote], especially against Indians, the main body must be foot. . . . In Indian expeditions I think there should always be a small body of *very select horse*. If the march is long, and without grain, I would have the horses habitually led till required for action. A small body of this kind would be worth ten times the number of ordinary men on broken down horses.[80]

This was a new approach to western Indian warfare and one with which few of Sumner's peers would agree, even in the interest of economy.

There were never enough mounts in the department, and dragoon companies often found themselves with fewer horses than men. Although the army considered Mexican horses too small for dragoon service, Sumner decided to experiment with a few of them, offering to pay as much as $55 a head, which was much below the price paid for mounts in the

States. He soon reconsidered and reduced the maximum he would pay for "ponies" to $40, less than most owners would accept.[81] He also bought some horses from the Navajos, although they were not a reliable source. The Navajos were reluctant to sell their animals and would part with only a few at a time, but Sumner considered Indian horses less expensive to keep and they were often remarkably cheap. However, local sources could not provide enough horses, and in 1852 he requested that 150 be sent from Fort Leavenworth.[82]

Colonel Sumner was undoubtedly astonished by the price of corn when he reached Santa Fe in 1851. In very short supply because of the drought, it was selling for as much as $15.00 per fanega, whereas at Fort Leavenworth and at other posts along the eastern edge of the plains it delivered for less than 50 cents a bushel ($1.25 per fanega). There are no records of corn purchased under contract in the department before Sumner became commander, although bids had been solicited as early as 1847. Sumner had no intention of paying the existing high price and issued instructions to buy corn only when it could be had for $3 per fanega or less. The drought eased in 1851, and in November a contract was made with John J. Lease of Las Vegas and Charles W. Kitchen of Tecolote "to deliver on a good road practicable for wagons, within sixty miles of Fort Union, two thousand fanegas of corn, each fanega to consist of two and a half bushels." The contract was to be filled by January 1852, at a cost of $2.96³/₄ per fanega.[83]

That was the only corn contract made in 1851. Fort Union, as general depot, had to be assured of a supply of corn sufficient to maintain draft animals. Sumner expected all other posts to raise the corn necessary to meet their own needs. Until this goal was met post quartermasters were instructed to purchase corn locally, staying within the prescribed limit of $3 per fanega. At Fort Union and at most of the Rio Grande Valley posts enough corn was available within a reasonable distance, but as new posts were established far from sources of production the difficulty of supply increased. Fort Defiance purchased corn wherever it could be obtained but still had to be supplied by government trains from the Rio Grande Valley. Fort Massachusetts hauled its corn from Red River (the present Questa), Arroyo Hondo, the Taos Valley, and even at times from Fort Union. The short-lived Fort Webster drew its corn from Fort Fillmore.

At most posts corn cost more than it did at Fort Union. In the early months of 1852 it could still be purchased in the Taos and Las Vegas districts at $3 per fanega, but by spring the usual increase in price occurred. In March it sold for $5 on the open market in Santa Fe, and the price was expected to rise to $6 by April.[84] The army purchased all of the corn available in the vicinity of Fort Fillmore, a mere 225 fanegas, for $3.50 and $4.00 per fanega. The animals at the post were placed on half rations of corn, and only fifty fanegas could be spared for Fort Webster.[85]

North of the Jornada del Muerto, in the region about Socorro, corn sold for as little as $3, although it was scarce; but at Albuquerque the price was $4 on the open market. By July the asking price in Albuquerque had risen to as much as $6, and Captain Daniel H. Rucker, post quartermaster, complained that a train sent from Fort Conrad had bought up all the corn as far north as Belen. Sumner simply announced that he would "not pay $6.00 a fanega for corn, where there is grass and nothing for the horses to do." He ordered that a grazing camp be established for half of the dragoon horses and reduced the corn ration for the rest to three quarts a day.[86]

Unlike hay and fodder contracts that were entered into throughout the year, most corn contracts were made in the late fall after the year's crop had been harvested. The rains were generous in 1852, and it was anticipated that crops of all kinds would be larger and prices lower. However, an early frost badly damaged the corn before it was ripe in the region from which Fort Union obtained most of its supply. When Captain Sibley asked for bids to furnish the general depot with 4,500 fanegas of corn he received only three replies. Edward F. Mitchell[87] of Las Vegas offered 400 fanegas at $4.41 per fanega. The Kitchen brothers offered 400 fanegas at $4.13 and 1,750 at $4.50. Moore and Rees, who before the frost had agreed to sell corn at $3.25 per fanega, made a bid identical to that of the Kitchens.

Sibley, noting that the bids of the Kitchens and of Moore and Rees added up to the total quantity called for, suspected collusion. He rejected all bids as "extravagant." At once he received revised proposals from the several parties. Mitchell now offered 500 fanegas, the Kitchens 1,800, and Moore and Rees 2,150, with the corn to be shelled and sacked at $4.13 for the entire quantity. Sibley again refused to consider the bids, stating that he would not agree to a price of more than $3.85. To Sumner he suggested that the matter be held in abeyance, hoping that the bidders would give in. Sumner readily agreed.[88]

Sibley won his point with only a few days waiting. The original bidders, now joined by Thomas Russell of Las Vegas,[89] agreed to provide the full amount of corn—"dry, sound, shelled & in sacks, free from dust and cobs"—within fifty-five miles of the depot, at the specified $3.85 per fanega. Sibley at this time came up with an innovation that was valid and undoubtedly saved the army money. A fanega, as the Americans found the term applied when they first occupied New Mexico, was a rather inexact measure. George R. Gibson described it as "nearly equal to two and a half bushels." However, he added, "the weights and measures in New Mexico . . . are badly regulated, uncertain, and without uniformity."[90] In its transactions the army soon began to specify that a fanega was 2¹/₂ bushels. Now Sibley wanted it determined by the weight of 150 pounds, but all who had corn to sell insisted that this was too high by 10 pounds. The contracts were signed in November with the fanega fixed at 140 pounds. The 140-pound fanega became standard in all subsequent contracts.[91]

Sumner succeeded in keeping the price paid for corn generally under $4 by refusing to pay what he labeled exorbitant prices and by reducing the corn ration. Whether it was wise economy may be questioned. Reports of broken-down public animals were common. To what extent this can be attributed to inadequate feed cannot be determined, but it was his successor's opinion that many dragoon horses had "perished for want of forage."[92] The same criticism was voiced more pointedly in the *Gazette* while Sumner was still in command of the department. When a party of recruits left Fort Leavenworth with 140 horses and arrived at Fort Union with only 10, the editor posed the question: "we should like to know whether they died of *economy*—a disease that has been rather more fatal to army stock in this Territory, than the colic or botts."[93]

When Sumner took command two flour contracts were in effect—Simeon Hart's for an unspecified quantity and Ceran St. Vrain's for 1 million pounds a year, to run through the fiscal year 1852–53—more than enough flour to supply the troops then stationed in New Mexico. This being the case, it is strange that when Sumner estabished Camp Vigilance,[94] a temporary encampment, at Albuquerque in April 1852, he purchased 100,000 pounds of flour from Antonio José Otero of Peralta.[95] Sumner's only explanation was that he "wanted the flour very much in Albuquerque." He paid Otero 8 cents per pound, St. Vrain's contract price at the time.[96] Otero's mill, originally the property of William L. Skinner, was erected at a cost of about $10,000 and was capable of grinding some 500,000 pounds of flour a year.[97] Otero acquired the mill in 1851 or early in 1852, and it was he who initiated the sale of flour to the army.

When the time came to negotiate new flour contracts in the fall of 1852 Sumner ordered that bids be called for, in the hope of inducing competition and thereby achieving a lower cost. He laid down certain specifications, including points of delivery and quantity, which he asked bidders to "propose for 1,600 men" (approximately 657,000 pounds). In anticipation of a good wheat crop on the post farms, he stipulated that the contractors accept "government wheat at market price."[98] Captain Bowen requested sealed proposals for 900,000 pounds of flour, one-fourth to be delivered in each quarter during the fiscal year 1853–54 at Taos, Santa Fe, and Albuquerque, and at Forts Union, Conrad, and Fillmore. Although Fort Union was the general depot, by far the largest quantities were to be delivered at Albuquerque (220,000 pounds) and at Fort Fillmore (230,000 pounds). The commissary department reserved the right to increase or decrease by one-third the amount required at any point. With transportation so important a factor, the bidder whose mill was closest to the point of delivery had a distinct advantage for that portion of the flour.

Actually, contracts were let for only 600,000 pounds, considerably less than the previous year. St. Vrain, predictably, received the contract for Taos and Fort Union, and Hart was given the contract to deliver south of the Jornada del Muerto. Otero drew the largest contract, 250,000 pounds to be delivered at Albuquerque or at his Peralta mill. A fourth contract, for only 50,000 pounds, went to Joseph Hersch of Santa Fe.[100] Two months earlier Hersch had acquired a mill on the Rio Chiquito (a small stream that formerly flowed down what is now Water Street), where, presumably, he ground the flour. The price paid by the government ranged from 7 cents per pound paid to Hersch to 10 cents per pound paid to Hart.[101] Sumner had achieved a reduction in the quantity of flour purchased, but he paid more for most of it than it had cost during the third year of St. Vrain's initial contract. By providing limited competition he may have encouraged the expansion of production facilities, but the four men who received contracts in 1853 furnished most of the flour purchased in the department during the rest of the decade.

Sumner planned to curtail the use of pork, thus reducing the cost of the meat component of the ration. As soon as he arrived in Santa Fe he ordered that fresh beef or mutton be issued 5 days in 7. He estimated that the cattle in the government herd would provide beef for 150 days and believed that more could be purchased in New Mexico to meet future needs.[102] His search for economy was aided when army headquarters ordered the fresh beef ration cut from 1 1/2 to 1 1/4 pounds per day. The reduction was strongly disputed by Captain and Brevet Major Lawrence P. Graham, Second Dragoons, commanding Fort Conrad, who argued that in making the reduction the Commissary General had in mind fresh beef of "good marketable quality," whereas that issued in New Mexico was "so lean and inferior, that the weight of the bone [was] altogether beyond the proper proportion."[103]

The beef cattle then in the department, either in the government herd or available for purchase, were generally inferior, were strictly range-fed, and often were draft animals that were permitted to graze for a month or two before they were slaughtered. Some 200 head driven from Fort Union to Fort Defiance in 1852 averaged less than 395 pounds on the hoof. Major Kendrick objected to the many undersized cattle, observing that "they consumed our hay and grass without getting fat, and some died from diseases engendered by their own poverty." He preferred large-framed cattle, "even if lean, to small ones tho' in better condition, we shall not then be called on to furnish materials for increase of bone, the very same that our soil is remarkably deficient in."[104] Of 325 animals driven under contract to Fort Fillmore in 1852, 55 were lost en route. Those that survived the trip were in such poor condition that they were not fit to slaughter for several months. It was the same story at Albuquerque where some of the beef cattle "were too poor to kill" and would probably cost more to put in shape than they were worth.[105]

The short supply of cattle in New Mexico caused a predictable increase in price; but the increase was uneven, depending in part on the availability in a given area and the desire of the owner to sell. Shortly after the Post of Los Lunas was established, Captain Ewell purchased ten head of cattle for $22 each and noted that more could be had in the vicinity at the same price.[106] Conversely, in what was obviously a seller's market, the commissary officer at Fort Fillmore bought the few beef cattle in the area at $40 per head. With the supply depleted he turned to mutton, purchasing sheep at Mesilla at the high price of $3 per head in order to have fresh meat to issue at the post.[107]

Sumner soon realized that there were too few beef cattle in the territory to meet the needs of the army; and a herd of 1,340 animals, accompanied by a detachment of recruits, was driven to Fort Union from Fort Leavenworth in the summer of 1852. Even with his penchant for economy Sumner could not spare the men to care for so many cattle, and he made a contract to herd them near the post for 40 cents per head per month.[108] From Fort Union the cattle were distributed, also under contract, to the various posts as needed. Small military escorts were provided to accompany the herds through areas considered subject to Indian attack. Sumner, however, refused to permit the employment of civilian herders at any of the other posts and ordered those who had been hired at Fort Fillmore discharged.[109]

In fact, among Sumner's first economy measures was an order to discharge all civilians, including agents, except for teamsters "temporarily employed with the moveable trains" and one clerk for each paymaster, assistant quartermaster, and the senior commissary officer. This was soon followed by an order providing that no clerk be given more "pay and emoluments" than a second lieutenant in the infantry.[110] Sumner's wholesale dismissal of civilian employees simply anticipated Secretary of War Conrad, who was amazed by the number of civilians working at western posts and expressed the opinion that "in most instances the duties performed by them might and ought to be performed by officers or soldiers." Hence, he prohibited the use of civilians in any capacity "for which soldiers could be detailed without manifest injury to the service."[111]

As was true of a number of the economy measures, the sweeping discharge of civilian employees was undertaken without first examining the real needs of the department or the effect it would have. Colonel Swords, when he made his inspection of most of the existing posts in the summer of 1851, found civilians employed at all of them, ranging in number from one at Taos to 134 at Santa Fe. He was particularly critical of an agent at Algodones who was paid $40 a month, lived in a house rented by the army, but had nothing to do and no stored property to supervise. Acting on Sumner's instructions, Swords summarily dismissed many of the quartermaster's employees. He estimated that the saving to the government at Santa Fe alone, "should it have been continued as a depot," would be about $45,000 a year, plus the cost of subsistence.[112] Once the general depot was transferred to Fort Union civilian employment was greatly curtailed. In the new location the sum paid to civilians working at the depot during the fiscal year 1851–52 was a modest $7,055.35.[113]

No doubt the number of civilian employees had been allowed to proliferate beyond the actual needs of the department. Sumner's comprehensive order, however, was unreasonable and could not be carried out without creating numerous problems. Because the army was dependent on the local population for fodder, corn, and fresh produce—at least until its own agricultural projects proved adequate—there was need for agents who knew the New Mexican people and could deal with them in Spanish. There was also the question of the efficient use of the relatively limited military force in the department. Could the troops build new posts, engage in farming and gardening, and also act as teamsters, blacksmiths, saddlers, expressmen, as well as fill all the other jobs previously held by civilians? Could they perform all of these duties and still carry out their primary function of controlling the Indians? The answer was no; and, in fact, Sumner's order was never fully implemented.

Henry Winslow continued to act as agent in Albuquerque, where he was called upon to do more, not less, for the army. Other agents were retained and some new ones were hired. Sumner, though reluctantly, authorized the employment of farm labor as early as the autumn of 1851, and this class of civilian employees steadily increased. A few other civilian jobs, such as those for teamsters and herders, were never entirely eliminated. Yet Sumner persistently restricted civilian employment, sometimes to the detriment of the service. An extreme example of this was his insistence that a civilian blacksmith at the Post of Taos be discharged, even though Taos was a dragoon station and there was no enlisted man competent enough to replace him.[114]

In his desire for economy Sumner resorted to a number of measures of dubious merit. Spoilage of salt meat had been a constant commissary expense. Sumner sought a remedy by ordering the erection of smokehouses at the newly established forts so that all salt meat could be hung up and further preserved, thus making it unnecessary to freight an additional supply from the East prior to the summer of 1853.[115] Unfortunately, the measure did not lead to a noticeable reduction in the quantity of salt meat condemned. In order to end what he considered an abuse of privilege Sumner placed strict limitations on the sale of commissary stores to officers, and he was extremely loath to approve expenditures for anything he did not deem entirely military in nature. Almost pathetic were the instructions directed to Captain and Brevet Lieutenant Colonel Horace Brooks, Second Artillery, in command in Santa Fe: "Send for the old Mexican guide [Rafael] Carabajal and tell him that he must send to this office as soon as possible the (10) Ten Dollars advanced to him last fall."[116]

In the conduct of his fiscal policy, Sumner sought to keep a close personal check on everything involving military expenses and, in the process, took into his own hands many of the matters normally delegated to staff officers and post commanders. The latter were instructed to send their estimates for quartermaster's supplies not to Major Sibley, as customary procedure dictated, but directly to Sumner, who altered them as he saw fit. As a result, Sibley admitted that even though he was the chief quartermaster officer in the department he knew neither the condition nor quantity of the stores at any of the posts.[117] It may be assumed that the same was true of the commissary department during the Sumner years.

Sumner was reasonably pleased with his own achievements. After his first year as department commander he reported that "the orders of the war department for the reduction of expenses have been rigidly carried into effect in spite of the most determined opposition from all classes."[118] It was not until Colonel and Brevet Brigadier General John Garland made his first report on the condition of the department as he found it that the fruits of Sumner's economy became more apparent.[119]

5

⟨≈⟩⟨≈⟩⟨≈⟩

New Mexico under General Garland

Colonel Sumner's reorganization of the department provided the basic pattern for troop distribution throughout the remainder of the decade. Most of his posts were relocated, some only a few miles from their original site, and additional posts were established. Prior to 1860, however, there was no sweeping revision comparable to that of 1851. During the two years of Sumner's command there was no change in the makeup of the troops in the department, although there was a modest increase in strength as a result of the number of recruits exceeding normal discharges and men lost by other causes. This was, in part, Sumner's own decision, for he consistently stated that the force at his disposal was adequate. His successors viewed their needs differently, and just as consistently they requested additional troops. During the rest of the decade there was a gradual growth in strength and various alterations in the composition of the troops in the department, the number of officers and men increasing from some thirteen hundred in the summer of 1853 to about nineteen hundred in the summer of 1858.

On July 20, 1853, General John Garland formally took command of the department when he forded the Arkansas River about seventy miles above the Cimarron Crossing. He was escorted by a small detachment of Third Infantry and a body of recruits, about two hundred officers and men, and was accompanied by the new civil officials for New Mexico, including Territorial Governor David Meriwether.[1] Also with the party was Colonel Joseph K. F. Mansfield, Inspector General's Department, who carried instructions to conduct a general inspection of the department.

General Garland retained command of the department for a longer period—from July 1853 to September 1858—than anyone else in its comparatively brief history, thus providing a degree of stability that the department had lacked previously. Garland differed from Sumner in temperament. He was less impressed by his own position, less concerned with minutiae, and more inclined to delegate authority to subordinates. In his relations with representatives of the civil government he was generally cooperative, and in his dealings with civilians he was more often conciliatory than peremptory. As a result, his period of command was less fraught with the minor crises that had marked Sumner's tenure. Meriwether, too, added to the continuity of leadership in New Mexico. He filled a complete four-year term as territorial governor, whereas no previous governor, civil or military, had served for as long as two years.

The limits of the Ninth Military Department had been redefined several times since it was first established in 1846. The modifications had been minor, the most significant change being the removal of the El Paso district shortly after the abandonment of the post at Coons' Ranch. On October 31, 1853, the Ninth Military Department was terminated when the army carried out a revision of the entire military geography of the United States. In its place the Military Department of New Mexico was created, to consist of the "Territory of New Mexico, except the country West of the 110th degree West Longitude."[2] At the time the limits were proclaimed the most westerly post in the department was Fort Defiance, and there were no civilian settlements in what was then part of the territory of New Mexico but is now Arizona.[3] Only relatively minor changes were made in the description of the department during the rest of its existence, but it should be noted that the western boundary of 110 degrees was not observed even though it was never officially moved.

The effect of Sumner's policies became clearer as soon as Garland began to assess the condition of the department, a process facilitated by Mansfield's inspection. Sumner's tendency to act with undue precipitousness created problems while he was in New Mexico and caused expenses after he was gone. Nowhere was this more apparent than in the posts he had established. All of them were poorly constructed and began to deteriorate even before they were completed, thus requiring constant repairs at additional cost. Five of the forts—Union, Defiance, Massachusetts, Conrad, and Webster—were criticized as being improperly located; three—Defiance, Massachusetts, and Webster—were difficult and expensive to supply; three—Union, Conrad, and Fillmore—were admittedly on private land, and even though only token rentals were paid for the reserves there was no assurance that this would always be true.

When Garland arrived in the department the Barclay and Doyle suits were still pending, and the future of Fort Union was uncertain. As soon as the court decided in favor of the plaintiffs he acted to reduce the importance of the post. Declaring that it was "entirely out of position for a depôt," Garland transferred the commissary, quartermaster, and medical stores to Albuquerque. That he contemplated abandoning Fort Union entirely seems probable, for he reported that he would leave "the present garrison there for the winter."[4] Only the ordnance depôt remained at Fort Union, and the post was relegated to a position of greatly decreased importance. At the same time, the economic position of Albuquerque, which became the center for military employment and purchasing, was significantly enhanced. As a result, some merchants, particularly those engaged in wholesale businesses, moved from Santa Fe to Albuquerque. One prominent Santa Fean predicted that unless something were done the town "will go to the dogs—literally" as "people are leaving this town quite fast" and business activity was stagnating.[5]

Although Garland deemed Albuquerque suitable as a central location for the distribution of stores to his scattered posts, he found it intolerable as a headquarters for the department. His opinion, it may be surmised, was based more on personal than on military considerations. Albuquerque was, he said, "the dirtiest hole in New Mexico" and had only been occupied "from necessity." Santa Fe was equally convenient as a place for the conduct of his official business and a much better place in which to live. Hence, in September 1854, he returned the department head-quarters to Santa Fe, from which Sumner had so expeditiously removed it some three years before.[6] Santa Fe was once again the center for economic decisions affecting the department.

The outcome of the Barclay and Doyle suits ended for the moment the question of the ownership of the land set aside as a reservation for Fort Union. In March 1854, the government signed an indenture with Barclay and Doyle for sixteen square miles of land—much less than Sumner had sought to appropriate—centered about the Fort Union flag-staff. The land was to be retained as long as the government desired to occupy it. Included in the agreement was the privilege of using "wood, timber, grass and water et cetera," and of crossing "all lands owned, or in the possession of said Barclay & Doyle except those now under cultivation." In return, the government bound itself to pay $1,200 a year for as long as it made use of the property. A clause provided that any claim which the government "may now or hereafter have" to the reserve was not prejudiced.[7] Garland considered the rent excessive and was unwilling to make major repairs to the post. The fort was built of green and unbarked pine logs, "laid on the ground without any durable foundation," and was already badly decayed. He investigated the title to the reserve and contemplated relocating Fort Union; he even toyed with the idea of purchasing Barclay's Fort, but, as it turned out, he did nothing.[8]

In his zeal to carry his instructions to economize into immediate effect, Sumner had neglected to examine the long-range implications of his decisions. The litigation with Barclay and Doyle was the most public result and was probably more symptomatic than typical of the situation that his successor faced. Garland believed that the department was in a most unsatisfactory state. Confronted with major expenses in a variety of areas, he was reluctantly critical of Sumner:

> my predecessor is an *old friend* and acknowledged throughout the army to be one of our most efficient and gallant officers in the *field,* he is also a man of untiring industry—but his energies have been misapplied, and he has left the Department in an impoverished and crippled condition, wanting in many of the essentials for undertaking a successful enterprise. His great, and sole aim appears to have been to win reputation from an economical administration of his Department; in this, he will be found to have signally failed, if all his acts are closely looked into—his economy run into parsimony, the results of which, was the loss of a vast number of horses and mules—he found here in abundance—a plethora of every essential for a military enterprise, and makes capital out of it. In order to make a fair exhibit of the expenditures in this department under his administration of it, it is but fair that he should be charged with everything which has been ordered here to supply his exhausted coffers—Qr. Mrs. stores, subsistence, ordnance, graneries &c., especially wagons and mules. I found a number of Dragoons mounted on the ponies of the country, to the exclusion of Dragoon horses, which should have been sent here, in place of those which perished for want of forage.[9]

Of the nine posts established by Sumner only two remained active for more than a decade. Fort Union was scheduled for abandonment in 1860; but it was saved by the Civil War and, once reprieved, continued to exist, although in a somewhat different location, until 1891. The Post of Albuquerque, abandoned in 1851 and reoccupied in 1852 (hence only partly attributable to Sumner), was garrisoned until 1867. Because he insisted on economy Sumner favored the use of wood for construction; yet, except at Fort Union, he refused to supply sawmills. The posts were built by the troops, who, in most cases, had the added incentive of providing themselves with shelter before the onset of cold weather. The result was hastily erected buildings, frequently made of unpeeled logs and topped with earthen roofs.

In 1852 Major Sibley described the buildings at the new posts as "in most instances built of logs with slight cost to the United States." He recognized the shoddy character of construction when he noted that at all the posts the buildings were "confessedly of a temporary character"; and he suggested that if the posts were intended to be permanent "sound economy would prescribe that the necessary buildings be permanent also."[10] None of Sumner's posts was more than two years old at the time of Colonel Mansfield's inspection, yet he recommended that three be relocated and that two others be provided with more adequate defensive works.

Garland acted promptly to rectify conditions in the department. Before the year was out he visited all of the posts except Fort Massachusetts in order to see at first hand what needed to be done. Fort Webster had already occupied two sites in less than two years. In its second location it was still incomplete, with one company and the sick housed in tents. The existing buildings were "made of logs and mud and quite indifferent." In addition to its makeshift construction, Colonel Mansfield criticized the fort as serving no useful purpose where it was. The roads over which Fort Webster was supplied ran through rugged country, some stretches without adequate water and grass during much of the year and constantly menaced by marauding Apaches. Moreover, the "huts" which constituted the fort were expected to "tumble down before the spring of the year." Garland issued orders early in November 1853 to break up the post and to transfer its garrison to the recently abandoned Santa Barbara on the right bank of the Rio Grande.[11]

The new post, Fort Thorn, was established on December 24, 1853. Although the troops were put to work erecting buildings they were not required to prepare the materials, as they had been during Sumner's tenure. Arrangements were made with civilians to make adobes at $8 per thousand and to furnish sawed lumber for $60 per thousand feet. An acequia some $3^{1/2}$ miles long was dug by the troops to provide water for all the needs of the post, including a post garden. Fort Webster had been expected to restrain the western Apaches but proved ineffective. Hence, to achieve economy and efficiency the line of defense in the Southwest was pulled back to the Rio Grande where, hopefully, it would afford greater protection to the settlements and would inhibit the theft of livestock.[12]

In describing Fort Conrad, Major Sibley wrote that the commanding officer's quarters and the smokehouse were "cotton wood frames filled with adobes," while the other buildings were built of "cotton wood poles, the company officers quarters being daubed with mud." When Mansfield examined the post he found it in an advanced state of dilapidation, with the quarters falling apart and the timbers rotting away. He recommended that it be relocated some ten miles to the south where it would be in a better position to intercept Indian raiding parties. Hugh N. Smith, who with Thomas Biggs claimed the land occupied by the post, offered to lease the existing reserve to the army for a "nominal sum." Although he doubted that the claim was valid, Colonel Chandler, commander at Fort Conrad, preferred a location opposite Valverde, where there was adequate wood, water, and grass as well as excellent land already cleared and broken for a post garden. The site was closer to the northern end of the Jornada del Muerto, hence in a better position to guard that difficult segment of the important north-south highway. [13]

When the courts upheld the Smith-Biggs title, Garland decided to move the post to the site recommended by Chandler rather than rebuild it. The site was presumed to be on the Pedro Armendáriz Grant; hence, a reserve running for about five miles along the west bank of the river and extending a mile back from it was leased in 1854, for the token sum of $1 for five years, from José R. García of Chihuahua, the heir of Pedro and Josefa Ortiz de Armendáriz. Work on the new post, soon designated Fort Craig, began in 1853, some time before the lease was signed. It was designed for two companies and solidly built of adobes. [14] On March 31, 1854, the garrison was withdrawn from Fort Conrad to occupy Fort Craig. The second of Sumner's posts had been abandoned.

Fort Massachusetts was permitted a somewhat longer existence. Mansfield criticized it on two grounds: it was too close to a spur of Blanca Peak for proper defense and too far from the areas of settlement to afford them protection. He proposed that it be relocated on Culebra Creek, "where access could be had to the troops by the population of the [San Luis] Valley, without the hazard of being cut off by the Indians." He also noted that all supplies must be brought from the Taos Valley or Fort Union "over roads in several points impassable for loaded wagons," one of the causes for the great shortage of stores. [15] In addition, the post was sickly, presumably because of an extensive marshy area in the immediate vicinity.

Garland initially intended to pull the troops back from Fort Massachusetts to the Taos Valley. Toward the end of October 1853 the garrison was withdrawn except for a dozen men left to guard public property, but the following March a company of dragoons was sent to reoccupy the post. The defeat administered to First Lieutenant John W. Davidson, First Dragoons, near Cieneguilla (now Pilar) later in the month, and the subsequent campaign against the Jicarilla Apaches, gave the post a temporary importance.[16] However, when Garland visited it in July 1854 he came away more than ever convinced that it was "altogether out of place." Despite the uniformly adverse opinions Fort Massachusetts remained occupied and continued to deteriorate rapidly. In the summer of 1856 Garland described it as "almost untenable from decay." At that time he selected a new site some eight miles to the south, but again the removal was postponed.[17]

The other posts established by Sumner remained where they were for the time being. This was not to say that none of them presented problems. On the contrary, extensive repairs were required and some were rebuilt entirely. The original buildings at Fort Fillmore were constructed of wood, except the quartermaster's and commissary storehouses, which were adobe, and the hospital, which was a combination of the two materials. Mansfield considered the quarters for both officers and men superior to others in the department, and Garland pronounced the post in a good state of preservation. Nevertheless, almost at once work began to replace the wooden structures with more substantial adobe buildings. When Lieutenant Colonel and Brevet Colonel Joseph E. Johnston, First Cavalry, inspected Fort Fillmore in 1859 he called it the best post in the department, "altho' ragged in external appearance."[18] One of the unusual features of construction was the flooring of square adobe bricks in the officers' quarters. Fort Fillmore, despite the praise so generally bestowed upon it, was destined to become a casualty of the Civil War.

Mansfield's only objection to Fort Defiance—which impressed him by the romantic wildness of its setting—was that it was within musket range of a ridge, a shortcoming that could be remedied by erecting blockhouses on the ridge itself. The original buildings were nothing more than pine logs topped by earthen roofs, except for the combination office, guardhouse, and smokehouse, which was built of stone. Some of the buildings required repairs within a year of their completion. Later additions to the post were more substantially constructed of adobe and stone. In 1859, however, four of the original log buildings were still in use, but all were much deteriorated, one to the point where it had to be propped up to prevent its collapse.[19]

Cantonment Burgwin, never intended to be permanent, had served a useful purpose in its early years. By 1855 the Jicarilla Apaches were largely subdued and, as a result, the post was rendered less significant. It was built of green pine logs set on end in the ground. In 1859 Colonel Johnston found the logs so badly rotted that he did not consider the post worth repairing. In fact, he wrote, "in some of the quarters this decay is perceptible to the sense of smelling." Both Fort Defiance and Cantonment Burgwin were abandoned as a result of the reorganization of the department ordered in 1860.[20]

Los Lunas, one of the two rented posts, was something of an exception. Almost nothing was spent on its maintenance until the latter part of 1856, probably more a case of neglect than a lack of need. At that time the quarters for the men, shops, storerooms, corrals, and stables were completely rebuilt, and a stone guardhouse was erected. The materials were purchased from civilians but the troops carried out the construction. If Los Lunas was badly deteriorated the same cannot be said of Captain Ewell's dragoon company, which had garrisoned the post since its founding. Company G, First Dragoons was undoubtedly the wealthiest and probably the most comfortably provided company in the department. When it was transferred from Los Lunas in 1856, it took with it a company fund of some $25,000 and what was described as "a large valuable Library," and it left behind a ninepin alley and a flourishing company garden.[21]

Albuquerque, unlike Los Lunas, was a constant expense. The buildings comprising the general depot required extensive additions and alterations, and some entirely new construction was undertaken. Facilities rented to quarter officers and men also needed numerous modifications and some additions. In 1854, when the garrison consisted of one company of infantry and one of dragoons, rental costs for the post were $3,654 for the year. Captain Easton was convinced that the government should build its own depot and other facilities on a site away from the town. The money spent for rent would soon repay the cost, the army would be protected against thefts (then prevalent in Albuquerque), and the demoralizing influence of the town on soldiers and employees would be obviated.[22]

The necessity for relocating and rebuilding so many posts may be laid in part to Sumner's hasty and penurious methods. The resultant cost exceeded the initial saving. In addition to relocating the two posts, Garland reestablished one of the posts that Sumner had abandoned. Colonel Sumner had insisted, unreasonably it would seem, on breaking up the Post of El Paso in spite of its strategic location and the reasonable terms on which Benjamin Coons offered to lease it. Mansfield stated categorically in 1853 that "a post is indispensable opposite the town of

El Paso," both to afford protection and to encourage settlement. "By a post here, the bottom lands of the river at this place would be occupied and cultivation extended down the river to Isleta,[23] and a trading town would soon spring up with an American population capable of self defence."[24] The War Department gave its approval, and in November El Paso District was transferred back to the Department of New Mexico. General Garland visited the area in December and selected Magoffinsville as the proper location for the post. He believed that the military's presence would put a stop to the filibustering activities "sometimes practiced by our restless border inhabitants," and it would provide protection against marauding Indians for the residents on both sides of the international border.[25]

Major and Brevet Lieutenant Colonel Edmund B. Alexander with four companies of Eighth Infantry was already en route from Fort Clark, Texas, to garrison the new post. Fort Bliss was established on January 11, 1854,[26] in facilities rented from James W. Magoffin. Because the existing buildings were inadequate to accommodate the command the troops were put to work in adding to them. Magoffin furnished the necessary materials, principally adobes. The original agreement provided eight buildings at a rental of $415 per month. Magoffin later offered to lease the post—including a ninth building (his own residence), corrals, and 320 acres of land—on more favorable terms. The offer was rejected, and by 1858, when the garrison consisted of only two companies, the rent had declined to $225 per month.[27]

The condition of the existing posts was only one aspect of Sumner's effort to achieve economy. After his departure other unusual expenses reflected his concern with immediate saving as opposed to long-range planning. Garland found the department with a greater deficiency of almost everything, more shortages than army policy normally permitted. Most of the posts had only a two- to three-month supply of subsistence stores, and some subsistence and quartermaster's articles, including clothing, were entirely depleted at the general depot. On hand at the depot was sufficient sugar to provide rations for the force then in the department for sixteen days. There was enough bacon for three-and-a-half days, but no rice or coffee at all. Other items of the ration were in greater supply, but none were adequate. Sumner had approved requisitions for some subsistence stores for the year 1853–54, but none had been delivered when Garland took command. When the trains from Fort Leavenworth began to arrive during the summer of 1853 they did not bring sufficient quantities of many items, in some instances because supplies had not been requisitioned. "The empty storehouses left by my predecessor," Garland wrote, "are not yet filled" because of the late arrival of supplies and the "limited means" of transportation available.[28]

By the time Garland reached his headquarters and gained some idea of the extent of the shortage in the department it was already long past the usual season to start trains across the plains. Yet Garland considered it essential that more stores be brought in, particularly in view of the fact that additional troops had already been assigned to the department. Hence, in September, three contracts were issued at Fort Leavenworth to transport stores "with all possible dispatch" to Fort Union. Because of the danger and difficulty of freighting on the high plains so late in the year—with the inevitability of a shortage of grass and the probability of cold weather—the contract price was $16 per hundred pounds, more than twice the cost under the freighting contract of 1851. In December a fourth contract was made at the same rate to transport two hundred thousand pounds of stores from San Antonio to the soon-to-be established Fort Bliss.[29]

There was to be no more skimping, nor was consideration again given to having the quartermaster's department handle transportation to New Mexico. Whatever temporary saving Sumner had achieved was offset by the cost of replenishing the stores he had deliberately depleted. In 1854 more reasonable transportation contracts were made, though still at a higher rate than in 1851, and all these contracts provided for freighting from Fort Leavenworth.

Table 3

Transportation Contracts for Freight Moved from Fort Leavenworth to Department Posts, 1854[30]

Destination	Cost per 100 pounds
Fort Union	$ 7.96
Albuquerque	10.80
Fort Fillmore	13.75
Fort Bliss	14.00

In 1855 the army drew up its first contract with the famed freighting firm of Russell, Majors, and Waddell.[31] The contract provided for the transportation to New Mexico of all goods destined for the department for two years. It differed in several respects from previous contracts, and the innovations were continued in all subsequent contracts. The price for freighting was based on 100 pounds per 100 miles, the rate to vary according to the season of the year and to be determined by the date the contractor was notified that the stores were ready to be loaded and moved out. The rate ranged from $1.14, for goods ready for shipment between May 1 and July 31, to $3.60, for supplies ready between December 1 and February 28. The high rate for the winter months reflected the fact that losses of draft animals were frequently great, and it was necessary to haul feed over the entire distance to sustain them. Transportation from Fort Union to other posts in the department was fixed at $1.40 from May 1 to August 31, and $1.80 for the rest of the year. The distance from Fort Leavenworth to Fort Union was considered, by mutual consent, to be seven hundred miles. Military escorts were to accompany all trains carrying less than fifty thousand pounds, the maximum weight permitted for ten wagons. The army reserved the right to provide part or all of the transportation if it so desired. Two months later a contract was signed for transportation from San Antonio to Forts Bliss and Fillmore for $1.70 per hundred pounds per hundred miles, the rate to apply throughout the year.[32]

Each subsequent transportation contract made through 1860 provided some reduction in base rates. The contract signed in 1861 was an emergency measure to go into effect if Russell, Majors, and Waddell could not meet the terms of their commitment, and contained a moderate increase.[33] The only modification of significance was the provision, first included in the 1858 contract, calling for a 10 percent surcharge for hauling hard bread, bacon, pine timber, and shingles.[34]

The last estimate of expenses prepared by the quartermaster's department during Sumner's command was for the fiscal year 1853–54. It provided for a total outlay of $167,552.60. Only two items were appreciable. Corn for feed slightly exceeded $100,000, and the purchase of mounts, remounts, and mules was placed at $30,000. Incidental expenses, presumably including rentals, were budgeted at $20,000, leaving $17,000 to meet all other costs. The estimate stipulated that the transportation of troops and supplies would be handled by government trains and that lumber for public buildings would be procured by the troops. Only twenty-nine civilian employees were provided: two clerks (one at $75.00 and one at $65.00 per month), a wagon master ($58.25 per month), an assistant wagon master ($30.00 per month), and twenty-five teamsters ($20.00 per month each). The sum of $1,500 was included to pay guides, interpreters, and expressmen, who were to be hired as required.[35]

By 1858, when Garland left the department, the number of civilian employees had increased many times over. The largest number employed was at the general depot in Albuquerque, followed by Forts Union, Buchanan, and Fillmore. No civilians were employed at Cantonment Burgwin. The wages paid were similar throughout the department.

Table 4
Wages Paid Civilian Employees in the Military Department
of New Mexico, 1858

Category	Pay per month	Category	Pay per month
clerks	$85	hostlers	$25
wagon masters	50 to 60[36]	messengers	20
carpenters	50	expressmen	100[37]
wheelwrights	50 to 55[38]	storekeepers	30
millwrights	50 to 85	yardmaster	40
blacksmiths	50 to 55	labor superintendent	40
saddlers	50	teamsters	25
strikers	30	laborers	20 to 30
sawyers	30	herders	10 to 25[39]
interpreters	45	ferrymen	10 to 45[40]
ambulance driver	25		

In addition to their wages, most employees received one ration per day. This single ration was commuted, in a few cases, at 20 cents. By far the largest category of employees was teamsters, who varied in number from month to month and were most numerous at the general depot. In the early years of the department few persons with Spanish surnames had been employed, except as herders and for such relatively specialized tasks as guides and interpreters. In 1858 Spanish Americans held none of the supervisory positions and none of the jobs requiring particular skills, such as those of blacksmith and wheelwright. Many of the teamsters and laborers were Spanish Americans, while some of the herders were not. A few of those classified as laborers were assistants to skilled personnel and, presumably, were themselves becoming more proficient in various skills.

In addition to the civilians hired at the posts, there was occasional employment in actual military service. Spies and guides were used with increasing frequency, taking part in all major Indian campaigns. The spies and guides were, for the most part, Spanish Americans and Indians, usually under the command of a Spanish American. A number of men

were called on to organize parties of spies and guides but none as frequently as Blas Lucero of Albuquerque.[41] In 1857 Lucero was retained
permanently at $40 per month, or, when actually on campaign, at $3
per day plus a ration. By that date standard pay for a captain or principal
guide had become $3.00 per day, and $1.50 per day was standard pay
for each of the men making up a company when called into service. The
army provided subsistence, but the spies and guides furnished their own
arms, mounts, and pack animals.[42]

There was a long tradition for the use of Indian auxiliaries in New
Mexico, firmly established by both Spain and Mexico. The United States
was equally ready to pit Indian against Indian. The first extensive use of
Indians by the army was in Colonel Washington's Navajo expedition of
1849. On that occasion they were compensated for their services in goods,
apparently furnished by a Santa Fe merchant who took a receipt and
power of attorney to collect the money due when Congress appropriated
it. As it turned out, the pay for all of the volunteers who participated
in the expedition was made available in 1851.[43] In the 1850s Indian
auxiliaries were sometimes paid as though they were serving as spies and
guides, and in some campaigns they served as unpaid volunteers. They
were often permitted to retain goods seized, which usually meant the
animals taken from the enemy.

Contention over the price paid for corn largely ended with Sumner's
departure. The failure of the military farming program left the army
dependent on civilian production and the vagaries of nature. By 1854
the imbalance caused by the expansion of flour milling and the subsequent
increase in wheat planting had been corrected. As a result, during a year
of adequate rainfall the army's corn requirement could be met at most
posts. Only at Albuquerque, where the transfer of the general depot
created an unanticipated demand, was the supply a temporary problem.
There, in the summer of 1854, it was necessary to purchase wheat to
issue as feed until the new corn crop became available in October.[44]

General Garland hoped that competition between suppliers would hold
corn prices at a reasonable level. To further this end he instructed his
post commanders not to compete with each other for corn and ordered
that Fort Conrad purchase no corn below the Jornada del Muerto and
that Fort Thorn acquire all of its corn from the area south of the Jornada.[45]
In December 1853, contracts were drawn up, without bickering, for the
delivery of 4,500 fanegas of corn at Fort Union for $3.50 per fanega.[46]
The first contract for supplying corn at a post other than Fort Union
was made for Cantonment Burgwin in the following year. In 1855 con-

tracts again were made only for Fort Union, but in subsequent years more of the posts obtained part of their supply by contract.

Fort Defiance purchased corn wherever it could, to the benefit of the western pueblos. In 1852 Robert Nesbitt arranged to buy at Zuñi 400 fanegas for the army.[47] The major difficulty in dealing with the Indians was that they would sell very little for money, preferring to trade for goods. As a result it was necessary to make use of the services of a civilian who traded with the Indians for their corn, often a long and drawn out process, "in the hope of selling to the Government at a great advance in cost price."[48] Major Kendrick reported in 1856 that as a result of the market provided by Fort Defiance, the Zuñis had increased their planting of corn and annually sold to the army a quantity worth about $4,000. He had given the Indians four iron plows and had instructed them in their use and expected a continued expansion of production. Both Kendrick and the Indians ascribed the growing prosperity of the pueblo to the proximity of Fort Defiance.

In the spring of 1852 Major Backus sent an expedition to the Hopi pueblos to open a wagon road, to ascertain "the number and locality of all their villages," and to learn if they could become a source of corn. Kendrick made a consistent effort to encourage the Hopis, as much for their own good as for that of the post. He suggested giving hoes and spades to the Indians, which they wanted, in order to enable them to cultivate more land and thus set an example "of much benefit to the Navajoes." By 1856 government trains regularly hauled all the corn that the Hopis had to sell.[49]

There was no particular pattern in the quantity of feed obtained under contract or in the price paid for it. There is reason to believe that some contracts were not recorded but, based on those that were, there was a general increase in the amount of corn purchased under contract through 1857. In the fall of 1857 contracts were let for more than 29,000 fanegas, more than twice as much as in any previous year, for delivery in the year 1857–58. Less than 12,000 fanegas were acquired under contract for the year 1858–59, but the contracts made for delivery in the year 1859–60 called for more than 25,000 fanegas.

In general, the price paid for corn, fodder, and hay varied more between posts than from one year to another. In most years the price was lowest at Forts Union and Bliss and highest at Forts Stanton and Buchanan. Quartermaster contracts were issued in more years and for a larger total quantity of corn for Fort Union than for any other post.

Table 5
Fort Union Corn Contracts, 1851–59

Year of delivery	Fanegas	Price per fanega
1851–52	2,000	$2.96³/₄
1852–53	4,500 (shelled)	3.85
1853–54	4,500	3.50
1855	5,000 (shelled)	1.80–2.40
1855–56	10,000 (shelled)	3.00
1856–57	5,300 (shelled)	3.10–3.28
	1,500 (cob corn)	3.00–3.15
1857–58	9,600 (shelled)	2.31–2.82
1858–59	1,500	3.00

At some posts the commissary department occasionally made contracts for corn. Such contracts were made at Fort Union in 1856 and 1858, both for 500 fanegas of cob corn. In 1856 the commissary paid $3.00 per fanega, the same as the quartermaster paid for part of the cob corn he purchased; but in 1858 the commissary paid only $1.69, much less than the quartermaster paid. Where a comparison is possible, the commissary, which purchased smaller quantities, usually paid less for corn. On November 21, 1857, the post quartermaster at Fort Stanton contracted for 2,000 fanegas of cob corn at $4.75. Four days later the same officer, this time in the role of post commissary, contracted for 500 fanegas at $4.40.[50] On the other hand, both departments paid the same amount, $3.20 per fanega, for corn delivered under contract to Fort Marcy in the year 1857–58.

Hay was still cut by the troops at most posts in 1853, but in Santa Fe, where such was not possible, some hay was purchased by the quartermaster for $30 per ton.[51] In 1854 the first contract for hay since 1851 was made for delivery at Cantonment Burgwin. Hay and fodder contracts were concentrated in the years 1851 and 1856–60. Hay was consistently cheaper at Fort Craig than elsewhere, ranging from $6 to $9 per ton, with Fort Bliss in second position. It was most expensive at Fort Stanton, $50 per ton in the summer of 1858, partly because of transportation costs. The prices are not strictly comparable because some contracts specified long tons, some short tons, and some simply tons. Fodder, rarely purchased under contract, was more expensive at Santa Fe and at the posts to the north. Because fodder was purchased most commonly on the open market, some competition developed between posts, creating petty annoyances and probably having some impact on prices. Garland ended the practice in 1856 by dividing the department into districts and assigning specific limits within which each post was permitted to purchase all varieties of feed.[52]

Unlike the flour milling industry, the business of providing feed for the army produced no particularly dominant figures. Between 1851 and 1860 thirty-two different individuals or partnerships held corn contracts and twenty-eight had hay or fodder contracts. William F. Moore and Burton F. Rees of Tecolote were the major corn contractors, holding a total of nine contracts and delivering corn in each year, 1853 through 1858. They sold more corn to the army under contract than anyone else; most of it was delivered to Fort Union but also at one time or another to Fort Marcy, Fort Stanton, and Albuquerque. Ceran St. Vrain held contracts during five years, all for Fort Union and Cantonment Burgwin; and the Kitchen brothers, twice in combination with someone else, held contracts during four years. On the other hand, eighteen individuals held only one contract; four held two contracts; and Henry Connelly held three,[53] one jointly with Moore and Rees. Several of the contractors were or had been associated with the army as sutlers or purchasing agents. Three of the major flour contractors were also corn contractors, but Simeon Hart and Joseph Hersch held only one contract each. Only one of the corn contractors was a Spanish American.[54] Some of the contractors were land owners and farmers, but most were not. It is reasonable to assume that a large part of the corn sold to the army under contract was not raised by the sellers but was acquired by them from the small farmers. As was true of wheat, the army provided the farmer with a good market for a crop previously raised almost exclusively for subsistence.

Most of the fodder contracts were for hay cut from native grass, with some specifying grama grass and some "bottom" grass. Because the process of filling a hay contract involved neither land ownership nor farming, the contractor had only to hire a crew of men and to go where grass could be cut. In some cases the grass was cured and stacked for the army to transport; in others it was delivered at the post. Five contracts for forage other than hay were issued, three of them in 1859. Three of these contracts simply called for forage, and one specified "wheat straw or forage." The fifth was for bran (mill feed), a by-product of gristmilling, and was held by Simeon Hart in 1859. St. Vrain sold bran to the army at both his Mora and Talpa mills, but none was sold under contract, and some of the other mill owners probably did so as well. Of the twenty-eight fodder contractors only three—Moore and Rees, Samuel Magoffin,[55] and John M. Francisco,[56]—held more than a single contract, and they had but two each. Four contracts were held by Spanish Americans: one in 1851, two in 1859, and one in 1861. Nine corn contractors received hay contracts; and Moore and Rees, the principal purveyors of corn, also sold the most hay, 800 tons in their two contracts.

The corn and fodder contracts were intended to assure a minimum supply at a reasonable cost. At no time did the army contract for a sufficient quantity of either corn or fodder to fill its needs. The December 13, 1856, issue of the *Gazette* carried an interesting article based on information provided by Captain Langdon C. Easton, then chief quartermaster in the department. The amount of corn consumed in the department during the current year came to 61,734 fanegas, and the amount of hay and fodder totaled just under 5,332 tons. If these figures are correct they indicate that 75 percent of the corn and more than 80 percent of the hay and fodder were purchased in individual transactions rather than under contract. Bearing on this was an advertisement appearing in a number of issues of the *Gazette* in the fall of 1857. The quartermaster at Fort Marcy, who earlier had asked for bids to furnish 5,000 fanegas of corn and 300 tons of hay, offered to purchase hay "at all times and in any quantity" for $1\frac{1}{2}$ cents per pound.

At all posts corn and fodder were bought in casual transactions, as they had been before contracts were issued. A majority of the sellers were Spanish Americans. At a number of the posts, the post sutlers sold corn to the army. Among the less usual vendors was the Reverend Joseph P. Machebeuf, who sold 591 *costales* at $1 per costal to Captain Ewell at Los Lunas in 1853.[57] At several posts retail merchants sold corn to the army in fairly small quantities, leading to the supposition that they had accepted the grain at their stores in lieu of cash.

Comparatively few private business records from the pre–Civil War period are available, but there are enough to disclose one method by which corn and other farm products passed from the hands of the producer into those of the middleman. Rafael Armijo, an Albuquerque merchant and a nephew of former governor Manuel Armijo, advanced money (or credit) to small farmers in return for liens on their future crops. In 1857 he paid $1 per fanega against the crop for the coming October. Most of the sums advanced were from $2 to $20, but in this way Armijo gained control of several thousand fanegas of corn at minimum risk.[58] Army contracts made for the Albuquerque depot in the fall of 1857 were for $3.70 to $4.00 per fanega; however, Armijo neither held a contract nor sold corn directly at the depot.

Persons holding contracts also sold corn and fodder to the army in individual transactions. The price paid for feed thus acquired was often less, sometimes much less, than that purchased under contract; although in years of poor crops it was higher. Over the years Fort Union received more corn under contract than any other post, but after Albuquerque became the general depot it also became the chief purchaser of corn, buying as much or more from individuals as it did by contract. This is, perhaps, best exemplified by purchases made in 1858, the year for which the greatest amount of corn was delivered under contract. At Albuquerque Moore and Rees had two contracts, calling for the delivery of 9,500 fanegas: 6,000 at $4.00 and the rest at $3.70 per fanega. In the five months for which records of casual transactions have been located, more than 9,250 fanegas were purchased from individuals who brought in corn to sell at the depot. The grain was paid for at a uniform price of $3.00 for cob corn and $3.50 for shelled corn. While a few of the purchases were quantities of 100 fanegas or more, most were for less than 30 fanegas and a few for as little as 3 or 4. More than 90 percent of the transactions were with Spanish Americans.[59]

In the last quarter of 1858 more than 250 tons of fodder were purchased at Albuquerque at a cost of $20 per ton. This too was acquired in small lots, usually of less than 2 tons, although in one instance the quantity exceeded 57 tons. In a majority of the transactions the fodder, probably cornstalks, was sold by the same persons who sold corn. Two sales of barley were made to the army in this quarter, both by Spanish Americans, the first record that has been found of army purchases of New Mexican barley. The amount was small, a total of 13,150 pounds, paid for at $3 per 120 pounds. Many of the individuals who sold to the government engaged in several transactions during the quarter.[60]

At no other post in the department were such large quantities of feed purchased from individuals as at Albuquerque, but at most posts there were some transactions. During the quarter no purchases were recorded at Fort Thorn and the only feed delivered at Fort Stanton was under contract.[61]

Prices were particularly high at Fort Massachusetts where the cost of corn delivered at the post was $6.00 per fanega, while that hauled by the army in its own wagons was only $3.75. Hay delivered at the post for $30 per ton, half again as much as that bought under contract for its replacement, Fort Garland, later in the year. Fodder, as distinguished from hay, cost $35 to $40 per ton, comparable to the price paid at other northern posts. This too was hauled by the army.[62] Fort Buchanan, for which no feed contracts were signed until 1859, was too distant to supply economically from the Rio Grande Valley. There the cost of corn was exceptionally high: 5 cents per pound, the equivalent of $7 per fanega. The post quartermaster bought almost 2,000 fanegas at that price during the first quarter of 1858. On the other hand, hay was purchased at the fairly reasonable price of $25 per ton.[63]

Table 6
Feed Quantities Purchased by Lots from Individuals,
Specified Months, 1858[64]

Post	Corn	Fodder	Hay
Fort Union (January)	37 fanegas	7 tons	—
Fort Craig (January)	223	2^2/$_3$	—
Fort Defiance (January)	264	9	—
Fort Fillmore (January)	175	—	10^1/$_2$ tons
Fort Buchanan (January)	1,083	—	—
Cantonment Burgwin (January)	243	51^1/$_2$	—
Fort Bliss (February)	—	—	48^3/$_4$
Fort Massachusetts (March)	232	8	—
Fort Marcy (March)	193	—	35

In addition to large quantities of feed, post quartermasters regularly bought a variety of other New Mexican products from individuals, particularly from those at the general depot in Albuquerque. The items most frequently purchased were tallow, at 20 to 30 cents per pound; charcoal, at 25 to 75 cents per bushel; lime, at 75 cents to $2.75 per bushel; and a surprisingly large number of buckskins, used as covers and sometimes made into sacks, for which the standard price was $1.00. *Jerga* was occasionally purchased,[65] usually several hundred *varas* at a time (each vara equal to approximately 33 inches), for 25 cents per vara. Less commonly purchased were tar, saw logs, lumber by the piece, coal, saddle blankets, small numbers of adobes, and firewood. At times imported articles—such as screws, nails, window glass, and letter paper—were acquired from local merchants to fill temporary shortages.

Prior to 1860, with the exception of two contracts, St. Vrain, Hart, Otero and Hersch furnished the army with all of the flour bought in the department. The exceptions occurred in 1857, a year in which Hersch did not have a contract, when James A. Donavant contracted to deliver 75,000 pounds of flour at Santa Fe, and in 1859, when Theodore W.

Taliaferro held a contract for Fort Buchanan.[66] While it cannot be said with certainty, it seems that in some years contracts were made by direct negotiation with purveyors rather than by competitive bids. Simeon Hart continued to manufacture a large part of his flour at Santa Cruz, Chihuahua, very probably much the greater part of that sold to the army.[67]

As was true in the case of feed, no particular pattern emerged in army purchases of flour.

Table 7
Flour Purchases by the Army, 1853–59[68]

Year	Contracted quantity	Price per pound
1853	600,000 pounds	7–10 cents
1854	820,000	$5^{45}/_{100}$–$9^{1}/_{2}$
1855	110,000	8
1856	1,176,000	$5^{1}/_{2}$–$9^{1}/_{2}$
1857	1,161,000	6–$12^{1}/_{2}$
1858	1,157,900	$5^{8}/_{10}$–$12^{1}/_{2}$
1859	546,000	$4^{99}/_{100}$–12

Only one contract was registered in 1855, and that was issued to Ceran St. Vrain. The quantities in Table 7 are those for which contracts were issued during the year, rather than for the amounts actually delivered. Deliveries were usually spread over a twelve-month period, either on specified dates or on demand. Many of the contracts included a clause permitting the army to increase or decrease the quantity, usually by one-third or one-half. The price of flour clearly reflected the distance of the delivery point from the mill. In all years in which Hart held a contract, his flour was the most expensive. The $12^{1}/_{2}$ cents per pound in 1857 and 1858 was for flour delivered by Hart at Fort Buchanan, and the 12 cents in 1859 was in the Taliaferro contract for the same post.

In 1858 Joseph Hersch constructed a steam-powered gristmill on his property on the Rio Chiquito in Santa Fe. The mill, the first of its kind in New Mexico, was driven by an engine originally imported for use in the placer mines in the Ortiz Mountains. According to the *Santa Fe Weekly Gazette*, it was capable of "turning out some hundred fanegas" of flour a day.[69] All of Hersch's earlier contracts had been small and limited to delivery at Fort Marcy; but in 1858 he received a contract for 266,500 pounds and in 1859 a contract for 320,000 pounds, the latter the largest contract held by a miller in that year. In both years he supplied some posts previously served by Otero and St. Vrain. However, when Colonel Johnston inspected the department in 1859 he reported that Hersch's flour was "indifferent—or bad." Early in 1860 Secretary of War John B. Floyd ordered that flour of the quality described not be accepted.[70] Hersch did not again receive a flour contract.

The military continued to spend more for feed and flour than for any other New Mexican products, but appreciable sums were spent for some other commissary stores. Beef cattle were imported, as they had been, over the Santa Fe Trail and in lesser numbers from San Antonio. At some posts civilian herders were hired to care for all of the public animals, including beef cattle; and at other posts herding was left in the hands of the troops. The government maintained its principal herd in the general vicinity of Fort Union, where Moore and Rees held the contract for herding beef cattle from 1854 through August 1858. Their initial contract provided for a payment of 32 cents per head per month for herding within seventy-five miles of Tecolote, with the cattle to be delivered at either Albuquerque or Fort Union. A separate contract was made with Michael Gleason to drive beef cattle from Fort Union to Forts Bliss, Craig, Thorn, and Defiance and to Albuquerque at $3 per head.[71]

In 1855 a new contract was given to Moore and Rees on terms somewhat more favorable to the government. The 32 cents per head for grazing was retained, but the contractors agreed to deliver the cattle to any post in the department for $1.50 per head. Moore and Rees provided two herders for each herd of one hundred cattle. If additional herders were needed the government paid for them at the rate of $18 per herder per month. The contract was to run indefinitely and actually was in effect for two years. In 1857 Major and Brevet Lieutenant Colonel John B. Grayson, who had been chief commissary officer in the department since August 1855, called for new proposals for herding cattle, "2,000 more or less," and specified that he would not entertain bids so low as to suggest that the security of the herd would be neglected.[72] Moore and Rees again received the contract. The cost for herding was reduced to 10 cents per head, which was apparently considered adequate to secure the desired attention; but otherwise the contract remained the same.

In 1858 the herding contract went to Dr. John M. Whitlock of Las Vegas and in 1859 to Whitlock and John L. Taylor.[73] Both contracts were at somewhat higher rates but were otherwise similar to the Moore and Rees contracts. The only contract for herding south of the Jornada del Muerto was awarded in 1857 to Henry Skillman,[74] for herding the cattle allocated to Forts Bliss and Fillmore. He was paid on a sliding scale, ranging from $1 per head per month, for fewer than 200 animals, to 50 cents, for 400 head or more. Skillman also held a contract in 1859 to drive some 800 cattle from Fort Bliss to Fort Craig at 87$^{1}/_{2}$ cents per head.

Although the government beef herds were made up largely of animals driven from Fort Leavenworth, cattle were increasingly available in the territory. Most of the privately owned herds were American cattle; many of them were work animals, either driven from the East or native-born of American stock. In 1854 Peter Joseph of Taos sold 60 head of the cattle he was grazing in the valley of the Rayado to the commissary at Cantonment Burgwin. He asked only $20 a head for American cattle averaging "over 400 lbs. nett weight," an unusually good bargain. Presumably, he was willing to sell so cheaply because some of his cattle had already been run off by Indians and he was fearful of losing the rest.[75] Cattle purchased on the open market at this time usually cost the army about $25 per head, but the price increased in the latter part of the decade.

For a good many years the army bought cattle at so much per head, regardless of weight. Later contracts specified so much per hundred pounds or even per pound, but this meant little because there were no facilities in the department to weigh live cattle. In an attempt to get around this, the Commissary General's Office issued regulations in 1859, providing that where cattle could not be weighed the largest and smallest animals in the herd would be butchered and the parts weighed, thus arriving at an average weight for all the cattle in the herd.[76] This was not a satisfactory solution in New Mexico where the cattle were usually examined and purchased at the owner's ranch or on the range where they grazed. There were still no facilities for weighing the butchered parts, and the owners objected to slaughtering animals when most of the meat would be wasted.

In general, the beef cattle purchased in New Mexico were in better condition than those making up the army's own herds. In 1859, when Colonel Grayson inspected the government herd at Fort Union he reported that never before had he "seen as many poor, old, broken down, diseased and miserable looking cattle in one herd, and in all truth they are not worth the herding." He condemned all but 63 cattle (how many that was he did not say, but apparently it was several hundred) and recommended that they be sold at public auction at Las Vegas. He considered it particularly necessary to dispose of the cattle because the medical officer at Fort Union believed the meat was causing illness among the troops.

At the same time Grayson proposed the purchase of 200 cattle from Henry Connelly and Dr. Stephen Boice of Las Vegas and 600 from Moore and Rees—all offered at $32.50 per head. He rejected a third herd, the property of John Dold of Las Vegas.[77] By 1859 the army seemingly was able to obtain as many cattle as it needed to supplement its own animals. Lots of cattle ranging from fifty to several hundred each were purchased in various parts of the department, but the country east of the Sangre de Cristo Mountains was the principal source. Privately owned herds grazed as far as a hundred miles down the Canadian River; and there were ranches on the Cimarron and Rayado, on the streams in the neighborhood of Fort Union, and on the Pecos more than forty miles below its junction with the Gallinas.

Of the other items constituting the ration, only salt was consistently purchased under contract. Just as consistently, it was described as too coarse and as containing impurities; therefore, some salt was imported from time to time from Fort Leavenworth for distribution to officers. The saving achieved by using New Mexican salt was not great. In 1854 James Cumming of Albuquerque[78] and Michael Gleason had the salt contract for the department depot: 600 bushels at $4.50 per bushel.[79] In the same year "good clean dry fine salt" delivered at Fort Leavenworth for $1 per bushel. In 1855 Cumming was given a three-year contract for 600 bushels per year. In an effort to improve the quality the commissary specified that 450 bushels were to be "superfine" at $5.25 per bushel. For the remaining 150 bushels of "coarse salt" it paid $2 per bushel. When the contract was renewed for one year in 1858 the quantity was increased to 697 bushels, all of it "pure refined salt" at $5.25 per bushel, with the salt to be delivered in "seamless sacks of two bushels or 140 pounds." If the army provided the transportation the price was reduced by 25 cents per bushel. A second contract was made a month later with Louis Zeckendorf[80] of Albuquerque to deliver 500 bushels of salt at the depot. The quality was not specified, and the price was only $1.25 per bushel. No salt contracts have been located for 1859, although bids were requested for 700 bushels of "pure refined" salt and 500 bushels of "washed coarse" salt.[81]

Shortly after he came to New Mexico, Colonel Grayson reported that flour, beans, and salt could be procured in the department for a price 35 to 40 percent cheaper than if freighted from Fort Leavenworth. He was having "a sample of very superior vinegar" analyzed, and if it proved satisfactory, local procurement of vinegar would lead to further savings.[82] The excellent quality of New Mexican beans had never been questioned, but no contracts were made for beans between 1851 and 1856. When the Regiment of Mounted Riflemen was transferred from the Department of Texas to the Department of New Mexico in 1856, Grayson drew up a contract the wisdom of which is open to question. Simeon Hart agreed to furnish 700 bushels of beans to be imported from Santa Cruz, Chihuahua, at the reasonable price of $1.60 per bushel plus the unreasonable transportation charge of $2.90 per hundred pounds per hundred miles. Grayson also ordered an additional 300 bushels to be delivered—part of it at Fort Thorn and part of it near Tucson—on the same terms, though not under contract. The beans, once the cost of transportation was added, were anything but a bargain and provided more than a two-year supply of very expensive beans for all of the posts in the southern part of the department.[83]

In 1857 a contract was given to Franz Huning[84] of Albuquerque to deliver 500 bushels of beans to the general depot for $2.60 per bushel. Thereafter several contracts were let each year for delivery at specified posts:

1858 (3 contractors)	648 bushels	$3.00–6.00 per bushel
1859 (7 contractors)	1,213	2.12½–4.00[85]

Huning also held a contract, with his brother Charles, in 1858. The only other persons to be given a bean contract in more than one year were Tomás C. de Baca, who held contracts in 1859, 1860, and 1861 (the last in partnership with two other suppliers),[86] and Ceran St. Vrain, who held contracts in 1858 and 1861. C. de Baca's contract for 1859, calling for 572 bushels, was the largest single contract for beans grown in New Mexico. It was also the contract providing beans at the lowest price ($2.12½ per bushel for 414 bushels delivered at the general depot).

Prices generally reflected transportation costs, with one marked exception. In 1859, when C. de Baca provided 158 bushels of beans at Fort Union for $2.25 per bushel, Henry Connelly also received a contract to deliver 120 bushels at Fort Union for $4.00 per bushel. The $6 paid for beans in 1858 included the cost of delivery at Fort Massachusetts. Aside from the C. de Baca contracts, the only bean contract with a Spanish American was made in 1860 with Manuel A. Otero.[87] As is evident in regard to other commodities furnished to the government, many of the contractors were not producers, although some of them raised at least part of the beans they sold. In addition to beans purchased under contract, the commissary continued to buy some beans in casual transactions. This was one product that New Mexico could supply in adequate amount and of which there was no adverse criticism.

Apparently the vinegar analyzed at Colonel Grayson's request was satisfactory. Beginning in 1857, contracts were issued for New Mexico vinegar.

Table 8
Contracts for New Mexico Vinegar, 1857–59[88]

1857 (1 contractor)	6,000 gallons	$1.30 per gallon
1858 (4 contractors)	11,208	0.70–1.00
1859 (3 contractors)	8,090	0.60–0.95

The first contract went to Charles P. Clever[89] and Michael Gleason, and it called for delivery at the general depot. Beginning in 1858 the partnership of Kessler[90] and Zeckendorf held the contract for the depot, amounting to more than 20,900 gallons over a three-year period. Aside from the contracts for the depot, there was one for Fort Craig, while the others were for the posts south of the Jornada del Muerto. Peter Deus and John May[91]—who earlier had been engaged in milling, distilling, and brewing in Santa Fe and now were similarly occupied in Las Cruces—supplied vinegar to Fort Fillmore in 1858, while May alone held a contract for Forts Fillmore and Bliss in the following year. Thomas H. Logan also held contracts in both 1858 and 1859.[92] The vinegar was variously described as "grape" or "pure grape" and in one contract as "wine" vinegar. Delivery was made in "well hooped" barrels. As was true of most other things, vinegar was expensive in New Mexico. During the 1850s "good cider vinegar" delivered at Fort Leavenworth for about 20 cents per gallon, so the saving was in transportation and in the lesser wastage.

Pickles and sauerkraut were the only other items purchased under contract by the commissary department in more than one calendar year. Some sauerkraut had been brought into the department but none was purchased locally until the spring of 1857, when Judge James J. Davenport,[93] then chief justice of the territorial supreme court, offered Colonel Grayson sixteen barrels at $1.25 per gallon. Grayson wanted the sauerkraut for issue during an expedition into the Gila Apache country because no fresh vegetables were available; and, as Surgeon William J. Sloan, medical director of the department, assured him, sauerkraut would promote health and prevent scurvy.[94] In the fall of the year a contract was signed with Charles E. Whilden of Santa Fe for 3,500 gallons of pickles and 2,500 gallons of sauerkraut, to be delivered at the depot during the final quarter of 1858. Whilden, who was employed as Grayson's clerk in the commissary department, was given generous terms. He was to be paid the price current in St. Louis, plus what it would have cost had the items been freighted to the department.[95] In 1858 a more reasonable contract was made to furnish sauerkraut at Forts Union and Garland and at Cantonment Burgwin—a total of 800 gallons at $1.61 per gallon. In 1859 bids were requested on 2,100 gallons of sauerkraut and on the same quantity of "mixed pickles."[96]

Records of occasional purchases, other than purchases of beef cattle, by the commissary department are scant. Components of the ration were sometimes acquired in New Mexico when shortages developed, as in 1853 when Preston Beck, Jr., sold more than 8,750 pounds of coffee to Captain Isaac Bowen at Fort Union.[97] In 1855, when the government trains failed to bring coffee from Fort Leavenworth, Colonel Grayson purchased 6,000 pounds in Santa Fe for the general depot.[98] The commissary also bought bacon and sugar in unspecified but limited quantities in New Mexico. Although these items were obtained from local merchants, all were imported. Undoubtedly, similar purchases for which records have not been found were made from time to time.

After the regular army took over the problem of securing specie to meet the expenses in the department was recurrent rather than chronic. There were even a few brief periods when money was abundant and drafts in demand, periods during which the army imposed a surcharge of usually 1 or 2 percent on drafts sold to merchants. Funds were commonly sent to New Mexico in the form of drafts, usually drawn on New York or St. Louis. The quartermaster's department seemed to have no difficulty in obtaining money for St. Louis drafts, but the commissary department considered drafts on New York more readily negotiable.[99] The commissary, quartermaster's, and paymaster's departments all spent comparatively large sums of money and competed with each other for the coin frequently required in their transactions. The pay department soon learned that army officers preferred to be paid in gold because it was "so much less cumbersome than the currency of the country, Mexican dollars."[100] However, the Spanish Americans and Pueblo Indians had a predilection for the silver with which they were more familiar.

Any unusual demand created problems that were intensified by the distance of the department from its sources of money. General Garland complained in 1857 that even though they were "repeatedly urged to do so," the heads of the various departments of the army did not send the needed specie to New Mexico, and the drafts sent in its place sold at a discount of 6 percent. This was all the more serious because the gold that had formerly come from California in exchange for New Mexico's sheep no longer flowed in, and Chihuahua silver had virtually been cut off as a result of the heavy export duty imposed by the Mexican government.[101] Simeon Hart sometimes provided funds for the use of the commissary department at the posts he supplied, presumably in exchange for drafts.[102] The periodic shortage of specie was undoubtedly annoying, but the situation was never again as bad as it had been in the early months of the occupation.

The construction of roads to facilitate the movement of army and civilian freight was accomplished very slowly. The army made minor improvements on some existing roads, particularly as posts were established away from centers of population. Most important, perhaps, was the work undertaken on the route between Taos and Fort Union, much of which ran across very rugged terrain and proved almost impracticable for loaded wagons as well as virtually impassable in wet weather. In the spring of 1853, at the request of Colonel Sumner, First Lieutenant and Brevet Captain John Pope of the Topographical Engineers examined the route and suggested a number of improvements.[103] During the summer, work was undertaken, as far as funds would permit. Some grades were eliminated, and the road was made "perfectly open and safe for loaded wagons," so that the trip between Fort Union and Taos could be made in four days, at least in good weather. However, Colonel Mansfield, who traveled over the road while the work was in progress, recommended an appropriation of $2,000 to straighten it and to reduce the length by twenty or thirty miles.[104]

Until the spring of 1853 the road from Albuquerque to Fort Defiance ran through Cubero to Zuñi, then north to the fort. In May, Major Kendrick strongly urged that the "Oso route"—which branched from the existing route fifteen miles west of Cubero and proceeded via Ojo del Oso to Fort Defiance—be developed for military use. It was about forty miles shorter, traversed no really difficult country, and saved at least two days between Fort Defiance and the general depot; it also made the corn of the Cubero district more accessible to the fort. Kendrick estimated that within a month sixty extra duty men could make the Oso route into an excellent wagon road at a cost of $324.[105] The Oso route soon largely replaced the Zuñi route as a military road, but it would be some time before it attracted much strictly civilian travel.

In July 1854, Congress appropriated $32,000 to repair and improve the existing road from Taos through Santa Fe to Doña Ana.[106] An additional sum of $16,000 was later made available for the road from Fort Union to Santa Fe. Captain Eliakim P. Scammon, Topographical Engineers, was sent from the East to supervise the work; but in October 1855, General Garland ordered him to suspend his activities and reported to the Adjutant General that the step was necessary because "of entire inefficiency on the part of Capt Scammon arising from drunkenness." Scammon, a native of Maine, had not served previously in the West and seemingly was incapable of coping with its arid and unfamiliar reaches. According to the charges brought against him, he spent most of his time in abject and filthy inebriation. The *Gazette* claimed, with not too great exaggeration, that he had wasted the funds without even starting the work. He was court-martialed in April 1856 and dismissed from the army.[107]

Scammon was not replaced until 1857, when Captain John N. Macomb of the Topographical Engineers was ordered to New Mexico, primarily to improve roads useful to the army. In the meantime, Congress had appropriated an additional $32,000 for the construction or improvement of roads from Fort Union to Santa Fe, from Albuquerque to Tecolote, and from Cañada to Abiquiu. After attempting to straighten out Scammon's muddled accounts, Macomb's first task was to widen the Santa Fe–Fort Union road and to reduce some of the steeper grades. He then turned to what was probably the most useful wagon-road construction undertaken by the army in New Mexico prior to the Civil War: the Albuquerque-Tecolote road. The road joined the Santa Fe Trail at San Miguel, and it shortened and otherwise improved the route over which military supplies from Fort Leavenworth reached the general depot. As funds permitted, work was carried out on other roads for which appropriation had been made.

The *Santa Fe Weekly Gazette* lauded Macomb for his accomplishments, stating that of all the government money spent in the territory none had done so much for the "general good and convenience" as that expended for the construction of roads. In his annual message of 1858 to the legislative assembly Governor Abraham Rencher[108] also praised Macomb and noted that the road work, though "ostensibly for military purposes," contributed appreciably to facilitate trade and communications in New Mexico. The benefits already secured were an indication, he added, of what might be accomplished in the future, were government appropriations more liberal.[109] As it happened, no further work of significance was done on New Mexico's roads prior to the Civil War.

In addition to facilitating travel and the movement of freight, road improvements contributed to the expansion of New Mexico's mail service. From no regular internal service at all in the years immediately following the Mexican War, fortnightly delivery reached most settled parts of the territory by 1858. Virtually all of the mail was carried over roads laid out or improved by the army. Some of the routes, although they carried mail to the intervening settlements, were primarily to serve the army. These included the mail routes to Forts Massachusetts, Stanton, and Defiance, and the routes between Tucson and Fort Buchanan.[110]

All of the more isolated posts, other than Fort Defiance, attracted some civilian settlement and promoted the development of agriculture in the areas they protected. This, in conjunction with the improved roads, eased the problem of supplying the posts. Citizens brought in larger quantities of corn and fodder to sell to the quartermasters. By the close of the decade of the fifties all posts other than Forts Defiance and Garland could obtain enough feed from the surrounding districts to meet their needs, and even the difficulty in supplying Fort Defiance had been alleviated. Unquestionably, the development of transportation routes had been of benefit to the military and had promoted the expansion of civilian production.

During the first few years following the Mexican War military purchases, primarily flour and feed, disrupted existing agricultural patterns in New Mexico. Before production had completely adjusted to army demands Colonel Sumner arrived to institute a program that involved undersupplying the department, and he also attempted price fixing as part of his effort to reduce costs. Not until the Garland years did the army assume what might be termed a normal role in New Mexico's economy. Following Sumner's departure the attempt to control prices other than by competitive bidding was largely abandoned. With the gradual buildup of troops and the expansion of both quantity and variety of purchases army expenditures in New Mexico increased several times over, but production adjusted to the army's requirements without interfering with the domestic economy.

6

⚜⚜⚜

Expansion and Contemplated Change

In August 1855, Governor David Meriwether drew up a treaty with the Jicarilla Apaches, bringing an end to a year and a half of sporadic hostilities. An area of about 250 square miles west of the Chama River was set aside for the Indians, and within a month many of them had settled on it.[1] Although the assigned land was at a considerable distance from any military post, the Jicarillas were so reduced in numbers and so destitute that it was not considered necessary to watch them closely. The Jicarillas would continue to be a minor annoyance, but they would never again pose a serious problem to the army. General Garland hoped to restrain the Mescalero Apaches in a similar manner.

The New Mexico Mescaleros were accused of some acts in which they probably did not participate. For a time after they signed a peace treaty in 1852 they caused very little trouble, but their kinsmen in Texas committed numerous depredations along the San Antonio–El Paso road, especially in the vicinity of Eagle Springs.[2] Chief Gómez and his band, operating out of the Davis Mountains of Texas, were largely responsible; but the White Mountain band of New Mexico, whose members had made a genuine effort to be peaceful and had even engaged in a little planting, often were blamed. When several members of a California-bound emigrant party were killed and much of their property taken in August 1853, army reaction was inevitable. General Garland made plans for a campaign against the Mescaleros and gave serious thought to establishing a post to control them.[3]

In December 1853, General Garland ordered Colonel Daniel T. Chandler to lead an expedition into Mescalero country, with instructions to note "everything interesting in a military point of view," including passes traversable by wagons and all sites suitable for a military post, particularly those along the Rio Bonito.[4] Chandler spent more than three weeks in the field without making contact with the Indians. He described the country in the general vicinity of the junction of the Bonito and Ruidoso rivers as an excellent location for a post, though somewhat lacking in better grasses for grazing; and he added that with a little labor a good wagon road could be laid out either to Fort Fillore or to Fort Craig.[5] However, Garland decided that he lacked the manpower to establish a new post at the moment.

The Mescaleros continued their occasional marauding, forcing renewed military action against them. Early in 1855 Garland reported that they were "in open hostility with us," had killed several men, run off a large number of animals along the Pecos, and appeared as close to Santa Fe as Galisteo.[6] In March he sent two columns, one from Fort Fillmore and one from Albuquerque, into Mescalero country to establish a camp at the junction of the Bonito and Ruidoso. The combined expedition included dragoons, infantry, one volunteer company, spies and guides, and twenty-five civilian employees of the commissary and quartermaster's departments—a total of about three hundred men. Supplies for three months were taken, including half rations of forage, and roads were opened by both columns from their respective posts.[7]

Lieutenant Colonel Dixon S. Miles, Third Infantry, who marched from Fort Fillmore, was first on the scene and set up what he called Camp Garland. He was soon joined by Captain and Brevet Major James H. Carleton, First Dragoons, with the column from Albuquerque. In May, General Garland visited the camp. He had intended to conduct a punishing campaign against the Mescaleros, but when Indian Agent Michael Steck intervened on behalf of his charges,[8] he contented himself with selecting the site for a fort in the valley of the Rio Bonito. Except for the volunteers, who were specifically excluded, the troops were put to work getting out the timber to erect a four-company post. The quartermaster's department provided a sawmill to assist in preparing the lumber. Garland expected the post, which he designated Fort Stanton, to "exercise the same influence over [the Mescaleros] as does Fort Defiance over the Navahos."[9] The permanent buildings were constructed primarily of stone and adobe, both available in the immediate vicinity. Colonel Johnston wrote in 1859 that "it is the only post I have seen in the department which has an appearance of durability."[10]

Fort Stanton was located east of the White Mountains at an altitude of about 7,500 feet. It was more than 100 miles by road from its closest neighbor, Fort Craig, and even farther, 175 miles, from the general depot in Albuquerque. The fort was built in an area where settlement had not yet taken place, an area of potential agricultural development once military protection was provided. All supplies had to be brought in over roads crossing one or more mountain ranges and containing some very difficult stretches. The cost of transportation made everything delivered under contract to the fort more expensive than at most of the other posts in the department. When a wagon road was opened in 1857 from Fort Stanton to join the Fort Union–Albuquerque road near Anton Chico, some reduction in cost was achieved.

As was usually the case, the establishment of the post provided protection and soon attracted a few settlers into the area. By 1858 they were located in the valleys of the Ruidoso and Bonito rivers, and particularly in the immediate vicinity of the fort. In that year it was estimated that the little farms produced about twelve thousand bushels of corn, as well as some wheat and oats. In the fall of the year the post commissary purchased 1,400 fanegas of corn at $2.75 and $3.00 per fanega and 100 tons of fodder at $20.00 per ton.[11] The feed, intended for the post's beef cattle herd, cost appreciably less than the corn and hay purchased under contract by the quartermaster's department at Fort Stanton in that year. In 1859 it was estimated that in years of normal rainfall and good crops enough corn would be grown in the vicinity of the post to supply all of its needs, and that an abundance of excellent hay could be cut in the area.[12]

Between 1846 and 1861 the only major change in the territorial extent of the department occurred as a result of the Gadsden Purchase Treaty, which transferred some 19 million acres of land between the Rio Grande and the Colorado River to the United States. Although the treaty was signed on December 30, 1853, and promulgated in Washington, D.C. on June 30, 1854, it had only a minimal effect on the department for some time. In August 1854, the purchased territory was added to New Mexico by act of Congress, and when the New Mexico territorial legislature met in December it extended Doña Ana County to include the entire area;[13] but these steps were not immediately implemented. The Gadsden Treaty provided that the United States pay Mexico $10 million for the territory, but the final $3 million was to be withheld until the boundary had been "surveyed, marked, and established." Captain and Brevet Major William H. Emory, Topographical Engineers, United States Commissioner for the survey of the new boundary, advised very strongly that the final payment not be made until the official demarcation had been formally accepted by both parties.[14]

The portion of the Mesilla Valley west of the Rio Grande, opposite Las Cruces and Fort Fillmore and extending to the south, was only a small part of the purchase; but it was the part that caused the greatest contention. As late as October 1854, Colonel Dixon S. Miles reported that the Mexican authorities still exercised jurisdiction over Mesilla, endeavoring to collect taxes and thoroughly confusing the inhabitants. United States citizens were determined to introduce goods, and the Mexicans were equally determined to seize anything on which import duties were not paid. The resultant tension threatened to lead to hostilities.[15] The Mesilla Valley could not be left indefinitely to serve as a center of friction. In November 1854 General Garland and Governor Meriwether went together to Franklin (now El Paso), Texas, where they accepted the hospitality of Simeon Hart rather than the more austere comforts of Fort Bliss. Meriwether conferred with Governor Angel Trías of Chihuahua, who "at once consented to deliver possession of the disputed territory" to the United States.

On November 15, General Garland, escorted by Colonel Miles and a portion of the garrison of Fort Fillmore, occupied Mesilla and hoisted the United States flag above the plaza. The military band played; Meriwether made a speech and distributed copies of a proclamation printed in Spanish, conveniently prepared before he had left Santa Fe; and the transfer was accomplished.[16] The only area affected was the Mesilla Valley, with an estimated population of about three thousand clustered principally around the settlements of Mesilla, Picacho, and Santo Tomás. Farther west in the Gadsden Purchase the closest European settlement was in the valley of the Santa Cruz River, in what is now Arizona. There the only significant population center was Tucson, protected by the Presidio of San Agustín de Tucson, which was garrisoned by about one hundred Mexican soldiers.

Fort Fillmore was well located to extend protection to the settlements in the Mesilla Valley, by definition the only settled portion of the Gadsden Purchase to fall within the limits of the Military Department of New Mexico. The Territory of New Mexico west of 110 degrees longitude, including the valley of the Santa Cruz River, was specifically assigned to the Department of the Pacific.[17] Following the signing of the Gadsden Treaty a few United States citizens began to move into the Tucson area, attracted by reports of mineral wealth that was still largely undeveloped because of the persistent Apache menace. One of the first companies formed to exploit the known mines was the Arizona Mining and Trading Company, organized in September 1854 in San Francisco, California.

When the company sought to reopen the Ajo copper mines it ran afoul of a group of Sonorans who claimed the property and threatened to take possession by armed force if necessary. Edward E. Dunbar, director of the mining company, appealed, and quite properly, to Brevet Major General John E. Wool, commander of the Department of the Pacific, for military protection. General Wool forwarded the request to Secretary of War Jefferson Davis, who set forth the position of the government:

> The boundary line not having been established the right to hold possession is still in the govt of Mexico and the Comg Genl of the Dept of the Pacific will notify the applicant that his proposed occupation of land to which the U.S. has no other claim than that to be derived from a treaty not yet fulfilled would be a trespass upon the territory of Mexico.[18]

As his party approached the Santa Cruz Valley in May 1855, Major Emory anticipated that the boundary survey would be completed within a few months. He was pleased to find that the southwestern portion of the Gadsden Purchase was more valuable than had been supposed, containing much land suitable for cultivation and being rich in gold, silver, and other metals. He advised Secretary of the Interior Robert McClelland that once an adequate military force was available to protect the area settlers would move in. Hence, as soon as the Mexican garrison was withdrawn from Tucson, it would be essential to send United States troops to guard the population, including the friendly Indians, against the Apaches.[19] In August, Major Emory informed General Garland that he expected to finish his survey before the month was out, and Emory suggested informally to the Mexican commander at Tucson that he remain there until the United States sent troops to replace him.[20]

The few Americans who had settled in the Santa Cruz Valley feared that they would be left at the mercy of the Apaches. In September 1855, the residents of Tucson petitioned General Garland, inaccurately predicting that the Mexican garrison was about to depart and asking him to send a force to occupy the town. The petition, written in Spanish, carried the names of two Anglos and sixty-nine Spanish Americans. Most of the signatures were in the hand of Frederick Goerlitz, who also wrote a letter to support the petition: "We are here about eight U.S. citizens living, some of us already for more than one year most anxiously waiting for the taking possession of this territory by the U.S. government. . . ." According to Goerlitz, sufficient wheat, corn, beans, and beef were available near Tucson to meet army needs, but all other supplies would have to be freighted in because local prices were prohibitive.[21] Emory had reported earlier that the army would be able to purchase flour and beef, and perhaps coffee and sugar, for less in Tucson than elsewhere in New Mexico or in California.[22]

Another Anglo, one who did not sign the petition, also asked that troops be sent because of the imminent removal of the Mexican garrison, and not only to protect the settlers already there but to promote further immigration and to encourage the development of mining. In his opinion the newly purchased territory was "far ahead of California" in good land, water, timber, and mineral resources—"but those Indians Indians Indians"![23] These pleas brought forth a bevy of reactions. Garland correctly stated that "it is believed Tucson is not in this department." Adjutant General Samuel Cooper pointed out that the transfer of the territory to the United States had not been completed, and so the request for troops was premature. Jefferson Davis noted that when the jurisdiction of the United States was extended over the area it would become part of New Mexico. "A garrison will [then] no doubt be necessary at or near Tucson."[24] He seemed to imply that the garrison would be provided by the Department of New Mexico.

The final installment of $3 million was paid to Mexico in February 1856, although the completed boundary maps were not exchanged until the following June. The Mexican garrison was withdrawn from Tucson in March, leaving the area, as the inhabitants had feared, without organized defense; but the establishment of a United States Army post was delayed until additional troops were sent to the department. The entire Regiment of Mounted Riflemen was transferred from Texas to New Mexico, with the first companies reaching Fort Bliss early in August and the rest arriving before the month was out. Late in July, in anticipation of their arrival, Garland ordered the regimental headquarters and three of the seven companies of First Dragoons then stationed in New Mexico to march to the Department of the Pacific. The four remaining First Dragoon companies, under the command of Major Enoch Steen, were "selected to take post at Tucson."[25]

Steen was directed to proceed with his command to Tucson and, once there, to determine "whether the Military under the Mexican government, had any claim to lands; barracks, or buildings used as such; storehouses &c. &c.; and if so . . . have them repaired, and occupy them until further orders." If there were no public buildings he was to choose a position suitable for the protection of the settlements in the Santa Cruz Valley, but not one on privately owned land unless it could be leased for a minimum of twenty years with an option to purchase. There he would erect a four-company post, to be constructed, preferably, of adobes. "The primary object of establishing a military post in this newly acquired territory," Garland informed Steen, "is to protect the lives, and property of its inhabitants, but in doing this, great care must be taken not to provoke hostilities with the neighboring Indian tribes."[26] All of this reflected the army's experience of the past decade in New Mexico.

Although all of the Mounted Riflemen were in the department before the end of August, Steen's departure was delayed until mid-October, while he awaited the arrival of supplies and the wagons and draft animals to transport his goods and baggage. Some of the commissary stores came from the general depot, but the flour and at least part of the beans were provided by Simeon Hart under his expensive 1856 contracts. Eventually all of the command assembled at Fort Thorn. Accompanied by a wagon train loaded with a six-month supply of stores and a herd of beef cattle, Steen advanced over a route laid out by Second Lieutenant John G. Parke, Topographical Engineers, in the course of his railway survey along the 32d parallel.

The march to the Santa Cruz Valley was uneventful, although many of the cattle did not survive; and the dragoons encamped near the Mission San Xavier del Bac, some nine miles south of Tucson, on November 14, 1856. In compliance with his instructions Steen first visited Tucson, where he found "no public quarters or lands, excepting a few miserable huts, unfit for use even taken in their best condition." Moreover, he considered the available forage and grazing entirely too scant and the country about Tucson unhealthful for both horses and men. Captain Ewell concurred, at least as far as horses were concerned. He reported that one-third of his company's horses came down with colic, and one horse died from grazing in the vicinity of "St. Zavier & Tuzon."[27]

Having rejected Tucson, Steen moved up the valley of the Santa Cruz, carefully examining the country as he advanced; and on November 27 he selected the unoccupied Calabasas Ranch,[28] about nine miles north of the Mexican border, as the most eligible site for a permanent post. Even though there was nothing in the general area to protect, Steen predicted that the presence of troops would cause ranches and settlements to spring up along the Santa Cruz and its affluents. As for the availability of requisites to support a post, he was optimistic. Grazing was excellent, and hay (native grass) could be purchased at $18 per ton. Little corn was raised north of the border, but Calabasas was "conveniently located" to obtain corn from Sonora. Flour and beef were plentiful, both at $6 per hundred pounds, and beans and salt cost much less than if freighted from the Rio Grande Valley. Supplies not procurable locally could be imported over a "fine wagon road" through the port of Guaymas. Fine timber for building and oak and mesquite for firewood were abundant within a distance of twenty miles, and there was a spring on the site to irrigate a post garden. Finally, the locality was "said to be healthy." Steen painted a most attractive picture, though not an accurate one, and he proposed to lease from the owner, Governor Manuel María Gándara of Sonora, sufficient land for a military reservation.[29]

It is difficult to understand why Steen decided that Calabasas Ranch was the proper location for a post. Both public land and buildings existed in Tucson, and if the buildings were dilapidated and inadequate for four companies the army could build a new post at Tucson as readily as it could build elsewhere. Calabasas was about sixty miles south of Tucson and not in a position to protect any of the Santa Cruz Valley's few inhabitants, although it would undoubtedly encourage new settlement. Steen also rushed into his decision without undertaking a proper investigation. What rights the government could acquire to the proposed site, to what extent the army could depend on supplies available locally (which really meant supplies obtained in Sonora), and whether the location was as healthful as it was purported to be were questions left unanswered. When the answers came in they were all negative.

Steen proceeded to establish a post which he first called Camp near Calabasas and then designated Camp Moore.[30] Some of the existing ranch structures were occupied, but they were inadequate for the four under-strength dragoon companies. Jacales were erected to quarter most of the men, but no beginning was made toward the construction of a permanent post. Two of Steen's companies were constantly in the saddle, attempting, and not too successfully, to curb Apache marauding; other men were required to guard the beef herd and to open roads. Captain Ewell laid out a new route to connect Calabasas more directly with the San Pedro River; and Steen planned to extend the route to Cow Spring, fifteen miles west of the Rio Mimbres, thus shortening the distance to Fort Thorn by one hundred miles. Believing that his command would be occupied indefinitely by these duties, he asked permission to let a contract for the construction of the post, since "eventually it will be the cheapest way."[31]

Some of the problems that beset the new post might have been avoided had it not been for the slowness of communications with department headquarters. Major Steen organized a monthly military mail between

Camp Moore and Fort Thorn, where it connected with the regular express service to Santa Fe. Even so, the announcement that he had selected Calabasas as the site for a post did not reach headquarters until after the new post had been established, and Steen apparently did not receive a reply until February 1857.

On October 11, 1856, in order to avail himself of a leave of absence, General Garland turned the department command over to Colonel Benjamin L. E. Bonneville, Third Infantry.[32] Thus it was Bonneville who informed Steen that Calabasas was not an acceptable site for a post. Bonneville pointed out that "the first object contemplated by the Department in sending troops to that region of country is frustrated, our settlements will gradually grow weaker, whilst the country around your present site will be filled up by settlers, but on the other side of the line, in the state of Sonora." He directed Steen to renew his efforts to find a suitable location close to Tucson or, if he could not, to assign a detachment to protect the town. As for supplies, Bonneville warned that it would be a mistake to depend on imports either from or through Sonora.[33]

Even before he had the benefit of Bonneville's advice, Steen began to have second thoughts about Calabasas. Gándara demanded far too high a price for either the lease or the sale of his property. Hence, Steen reexamined "all of the known points of the 'purchase'" in an effort to find a more suitable location for the post. He still considered Tucson to be an impossible station for mounted troops. Moreover, it was neither a center for production nor for consumption. It had, in his unflattering opinion, been "built for no other reason than that there was protection [the presidio], and now requiring protection because it has been built." The Mission San Xavier, as well as having all the shortcomings of Tucson, was claimed by the Pima and Papago Indians, who would not willingly lease it to the government. He rejected all other sites in the vicinity of Tucson because they lacked the essentials for building and maintaining a post.[34]

Captain Ewell strongly recommended the valley of the Sonoita River as encompassing the only good sites for a post west of the San Pedro River. Near the source of the Sonoita there was an abundance of wood, grass, and water for both a post and a garden. Fine building timber could be obtained within a dozen miles. The area, of course, was "healthy." It was some forty miles from Tucson, closer by twenty miles than Camp Moore, and it was also nearer to the country of the hostile Apaches. Ewell neglected to mention that the direct approach to Tucson was blocked by the intervening Santa Rita Mountains. A post on the site, he wrote,

> would hasten the settlement of the Sonoita & San Pedro waters by respectable people & afford protection to the mines opened & to be opened around Calabasas, we will soon be supplied with forage, beef, flour and beans from our vicinity. We are on the Indian pass with the settlements in our rear & the Indians forced to approach after a robbery, to return to their own country.

Ewell predicted that the post "would consume all the forage raised at Tuczon & the only sufferers by our absence would be the whiskey sellers & those who hope to profit from the dissipation of the Soldiers."[35]

Steen agreed unreservedly with Ewell's selection, and he specifically proposed as the only location reasonably satisfactory for a post the Ojos Calientes, which he described as "two clusters of springs, each having an abundance of water, situated within one and a half miles of each other." The site was on the road newly opened to the San Pedro River, and no grants had been made in the area, nor were there any known claimants to the land. To bolster his selection of the site rather than of one closer to Tucson, Steen claimed:

> As a center from which to protect the natural agricultural portions of this country, it is the only one, that in pursuance of the policy of protection by placing troops in the settlements, could be selected. The valleys of the San Pedro, the Babacomeri, the Sonoita and the Santa Cruz, any one of which far surpasses, in an agricultural point of view, the country about Tucson, will, in a few years, instead of being as heretofore devoted almost exclusively to grazing, be settled by a population chiefly of Americans, capable of defending itself against Indian depredations. The amount of grain raised in our own territory near the post during the present summer will far exceed that which could by any probability be raised in Tucson, were it completely protected, and, in a short time the resources now developing and to be developed in our own territory, will be ample for all the requirements of the post.

If Tucson were occupied by the army, reasoned Steen, agricultural production there would decline to the extent that water was diverted for the use of the military post. He also made what he apparently considered a telling point. Already a number of Americans, "whose only calling is labor," had settled in the vicinity of Camp Moore with their wives and children. If the post were moved to Tucson "they would at once abandon their improvements" and move to California. As it was, the majority of the Americans to be protected in Tucson were those "recently driven out of California by the Vigilance Committee."[36]

If Steen's impression of Tucson was unflattering, the citizens of the town were equally caustic in expressing their opinion of Steen. Obviously influenced by the belief that a military post should be a source of income to the community, they claimed that Steen's disposition of the troops was a positive detriment. So much corn had been consumed as feed by army mounts that there was a serious shortage of breadstuff for the local population. The army had "retired to the extreme edge of the Territory," where it offered no protection and was too far away to afford employment for those deprived of their food. But this was not the greatest damage inflicted by Steen's "stuborness or indisposition" to carry out the instructions of the War Department. By locating the post either at Calabasas or on the Sonoita he would force the Apaches, on their marauding expeditions into Mexico, to pass closer to Tucson, thus making it "more dangerous for a small number of persons to travel (even in the immediate vicinity of Tucson) than in former days." True, the site on the Sonoita was closer, "according to a tape line measurement"; but by road, and a very poor road at that, the distance was at least as great.

The citizens of Tucson then turned their attention to Steen's motives. The residents claimed that he was influenced by private interests because he and his fellow officers devoted their attention to farming at Calabasas (and how Sumner would have rejoiced):

> It appears to your petitioners that if Major Steen has been sent to this position of the Territory for the purpose of turning the "Sabre" into the Ploughshare, and teaching the soldiers under his command the science of agriculture, then he has taken an admirable position, but on the other hand if he was sent here to protect the lives and property of the citizens of the "Gadsden Purchase," then he has gone wide of the mark, some protection it is sure he affords the state of "Sonora" but none whatever to his countrymen.

As Steen had provided neither protection nor (more particularly it would seem) economic gain to Tucson, the petitioners urged that he be forced to fulfill his proper function or be replaced by someone who would.[37]

The first troops to occupy the site of what would soon be called Fort Buchanan arrived on March 5, 1857. However, they were pulled out almost at once to participate in Colonel Bonneville's campaign against the Apache Indians. Not until June 3 was a company sent to begin the construction of Fort Buchanan.[38] The new post was located "at the head of a small valley, in the extensive broken foot hills of the south-eastern slope of the Santa Rita mountain." A general plan was drawn up in Santa Fe, but it was only vaguely followed. As the post developed, it turned into something "built more like a village than a military post," extending "down the slope of a low ridge even into the valley."[39]

Asserting that field duties would hamper the ability of the troops to engage in construction, Steen requested permission to hire civilians to erect quarters before winter set in. Garland, unimpressed, authorized only a mason, a carpenter, and a blacksmith. In addition, a civilian was employed at a salary of $50 per month to put up a sawmill and was retained for a short time to operate it. Later an agreement was reached with a number of Spanish Americans to make adobes at $4 per thousand, and some fifty thousand adobes were made before the arrangement was discontinued.[40] By the end of 1857 the quarters and barracks were nearing completion and the post hospital was ready for use. The entire command, according to Steen, would shortly "be housed and comfortable with but little expense to the Government."[41]

Undoubtedly, the condition of the post was influenced by the uncertainty of its future. Almost from the moment of the fort's establishment there was talk of relocating it. Captain and Brevet Colonel Isaac V. D. Reeve of the Eighth Infantry, who took command of Fort Buchanan in the spring of 1859, was highly critical: "It occupies ten times the ground it ought to, being on & around a side hill of considerable abruptness— and does not admit of any considerable improvement in a military point of view—the buildings being located with great irregularity & irrespective of defence."[42] Colonel Joseph E. Johnston, who in the autumn of 1859 subjected Fort Buchanan to its only general inspection, described the sorry condition of the buildings. Some of the officers' quarters were built of adobe, but most of the structures were "of logs, or wooden slabs, set on end in the ground & the intervals closed with mud—most of which, however, has fallen out. They are too open for winter & not sufficiently ventilated for summer. Fortunately very little labour, or, it is to be presumed, money, has been expended upon them."[43]

It remained for Assistant Surgeon Bernard I. D. Irwin to provide the least flattering picture of the "scattered, ill looking, temporary buildings of the post," erected without thought of permanent occupation and surrounded on three sides by "a swampy morass." The buildings were neither neat nor comfortable.

(TOP) Fort Fillmore, New Mexico. (From *The Illustrated London News*, December 2, 1854.)

(BOTTOM LEFT) Colonel John Macrae Washington, military governor of New Mexico, 1848–49. (Courtesy, Museum of New Mexico.)

(LEFT) General Edward R. S. Canby. (Courtesy, Museum of New Mexico.)

(RIGHT) Colonel Edwin Vose Sumner. (Lithograph by Alonzo Chapel; Courtesy, Museum of New Mexico.)

(TOP) Pueblo of Laguna, New Mexico. (Drawn by Captain Seth Eastman, 1847, from a sketch by R. H. Kern; Courtesy, Museum of New
Mexico.)

(BOTTOM) Pueblo of Zuñi, New Mexico. (Drawn by Captain Seth
Eastman, 1847, from a sketch by R. H. Kern; Courtesy, Museum of New
Mexico.)

(TOP) Hospital at Fort Marcy in Santa Fe, New Mexico, ca. 1875. (Courtesy, U.S. Army Signal Corps Collections, Museum of New Mexico.)

(BOTTOM) Company Quarters, Fort Craig, New Mexico, ca. 1865–68. (Courtesy, U.S. Army Signal Corps Collections, Museum of New Mexico.)

(TOP) An artist's conception of the valley of copper mines as it may have been viewed in 1853. Fort Webster originally occupied the triangular structure in the foreground. (Courtesy, Museum of New Mexico.)

(BOTTOM) Cantonment Burgwin, New Mexico, March 1857. (Drawing by Major William W. Anderson; Courtesy, Museum of New Mexico.)

(TOP) Fort Thorn, New Mexico. (Courtesy, U.S. Army Signal Corps Collections, Museum of New Mexico.)

(BOTTOM) Fort Union, New Mexico, 1856–61. (From Du Bois and Heger, "Campaigns of the West"; Courtesy, Museum of New Mexico.)

	58.			
	Captain Francisco Gonzales			
	Bought of Spiegelberg Bro.			
	Sutler for N Mex Volunteers			
1861				
Oct 2	Bottles Ale	1	50	
2	" Champagne	3	00	
1	" Brandy	2	00	
1	" Champagne	1	50	
1	Broom		75	
1	Bottle Brandy	2	00	
1	" "	2	00	
4	" Beer	3	00	
1	" Brandy	2	00	
	Brandy		50	
	order	3	12	
1	Trunk	5	00	
1/2	Bottle Champagne	1	50	
1	Bucket	1	00	
2	Combs		50	
	Oysters + Pigeon	3	50	
1	ps Lunch	0	50	
2	Cans Grouse	3	50	
1	Bottle Ale		75	
	Whiskey		50	
	Cash	5	00	
1/2	pints Whiskey		75	
1	quart "	1	00	
	Cards		37	
1	Can Grouse	1	75	
1	Hat	4	00	
1	Can Duck	1	75	
1	Shoebrush		37	
1	Bottle Gin	2	00	
		61	11	

Copy of the ledger of purchases in October 1861 by Captain Francisco
Gonzales at Spiegelberg Bros., sutlers for the New Mexico Volunteers.
(Courtesy, Michael Stephen Martinez Memorial Collection, Rio Grande
Historical Collections, New Mexico State University Library.)

The chinking remains only long enough to dry, shrink, and tumble out, never to be replaced, lest it should destroy a new system of ventilation which its absence has established. During the wet weather the mud roofs are worse than useless—save it be for the purpose of giving dirty shower baths to the unhappy occupants. . . . The picket lines used for stabling purposes are in front of and close to the barracks. Stables, corrals, pig-pens, root-houses, open latrines, and dwellings, are indiscriminately scattered all over the camp, wherever the fancy of the owner prompted him to squat. The physical nature of the ground renders anything like uniformity or regularity impossible.[44]

The hospital, constructed of adobes with a raised earthen floor, was the only building considered adequate by Colonel Johnston; but Surgeon William J. Sloan stated flatly that it was "equally [as] primitive and unsuitable" as the others.[45] It is clear that Fort Buchanan was the least prepossessing military post in the department, though not necessarily the most uncomfortable.

The problem of supplying the post began as soon as Steen's command reached the Santa Cruz Valley, and to this problem Steen contributed. The train which accompanied him from the Rio Grande brought a six-month supply of commissary stores, as well as all other supplies deemed necessary for the support of four dragoon companies. General Garland hoped that some items of subsistence could be obtained in the vicinity of Tucson, but he was prepared to freight everything required by the post from the Rio Grande Valley for an indefinite period. A wagon train loaded with stores for Elias Brevoort,[46] the post sutler, left Fort Thorn under escort in November 1856, and a quartermaster's train followed in February 1857.[47]

Shortly after Camp Moore was established, Steen recommended that no more flour, beef, salt, or beans be sent from the general depot because, he claimed, they could be secured more advantageously locally.[48] As a result, plans to send an additional six-month supply of flour to Camp Moore were dropped. However, almost as soon as this was done, Steen approved an estimate for commissary stores, including 176,000 pounds of flour, 200 bushels of beans, 250 bushels of salt, and 450 head of beef cattle. Then, to add further confusion, he announced that beef cattle and beans could be purchased more cheaply at the post than in the Rio Grande Valley. However, in his estimate of commissary funds required for the first quarter of 1857, the only items for which he requested an appropriation were fresh beef and sheep. Cattle could be purchased for

$18 per head, less than in the more eastern part of New Mexico, but sheep cost a relatively expensive $3 per head. The total sum requested by the commissary for the quarter was $7,618, including $5,000 for meat animals and $1,000 for cattle feed.[49]

Whatever hope there was of obtaining a significant quantity of commissary stores close at hand was destroyed when a power struggle flared up between Manuel María Gándara and José de Aguilar in Sonora, shortly after Camp Moore was established.[50] As Bonneville had predicted, it was unwise to place too much reliance on a foreign source for necessities. Steen, who a short time before had been so sanguine, now reported that the grain in Sonora had been burned in the fields and that other supplies on which he had counted had been destroyed.[51] On March 3, 1857, he informed Garland that it would be impossible to make contracts for flour until the new wheat crop was harvested. Hence, it was "of the greatest importance that the flour estimated for and required . . . be at once forwarded." Four days later he fired off an express announcing that he had just arranged to purchase a three-month supply of flour at 11 cents per pound, presumably in Sonora, and that he could get additional flour at 9 cents. Again he asked that no more flour be sent, "even if estimated for and approved."[52]

Colonel Bonneville was unable to understand Steen's constant "uncertainty and wavering" and suggested that Steen "be more fixed in [his] actions in the future."[53] In view of the unsettled conditions in Sonora and Steen's vacillation, Colonel Grayson decided to send 75,000 pounds of flour and 120 bushels of salt to Camp Moore. The salt came from the general depot, but the flour was from Hart's Santa Cruz mills. Hart furnished the train, eighteen wagons and each drawn by a ten-mule team. Thirty-five of his employees, "but few fighting men amongst them," handled the train, and the army provided a small escort between Fort Thorn and Camp Moore.[54] Obviously, this was expensive flour.

The contracts with Majors, Russell, and Waddell, drawn up in 1855 (for two years) and in 1857, provided for delivery at any of the posts in the department. In the winter of 1857 the *Gazette* reported that there were between eighty and ninety of the contractor's wagons engaged in hauling army stores to Tucson. These were drawn by oxen, six teams to the wagon, with each wagon carrying a load of 5,600 pounds.[55] However, this was not the usual situation, because most of the transportation between the Rio Grande and the Arizona post, except for Hart's flour and beans, was handled by quartermaster's trains.

Generally speaking, Fort Buchanan was adequately supplied, although the cost remained high. Initially, at least, there was little difficulty in obtaining funds for the post. Drafts on St. Louis banks were all but useless, but drafts on the New York sub-treasury were readily exchanged in Sonora, either for stores or for such United States money as was available. On the other hand, "small coinage," dollars or smaller currency, was not to be had. Mexican coin commanded a premium of 8 to 10 percent in San Francisco and was too expensive for army use; hence, the post was dependent on what it could obtain from department headquarters.[56]

In the spring of 1858, Major Steen and two of the dragoon companies stationed at Fort Buchanan were transferred to the Department of the Pacific.[57] This left only two companies of the regiment in New Mexico and elevated Captain Ewell to the command of Fort Buchanan. In October Ewell reported that he had on hand more than a year's supply of flour and more than a two-year supply of bacon for the reduced garrison. He proposed that he be allowed to purchase additional flour locally, should it be needed. This was now feasible because William and Alfred Rowlett had erected a small, modern gristmill on the Santa Cruz River adjacent to Tucson, which had commenced operation in 1857 or 1858. Ewell also suggested that it might be wise to dispose of part of the bacon before it deteriorated in weight and quality.[58]

Simeon Hart had already been given a flour contract, to run to September 1, 1859, for the delivery of 110,000 pounds to Fort Buchanan at $12^{1/2}$ cents per pound. Of this price, 3 cents represented the cost of transportation from Fort Thorn.[59] The flour contract could not be cancelled because it was already in effect. As to the bacon, Ewell was told to keep it, for it would be difficult to replace if needed and, if properly cared for, it would be better, even after a year, "than any bacon made in New Mexico."[60] Of course, almost no bacon was made in New Mexico.

Except for the flour provided by Hart, no supplies were purchased under contract specifically for Fort Buchanan prior to 1859. Necessary stores were hauled, primarily, either by quartermaster's trains from the depot at Albuquerque, via Fort Thorn, or by the quartermaster at Fort Buchanan, who sent his own wagons to pick up stores deposited at Fort Thorn or at Fort Fillmore. As a result, Fort Buchanan had more transportation facilities than most of the other posts in the department. Just before the garrison was halved in 1858 there were twenty-two wagons with the requisite teams and equipment at the post. It was also one of the few posts authorized to employ a civilian wagon master.[61]

Almost everything purchased at Fort Buchanan was a little more expensive than elsewhere in the department. The same was true of stores
freighted to the post. The fort's closest neighbors in the department were
some 250 miles distant (actually, it was closer to Fort Yuma, a post in
the Department of the Pacific, than to any post in New Mexico), and
it was located almost twice as far from the general depot as any other
post in the department. Fort Buchanan would have been even more
expensive to maintain had it not been for the increase in local production.
Quite clearly, the presence of the military attracted settlement and encouraged the development of agriculture as well as mining. Even in the
short time Camp Moore was occupied, some ranching sprang up along
the upper Santa Cruz Valley. Tubac, abandoned in 1848 in the face of
Apache incursions, was reoccupied in 1856 and became headquarters for
the Sonora Exploring and Mining Company.

When Colonel Bonneville visited Fort Buchanan in 1858 he found
that below the post, wherever the valley of the Sonoita widened, farms
had been opened. The industrious Pima Indians were a source of corn
and beans, and they sold so much of their crop in 1859 that they were
themselves virtually destitute. Bonneville noted that the laborers employed in the mines were "all Mexicans from Sonora"; and in remarking
that most of the supplies for the civilian population also came from
Sonora, he declared this would continue "until all the lands on the Santa
Cruz and San Pedro rivers are brought into cultivation to the full extent
of their waters."[62] Apparently all of the fresh beef consumed at the post
came from cattle acquired in the immediate vicinity; at least there are
no records of herds driven from the Rio Grande. The commissary purchased a small quantity of flour locally, which was presumably the product
of the Rowletts' Tucson mill. Even so, for the time being Fort Buchanan
remained dependent on the general depot and on Simeon Hart for the
great bulk of its commissary stores.

The expansion of feed production was important to the army and to
the economy of the area. After the garrison was reduced to two companies, Captain Ewell stated that more corn was raised in the district
than could be consumed at the post.[63] In the first quarter of 1858 the
quartermaster bought from individuals almost 280,000 pounds of corn
and 115 tons of hay. He paid 5 cents per pound, the equivalent of $7
per fanega, for both corn and a small quantity of barley. This was a price
considerably higher than was paid at any other post in the department
at the time. It is not clear that the barley was grown in the vicinity, but

the price implies that it was not transported a great distance. Hay varied in price from one month to another at Fort Buchanan, moving through the narrow range of $25 to $27 per ton, no more than was paid at most of the other posts.

The total sum expended for local products by the quartermaster's department at Fort Buchanan during the first quarter of 1858 was $17,298.68, which was paid out to thirteen different suppliers, and, in addition to feed, included lime, charcoal, and adobes. Adobes at this time cost the much higher price of $14 per thousand.[64] As long as Fort Buchanan was garrisoned by four dragoon companies the quartermaster issued an average of almost 160,000 pounds of corn monthly. Hay consumption varied between 49 and 93 tons during the months for which records are available, the amount decreasing as the season advanced and as grazing improved. The post employed two expressmen, one wagon master, one blacksmith, one interpreter, and varying numbers of teamsters and herders. When scouting expeditions were made into Apache country civilian guides were hired at wages ranging from $2 to $5 per day, but there was not the consistent use of spies and guides that there was elsewhere in the department. The total amount paid to civilian employees was less than $1,000 per month.[65]

In the autumn of 1857 Garland finally acted to accomplish something that he had proposed since his first days as department commander. He ordered one of the two companies stationed at Fort Massachusetts to withdraw to Cantonment Burgwin as soon as cold weather arrived; and the first frost came very early at the foot of Mount Blanca. One commissioned officer and all of the mechanics in the company were left behind to assist in constructing a new two-company post that was to be located between Ute and Trinchera creeks, about eight miles south of Fort Massachusetts but still some fifteen miles north of the closest settlement. However, the new post would be built away from the foothills and upon the valley floor, where it would be in a much better position to offer protection to the settlers.[66]

The new post, still under construction, was occupied on June 24, 1858. A civilian was hired at $85 per month to set up a sawmill and to supervise the cutting of lumber; and John M. Francisco, the post sutler, provided adobes under contract.[67] All buildings were constructed of adobes, and only the officers' quarters and the commissary storehouse had wooden floors. When Colonel Johnston inspected the post in August 1859 it was nearing completion, and he described the buildings as "adequate." He also remarked that it was connected to Albuquerque and Fort Union, "the two points from which military stores are received—by roads in many places barely practicable."[68] Two distinct benefits were derived from the relocation. Even though the fort was located at an elevation of just under eight thousand feet, the post garden was more successful than the garden at Fort Massachusetts had been, and there was a notable improvement in the health of the garrison. The post was originally referred to as the New Post of Fort Massachusetts, but it was soon designated Fort Garland.

General Garland gave some thought to establishing or relocating other posts, particularly if additional troops were assigned to the department. By 1858, William Pelham,[69] surveyor general for the territory, had pushed the survey of public land down the Canadian River Valley toward the Texas boundary, where he reported that the country had excellent agricultural potential. At the same time, preparations were under way to open a mail route from Neosho, Missouri, to Albuquerque. To protect the mail route and to encourage settlement Garland recommended the establishment of a four-company post near the junction of Ute Creek and the Canadian River in Kiowa-Comanche country.[70] This he proposed as a replacement for the badly run-down Fort Union, which he believed no longer served a useful purpose where it was, not to mention the excessive rent paid for the reservation.

Fort Buchanan also continued to be a candidate for change. In addition to public dissatisfaction with its location, its shoddy construction, and its unhealthiness, there was a more compelling consideration: the projected Butterfield Overland Mail. That the overland mail would require protection from the Apaches seemed probable, and that Fort Buchanan was improperly located to provide such protection was certain. Captain John W. Davidson, who conducted a minor campaign out of Fort Buchanan against the Coyotero Apaches early in 1858, suggested that a post established at the junction of the San Pedro River and Aravaipa Creek would control the Coyoteros and thus would protect the settlements, the mail route, and eventually a railroad. As was almost always the case in such proposals, Davidson asserted that all necessary facilities for building and maintaining a post were available near the site and claimed that "an enterprising officer having four companies under his command, at this point, could subdue the Coyotero nation within a year." Major Steen agreed and predicted that if Fort Buchanan were relocated "large settlements" would be made in the valleys of the Gila and San Pedro, and within a year corn would be less expensive than in the Rio Grande Valley.[71] Garland was ready to make the move, but when two of the four companies stationed at Fort Buchanan were ordered to California he did not pursue the matter.[72]

Fort Thorn, although otherwise satisfactory, was unhealthful. Fevers, described by Surgeon William J. Sloan as malarial, were prevalent at the post throughout much of the year.[73] The sickly nature of Fort Thorn was attributed to its location. James L. Collins, who was appointed Superintendent of Indian Affairs for the territory in 1857, hoped to settle all of the Apaches, including the Jicarillas and Mescaleros, near the Gila River. He urged Garland to move the post to a point near the headwaters of the Gila, so that it would provide protection for an Apache agency. Garland agreed to give serious consideration to the request.[74] Scheduled for possible relocation, then, were Forts Thorn, Union, and Buchanan. Although Garland made none of the changes his proposals had their influence on future planning.

During his tenure as department commander Garland established two entirely new posts, reestablished the post opposite El Paso del Norte, and relocated three of Sumner's posts. A line of posts protected the full length of the Rio Grande that lay within the jurisdiction of the department; and there were posts located in the country of all Indian groups considered hostile, except in that of the Comanches. True, the western Apaches were, for the most part, unaffected by the presence of the military; but, throughout the department, posts were located within, or close to, all significant areas of settlement. What had been accomplished did not represent a change in the pattern of troop distribution laid down by Colonel Sumner, but it was instead an expansion along the same lines.

General Garland was not well in the summer of 1858 and, obviously concerned abut the state of his own health, he summoned Colonel Bonneville to Santa Fe to replace him while he took a "temporary absence" to visit the East. On September 15, 1858, accompanied by Assistant Surgeon Jonathan Letterman, Garland left Santa Fe after placing Bonneville in command of the department.[75] Garland fully expected to return to New Mexico and, as a result, Bonneville was permitted to retain the command longer than might otherwise have been the case. Bonneville provided an active administration, yet one that followed, in most respects, the general policies of his predecessor.

In March 1859 Bonneville ordered the abandonment of Fort Thorn and the removal of most public property to Fort Fillmore. Window casings, doors, and other salvageable materials were recovered from most of the buildings. The hospital, "in complete order," was left in the care of a civilian, Ammon Barnes, who operated the ferry at the San Diego crossing; and one storeroom remained intact for the use of parties passing up and down the river. [76] Because the intent was to establish a replacement for Fort Thorn, Collins again asked that it be located near the headwaters of the Gila. [77] In June, Bonnevile ordered a detachment of twenty Mounted Riflemen to the Santa Rita copper mines, which were again being worked; there, the Riflemen were to provide a token protection until the new post could be established.

After conferring with Doctor Michael Steck in regard to a suitable site, Bonneville sent three companies, under the command of Captain and Brevet Major William H. Gordon of the Third Infantry, to select the specific location for "a permanent encampment" situated toward the southeastern end of the Burro Mountains and close to Mangas Coloradas Spring, where it would occupy a site "overlooking and commanding the valley of the Mimbres on the east, and an outlet westwardly towards the Rio Gila." [78] Major Gordon spent several days examining the area before selecting Ojo del Lucero (a spot no longer identifiable) as possessing the best attributes for a post. Assistant Surgeon George E. Cooper, who accompanied the command, provided assurance that the region was healthful. [79]

First Lieutenant George W. Howland was left, with a company of Mounted Riflemen, to establish the camp. He commenced erecting stone stables and "made every arrangement for the winter." He praised the site: plentiful grass and wood; excellent pine timber within twelve miles; and an abundance of water for the post, including water for a garden. Indians came into the camp in large numbers each day, and Howland reported they were pleased that the government was taking an interest in their welfare. However, on September 19, Bonneville ordered the company "temporarily stationed" at the Burro Mountains to return to Fort Fillmore to participate in his contemplated campaign against the Apaches. [80] The post had existed too briefly to have any lasting effect on the area.

Bonneville visited Fort Buchanan in the summer of 1859 and agreed that it was "entirely out of position." The buildings were in such poor condition that if the post remained where it was it would have to be completely rebuilt. He recommended that it be replaced by two posts: one located northeast of Tucson at the base of the Santa Catalina Mountains, and the other situated in the San Pedro Valley a few miles north of the overland mail route.[81] Surgeon Sloan, who prepared a comprehensive report on the health of the post and the adjacent country, called the causes of disease at Fort Buchanan "exciting." He believed that the health of the troops would be measurably improved if they were moved to a "high, dry, airy plain" about one mile north of the existing post.[82] However, for the moment, Fort Buchanan remained unmoved and unrepaired.

While Bonneville was absent on his southern tour, the Comanche Indians drew attention to themselves. Increased travel along the Fort Smith (Canadian River) route and the continuation of the public land survey down the Canadian Valley aroused Comanche distrust, and they let it be known that they did not intend to allow settlement in their country. The need for a post was reemphasized when Comanches seized the members of a small survey party and then released them a few hours later, after the captives had agreed to discontinue their work.[83] Both Bonneville and Collins questioned the wisdom of pushing surveys into areas so far beyond the frontier of settlement, but they believed that it was necessary to keep open the Fort Smith route and to protect the short-lived Neosho-Albuquerque mail line.[84]

John S. Phelps, a Missouri congressman and a long-time proponent of improved wagon roads and mail service between his state and New Mexico, arrived in Santa Fe, in July 1859, to accompany Collins to a council with the Kiowas and Comanches. Collins requested a military escort and, at the same time, invited Bonneville to join the party, both for the effect his presence would have on the Indians and, "much more," for his interesting company.[85] The proposal appealed to Bonneville, not only because it provided an excursion into a part of the department he had not yet visited but because it would permit him to examine the valley of the Canadian for a site suitable for a post to replace Fort Union.

Earlier in the year, as a result of an appropriation of $13,400 to rebuild the quarters and storehouses at Fort Union, Garland had appointed a board of officers to determine whether the sum was adequate to accomplish the desired work. However, the board recommended that instead of attempting to renovate the badly deteriorated post it should be moved abut four miles east of the existing site and there be completely rebuilt. Because most of the stores freighted from the States were transshipped at Fort Union, thus requiring the maintenance of government trains at both Fort Union and Albuquerque, Bonneville considered it more logical to select an entirely new site, a place preferably on public land, where the general depot, the ordnance depot, and a garrison to protect both depots could be consolidated. Hopefully, this would bring about a re-duction in expenses, notably in the quartermaster's department.[86]

Primarily as a result of Bonneville's proposal, Colonel Johnston was specifically directed to determine whether Fort Union should be rebuilt or relocated.[87] Johnston inspected Fort Union on July 7 and 8, and he found the buildings, except for the magazine and quartermaster's store-house, in such poor condition "that none of them are worth repairing." Even the storehouse, "from careless construction or bad materials, [was] an unfit depository for valuable property." After examining the post and the proposed site adjacent to it, he pronounced the latter much the better of the two; however, neither was useful for the protection of the frontier, particularly for protecting the ranches expanding to the south and east. He and Bonneville agreed that it would be far better to move the post into the area where the Comanches perpetrated their depre-dations. Admittedly, this would delay the removal of Fort Union, but it was already too late in the year to commence erecting a post to be built primarily of adobe.[88] Johnston joined the Comanche council party so that he could pass judgment on the sites along the Canadian.

The party left Santa Fe on July 18, picked up an escort of 130 soldiers at Hatch's Ranch,[89] then moved down the Canadian as far as the mouth of Ute Creek. The Indians, although they had been informed that Collins was coming to engage in peaceful talks, were made cautious by the presence of so many soldiers. Apparently fearful that they were to be punished for their past misdeeds, they departed before Collins arrived. No talks were held, nor was a post site selected. Unlike earlier official assessments of the intrinsic value of the Canadian Valley, Bonneville and Collins found the country through which they passed "perfectly worth-less." Phelps, with a small escort, went on to Missouri, and the rest of the party returned to Santa Fe.[90]

Colonel Johnston resumed his tour of inspection, concluding it as far as the Department of New Mexico was concerned at Fort Bliss on October 12. He had inspected the twelve existing posts and was critical of six of them. He recommended that Forts Buchanan and Union be replaced by new posts in more favorable locations; and he proposed that Cantonment Burgwin and Los Lunas be abandoned, for neither served a valid military purpose, in his opinion. When it came to sites for new posts he was less specific. Of Fort Buchanan he said only that it should be moved to a new location less prone to sickness. For Fort Union he proposed a site

near the Pecos, "where the Comanches commit most of their depredations." He found no fault with Santa Fe as department headquarters, but
he saw no need to maintain garrisons either there or in Albuquerque,
noting that the troops would be far more useful on the frontiers. Although
he suggested various improvements at the other posts, he did not object
to their locations, nor did he question their contribution to defense.[91]
Johnston's reports played their part in the decision to carry out a far-
reaching reorganization of the department.

7

⁕⁂⁕⁂⁕

The Reorganization of 1860

On October 25, 1859, from his camp at Cottonwood Springs, a few miles west of the New Mexico boundary on the Santa Fe Trail, Colonel Thomas T. Fauntleroy, First Dragoons, took command of the department.[1] Eight days later he arrived in Santa Fe. Fauntleroy was irascible and contentious, often to the point of petulance, and quick to take umbrage at fancied slight. He came to the department at a time critical for the nation and for the army, as the events leading ever more quickly toward the outbreak of civil conflict tended inevitably to overshadow all purely regional matters. Fauntleroy provided, almost against his will, an active administration. When left to his own devices he was probably the least effective commander in the department's history, except for those whose tenures were too brief to have genuine influence.

Fauntleroy had sought command of the department in 1853, basing his request on the fact that five companies of his regiment were stationed in New Mexico, whereas none of Garland's Eighth Infantry was stationed in the department. With somewhat more logic, he pointed out that in the three years during which he had been colonel of the First Dragoons he had seen only one of his companies and that his proper assignment was where most of them were stationed. His request earned him a "pointed rebuke," not so much for his remarks as because he had "violated military propriety and discipline" by failing to forward them through proper channels. Even if the effort did not gain him a departmental command it did secure his transfer to New Mexico where he served for about two years, from 1854 to 1856, before he was ordered to California with three companies of his First Dragoons.[2] Now, three years later, he was back to occupy the position of command previously denied to him.

As soon as he settled down in Santa Fe, Fauntleroy suggested a complete reorganization of the department that would involve the relocation or abandonment of many of the existing posts. In doing so, he drew on knowledge he had gained during his earlier tour of duty in New Mexico and on the recommendations of other officers, notably Garland, Bonneville, and Johnston.[3] A month later he submitted a more comprehensive plan to the War Department and asked for an early and favorable decision on its implementation "as being essential to the efficient conduct of the Department." Of the twelve existing posts, Fauntleroy's proposal left only four—Garland, Craig, Stanton, and Fillmore—where they were. It called for the relocation of Forts Union, Defiance, and Buchanan, and a new site for the Post of Los Lunas. Forts Marcy and Bliss, Cantonment Burgwin, and the Post of Albuquerque would be abandoned. This was the first suggestion that Bliss be abandoned and Defiance moved, but the other recommendations had been made before, although not necessarily in the same detail.

For some time it had been conceded that Fort Union should be moved to a new location where it would again become the general depot for the department. Fauntleroy, however, had more elaborate plans for its disposition; namely, to replace it with two posts. One would be in the valley of the Canadian River, near the base of the Raton Mountains, where it would guard both branches of the Santa Fe Trail and afford protection to emigrants going to the Colorado gold fields by the southern routes. According to Fauntleroy, "ample & cheap" supplies for the post could be brought from Taos and Rayado, while the region itself was the best in the department for the proper maintenance of horses. He advocated the establishment of a second post, lower on the Canadian, to serve as the general depot—where the commissary, quartermaster's, and medical depots, then at Albuquerque, and the ordnance depot, then at Fort Union, would be consolidated—and to defend the road from New Mexico to Fort Smith and Neosho. From the information available, he considered the mouth of Ute Creek to be the most suitable site. The mouth of Ute Creek had been considered as a possible post site as early as 1854, and the reasons advanced were always the same: protection of routes and reduction of transportation costs.

Los Lunas, originally established as a grazing camp, had never been of great military significance. Now Fauntleroy proposed that its garrison be moved to the vicinity of Jemez, where it would serve to curb Navajo incursions and thereby "be greater in its value than Albuquerque & Los Lunas combined." As a further measure to control the Navajos he had an even more startling suggestion: the relocation of Fort Defiance. From the time of its establishment Fort Defiance had been generally praised for its usefulness, and despite the high cost of transportation necessary to maintain it, its position had not been seriously questioned. Fauntleroy wanted to relocate it at the Ojo del Oso, some forty miles closer to Albuquerque and a little to the north of the wagon road from Albuquerque to the Colorado River—the road laid out in 1857 under the auspices of the War Department by Edward Fitzgerald Beale and his famous camel corps.[4] "I know of no change," Fauntleroy wrote, "that would so much contribute to the efficiency of a post & its economical supply."

If Fort Defiance were permitted to remain where it was, Fauntleroy urged that a separate post be constructed near Inscription Rock on the road between Cubero and Zuñi Pueblo. In either case, the principal post for the control of the Navajos ought not to be within their country but on its eastern fringe, as described in the treaty of 1858. The first article of the treaty, which was never submitted for ratification, laid down the eastern boundary beyond which the Navajos were not to plant, graze, or otherwise make use of the land. The line passed through Ojo del Oso.[5] Fauntleroy was convinced that it would be more effective to establish posts at both Inscription Rock and Ojo del Oso than it would be to retain Fort Defiance.

In the south, Fauntleroy recommended moving Fort Buchanan closer to Tucson, as Bonneville had suggested earlier. In addition, he advocated two entirely new posts. One would be located in the Mimbres Valley, "perhaps . . . the finest valley in Arizona," where it would protect the Butterfield Overland Mail route, the adjacent mining regions, and the settlements along the Rio Grande that were "to some extent exposed by the abandonment of Fort Thorn." Once established, the presence of the post would induce settlers to move into the valley, thus further enhancing the usefulness of the post. The other post would be situated at the point where the overland mail route intersected the San Pedro River, a strategic position for operating against the Apaches. The three posts, Fauntleroy asserted, would protect the southern lines of travel and communications. Although none would be in the immediate vicinity of the Arizona mines that disadvantage could be overcome by periodically sending detachments to patrol the mining districts, and thus their operations would deter Indian interference.

The reorganization would be practicable only if the force in the department was greatly strengthened and only if most of the additional troops were mounted. Specifically, Fauntleroy asked that a battery of light artillery and his entire Regiment of First Dragoons be transferred to New Mexico. Also, for the health of the troops and for the economy of the service, enough beef cattle should always be available so that salt meat could largely be eliminated from the ration. He had consulted in regard to the comparable benefits of fresh beef and bacon with Surgeon Sloan, who assured him that as long as the cattle were in prime condition beef was the more healthful. However, Sloan warned, "at some posts and at certain seasons, when grass is deficient, the beef has often been utterly unfit for the healthy subsistence of the troops."[6] Fauntleroy was convinced that cattle could be maintained in good condition almost anywhere in the department, to be slaughtered as they were needed. They could be driven from post to post at less expense than it cost to freight salt meat; and they could be taken along, "to a considerable extent," on expeditions into Indian country. Fauntleroy made a further suggestion, admittedly outside of his jurisdiction, that posts be established at the point where Beale's road crossed the Colorado River and on the Arkansas River near Bent's Fort.[7]

Fauntleroy's proposals were of major importance, if only for the impression they made in Washington. Not only did they include virtually all of the recommendations set forth during the past several years, usually in piecemeal form; they presented a comprehensive plan for the reorganization of the department, touching on all of the existing posts and emphasizing efficiency and economy. Very probably it was the inclusive and reasonably detailed nature of his plan that provided the principal appeal. Even though the cost of the reorganization would be considerable, General Winfield Scott thought "favourably of all the propositions" and added that Colonel Johnston's inspection reports tended to reinforce many of Fauntleroy's proposals. He also instructed the Commissary General's Department to give special attention to the recommendation regarding beef cattle.[8]

The reorganization plan had an added advantage: it was opportune. New Mexico's comparative isolation was disappearing; and the military department was involved increasingly in events outside of its own limits, more so than at any time since the Mexican War. The number of travel routes crossing New Mexico—both north into the newly opened Colorado mining districts and west to the Pacific coast—multiplied, and each road demanded protection. The Butterfield Overland Mail had its own particular defensive needs during the brief period that it traversed southern New Mexico through the heart of Apache country. Also, it was believed that the projected transcontinental railway would probably be built across southern New Mexico, and the protection it would require entered into the military thinking of the day. To a great extent the Department of New Mexico was called upon to guard segments of routes that were of at least as great importance to other areas as they were to New Mexico. This was reflected to some degree in Fauntleroy's reorganization plan.

Another factor in favor of the reorganization was the availability, close at hand, of a large body of troops. The hostile phase of the Mormon War ended early in the summer of 1858, but the peace that followed was restive as each side continued to distrust the other. With such a residue of suspicion, it is not surprising that the number of troops stationed in Utah Territory remained high, exceeding three thousand for a time in 1859. However, in his annual report for that year, Secretary of War John B. Floyd, even though he retained his antipathy toward the Mormons, admitted that there was no necessity for so large a force.[9] From Utah would come the troops to build up the Department of New Mexico.

One of Fauntleroy's recommendations had been carried out months before he had made it. Fort Mojave was established on the east side of the Colorado River crossing on April 19, 1859. Although it was on the far western limits of New Mexico Territory, it was attached to the Military Department of California. A post was established on the Arkansas River, near Bent's New Fort, on August 29, 1860. Originally called Fort Wise, it was designated Fort Lyon in 1862.[10]

On March 12, 1860, with the approval of the Secretary of War, General Winfield Scott issued a wide-ranging order, including provisions for the complete reorganization of the Department of New Mexico. The order called for the relocation of three forts and for the establishment of two entirely new forts. Fort Buchanan was to be moved to the junction of Aravaipa Creek and the San Pedro River, and Fort Defiance would be transferred to the Ojo del Oso. To replace both Fort Union and Albuquerque and to serve as the general depot for the department, a post was to be established at or near the point where the Fort Smith road crossed the Gallinas River a short distance above its junction with the Pecos; or, preferably, if a suitable location could be found, the post would be situated farther to the east, on or close to the Canadian River. Forts Garland, Bliss, and Stanton would continue as active posts, and "all other posts, now occupied, in the Department of New Mexico" were to be abandoned.

Almost two-thirds of the force stationed in Utah was transferred to New Mexico. Three companies of Tenth Infantry and two of Second

Dragoons were assigned to Fort Garland. Four companies of the Seventh Infantry Regiment were ordered to take post "at the Gila copper mines." The other six companies of the regiment were ordered to take post "near the mines of Arizona." Both of these were new posts for which neither names nor specific locations had been selected. Finally, the entire Fifth Regiment of Infantry was ordered to relieve the Third Regiment in New Mexico, with the latter going to the Department of Texas. Despite Fauntleroy's expressed preference, only two of the companies were mounted, but the overall increase of fifteen companies was considerably greater than he had requested. The order provided for the reduction of the number of posts in the department from twelve to eight. As only three of the existing posts would remain where they were, this necessitated the construction of five new posts.

The order also called for more direct transportation from the East to many of the posts. In the future, stores for Fort Bliss and the three posts in the "Gila country" were to be freighted "through Texas or from the Missouri and Arkansas frontiers," and, in either case, delivered at the posts for which they were intended. Fort Garland would be supplied directly from Fort Leavenworth via Sangre de Cristo Pass, making use of a route laid out under Bonneville's direction in the summer of 1859.[11] Stores for the other posts and "for all contingent purposes" would "be sent from the Missouri and Arkansas frontier to the depot at Fort Butler for distribution." This meant that the general depot would normally be responsible for supplying only two posts other than itself, thereby presumably reducing drastically the expenses of New Mexico's quartermaster's department.

The troops going to and leaving New Mexico served a useful function even while en route to their new stations, engaging in some exploration and improving for future military traffic the routes over which they passed. The dragoon companies destined for Fort Garland, as well as the Seventh Infantry Regiment, crossed southern Wyoming, proceeded along the eastern front of the Rockies, and entered the San Luis Valley by way of Sangre de Cristo Pass. This involved no exploration but it did test the feasibility of the route, particularly that part of the route across the mountains.[12]

The departure of the remaining troops for New Mexico was delayed because Lieutenant Colonel and Brevet Colonel Charles F. Smith, who commanded the Department of Utah, considered it necessary to improve the road through Spanish Fork Canyon before a large force, encumbered by baggage trains and supplies, moved over it. Hence, the thirteen infantry companies did not march until June 1, 1860. They went forward together up the Spanish Fork, then across to the Green River, where they were further delayed by high water at the crossing, before going on the Grand (Colorado) River.

A company selected to explore the Old Spanish Trail to Santa Fe was detached on June 24, just below the mouth of the Dolores River. Its object was to ascertain the most direct route suitable for wagons or, if not for wagons, for pack trains.[13] When First Lieutenant Donald C. Stith of the Fifth Infantry, commander of the company, crossed the Grand River, he was, for all practical purposes, temporarily lost. He followed an Indian path—in the mistaken belief that it was the Old Spanish Trail—over mountainous, exceedingly rough country, where even the pack mules sometimes lost their footing. Stith eventually struck the Old Spanish Trail where it forded the Mancos River. From that point he passed through well-known country, arriving at Santa Fe on July 20. An excellent wagon road could be laid out from Abiquiu to the Mancos River, but even though he had not been over it, he doubted that wagons could be used on the Old Spanish Trail beyond that point.[14] The rest of the Utah column followed an already existing route, making some minor improvements on it as it advanced.

Eight companies of the Third Infantry, when they left New Mexico, took the well-traveled road east from El Paso. The other two were ordered to march to Texas via the Pecos Valley.[15] The valley had been examined previously in segments by the army; and First Lieutenant Henry M. Lazelle, Eighth infantry, in connection with his duties as commander of the escort for the Texas–New Mexico boundary commission, had conducted a train of twenty-two loaded wagons down the east side of the Pecos River, from Anton Chico to Fort Lancaster, Texas. Colonel Bonneville was assigned to lead the two Third Infantry companies. Two Spanish Americans were hired at Anton Chico for $3 and a ration each per day to guide the detachment from the mouth of the Gallinas to Fort Lancaster. Actually, Bonneville's expedition proved to be little more than a summer outing and it provided no new information of significance. It reached its destination of Fort Clark, Texas, on July 28.[16]

By August 26 all of the companies transferred to New Mexico had reported to department headquarters. There were now more troops in New Mexico than at any time since 1848. The large buildup of troop strength and the cost of the extensive reorganization already under way appreciably increased the expenses of the department. More freight was hauled into New Mexico for army use in 1860 than at any time since the close of the Mexican War. The freighting contract signed with Russell, Majors, and Waddell for the years 1860–61 took into account the projected redistribution of troops and provided for transporting military stores from Fort Leavenworth, Fort Riley, or Kansas City, Missouri, to Fort Union "or the depôt which may be established in that territory." Also, if required to do so, the freighting firm undertook to deliver goods directly to Forts Fillmore, Bliss, or Garland, "or to any posts or depôts that are now or may be established in Arazona [sic] or the Gila country." The rates were based, as they had been for a number of years, on the month in which the goods were turned over to the contractor, and they ranged from $1.40 per hundred pounds per hundred miles in May to $1.60 for the same weight and distance in September through February. A separate contract was drawn up for transportation from Fort Union, or from the depot to be established, to all of the other posts in the department except Forts Bliss and Fillmore. The rate varied from $1.00 to $1.60, and was again based on the month.[17] However, most internal transportation was handled by the military department's quartermaster's department, and the number of civilian teamsters continued to increase.

Beginning in 1859, the Southwest was plagued by drought. Two years of extremely scant rainfall led to very poor crops and caused the price of corn to double in 1860. The drought also stunted the growth of native grasses, resulting in inferior grazing and some increase in the price of hay. Colonel Fauntleroy reported in 1860 that grass was virtually nonexistent, that hay was unobtainable at some posts "at any price," and that corn sold for a "frightful price everywhere."[18] The high cost of feed added to the expense of transportation, and the shortage of feed of all kinds contributed to the run-down condition of public animals.

In the autumn of 1859 a large quantity of corn, more than 25,000 fanegas, was purchased under contract for delivery during the following year. The average price was about $4 per fanega, an increase of $1 from the previous year. Only one contract was registered in 1860, partly because of the scarcity of corn throughout the department and the ensuing increase in price. Joseph Magoffin agreed to deliver 2,000 fanegas of shelled and sacked corn at Fort Bliss for $7.50 per fanega.[19] However, most of the corn purchased by the army during the period from October 1860 to October 1861 was acquired on the open market. Major James L. Donaldson, who had been chief quartermaster of the department since 1856, estimated in November 1860 that the lowest "average" price he would have to pay would be "not less than six cents per pound" ($8.40 per fanega).[20]

James L. Collins was faced with the same problem in securing corn for issue at the Indian agencies. In October 1860 he paid $6.50 per fanega, plus another dollar to have the corn ground into meal, but at that price it was impossible to obtain an adequate supply. A month later the small amount of corn offered on the market sold for $7.50 to $8.00 per fanega. As winter progressed the price continued to advance. By the end of January 1861 the price of corn in Santa Fe had reached $9 to $10 per fanega, "and indeed it cannot be bought now at those prices." Collins remarked that "at the present price of corn and fodder a mule will soon consume the amount of its own price."[21]

Contracts were made in 1860 for the delivery of hay or fodder at Forts Union, Craig, and Stanton, and at Taos. The total quantity specified was only 700 tons, but the contract for Taos, which was for wheat straw and fodder, was simply "as required." The price was generally a little higher than it had been previously, but the principal difference was in two contracts let by the commissary department at unusually high prices. William F. Moore was given a contract to supply 50 tons of hay at Fort Union at $50 per ton, more than 25 percent higher than had ever been paid at the post before. In October, Jesús García signed a contract with the post department at Fort Craig for 50 tons of hay at $20 per ton; yet four months earlier Esquipula Vigil had contracted with the quartermaster at Fort Craig to deliver 200 tons of bottom-grass hay at $9 per ton.[22] However, as in past years, most hay and fodder was purchased at the posts in individual transactions.

The flour contracts let in 1860 reflected both the poor crop conditions and the increased demand. That flour would be expensive was anticipated. It sold on the open market in Santa Fe in October for $10 per 100 pounds, and so short was the supply that several wagon trains brought flour from Missouri to be sold to the civilian population.[23] Contracts issued in 1860 provided for almost 1,100,000 pounds of flour, more than twice as much as had been purchased under contract in 1859. The prices generally were the highest paid in the department at any time prior to the Civil War, ranging from 7⁸/10 to 20¹/2 cents per pound. For the first time the distance of the point of delivery from the place of manufacture was not always a determining factor. Only the contract for Fort Buchanan was at a lower price per pound than in the previous year, and it was drawn up in Washington with a contractor completely unfamiliar with the conditions he would encounter in the department.[24]

The cost of other commissary supplies purchased in the department did not increase as drastically as the price of flour. Fewer beans (only

687 bushels) were purchased than in the previous year, and the price paid, $3 to $4 per bushel, was only slightly higher. Only one contract was issued for vinegar, for 5,000 gallons (as opposed to 8,090 in 1859) at a cost of 95 cents per gallon. The 800 bushels of "pure refined salt" purchased at $2.99 per bushel, for delivery at the general depot, cost little more than half as much as salt of similar quality in 1859. Salt, of course, was available in any amount and was unaffected by the drought. The only beef purchased under contract in 1860 was at Fort Buchanan (at .0792 cents per pound), for which there are no comparable figures.[25]

Fort Garland was the first post to feel the impact of the buildup of troops. The five companies assigned to garrison Fort Garland all reached their destination in the latter part of July. Because the post was designed to accommodate only two companies, work commenced at once to expand quarters and storerooms. All available troops were assigned to extra duty, to procure building materials and to work on construction. Four mechanics were hired at $2.50 per day, and eight laborers were hired at $25.00 per month, for the specific purpose of repairing the post's sawmill and erecting a building to protect it from the weather. An additional nine civilians, "lumber men," were employed at $25.00 per month to get out timber.[26]

Despite the increased number of troops at Fort Garland there was no immediate need for additional commissary supplies. Already on hand or allocated to the post was sufficient flour to meet all requirements until the following May, and until additional storage space was constructed there would be no room for more flour. The garrison had brought its own beef supply, in the form of more than four hundred oxen that had hauled the wagon trains accompanying the Seventh Infantry from Utah. Major Edward R. S. Canby of the Tenth Infantry, commander of the post, expected that after a few months of rest and grazing they would make fine beef.[27] There was so much bacon in the commissary storehouse that Fauntleroy ordered 40,000 pounds of it transferred to the general depot.[28] The only supply problems facing the post were the expected difficulty in obtaining sufficient corn from the Taos Valley and the great shortage of money in the area, with the unavailability of funds making it particularly difficult for the quartermaster's department to pay civilian employees. For the expected corn shortage Canby had a solution: feed the public animals wheat and bran, both of which were available and were cheaper than corn.[29]

Fauntleroy took the preliminary steps toward reorganizing the department before the troops from Utah arrived. In April, since there was no question in regard to the new location of Fort Defiance, he ordered Brevet Second Lieutenant Orlando G. Wagner, Topographical Engineers, to Ojo del Oso to lay out a ten-mile square reserve, centered about "East Bear Spring." At that time Fauntleroy assigned two companies of Eighth Infantry to form part of the garrison for Fort Butler, the replacement for Fort Union and the only new post for which a name had been specified by the War Department. The companies were directed to take post at Hatch's Ranch and to await further instructions. [30]

Unclear in the general orders were the locations of three of the new posts. The site of Fort Butler was suggested but it was left to Fauntleroy's determination, and the sites for the other two posts were indefinite. One was to be located "near the mines of Arizona." That, Fauntleroy decided, meant the silver mining district east of the Santa Cruz River. The other was to be built at the "Gila copper mines." The only copper mines then worked in the area were the Santa Rita mines, about thirty miles from the nearest point on the Gila River. Fauntleroy concluded that they were the mines referred to in the orders. In both cases his interpretation was accepted by the Secretary of War. Having defined the general locations, Fauntleroy assigned the troops intended to establish the posts. [31]

Eight companies of the Fifth Infantry, under the command of Captain and Brevet Lieutenant Colonel William Chapman, were ordered to Ojo del Oso to begin constructing the post soon to be named Fort Fauntleroy and to make the preliminary preparations for the abandonment of Fort Defiance. The other companies of the Fifth were stationed, one at Albuquerque and one at Fort Stanton. Lieutenant Colonel Pitcairne Morrison, with two companies and the regimental headquarters of the Seventh Infantry, was instructed to establish the new post near the mines of Arizona; and Major Isaac Lynde and two companies of the Seventh were ordered to take post in the vicinity of the Mimbres River. It was left to the discretion of both officers to select the specific sites. The remaining six companies of the Seventh were distributed among existing posts. Finally, Fauntleroy issued instructions to move Fort Buchanan to the junction of Aravaipa Creek and the San Pedro River. [32]

There was no public objection to the relocation of Fort Defiance, despite the praise so often accorded it in the past. James L. Collins went so far as to say that it would have been more useful had it always been at Ojo del Oso. [33] Fort Defiance, of course, was not on any regular route of travel and was at a considerable distance from the closest settlements. Its relocation would not have an adverse economic effect on any of them. In fact, the new site was closer to Zuñi Pueblo as well as to the principal areas of production, though it was still too distant to attract many casual vendors. Only the Hopi pueblos were placed at a disadvantage as a source of supply.

News of the impending abandonment of posts in the Rio Grande Valley, however, caused immediate complaint. The citizens of Doña Ana County sent a petition bearing more than five hundred signatures to Secretary of War Floyd, protesting against the breaking up of Fort Fill-more. The petition asserted that "the industrious but poor pioneers who have brought their all to this Valley and under the protection of our Troops have made it the Grainary [sic] of the Southern & Western New Mexico" depended on the presence of the fort both for protection and as a market for their products. Without it farms, ranches, and mines would inevitably be abandoned.[34]

Captain and Brevet Major John T. Sprague, Eighth Infantry, com-mander of the post, spoke to the point with equal pertinence. Hugh Stephenson had acquired an interest in a silver mine in the Organ Mountains in 1848. The mine had produced steadily, if not spectacularly, and the ore was smelted in a furnace located near Fort Fillmore. The miners feared the Apaches, and if the post was abandoned the mines undoubtedly would be deserted. Sprague warned that the whole stretch of the Rio Grande Valley protected by Fort Fillmore would be "decimated by Apache Indians" and that its promising agricultural and ranching activities could not be maintained. The audacity of the Indians, "even while a strong force of mounted men" garrisoned the post, led him to predict that "they will in less time than six months depopulate the valley, and destroy effectually all enterprise and industry."[35] Sprague was not exactly a disinterested party. He, as well as many of his fellow officers, had invested in mines in the Southwest. In 1858, when Stephenson sold his interests in the silver mine, Sprague was one of the purchasers. He divested himself of his share within a few months, but in 1859 he acquired an interest in the Stephenson Smelting House and 160 acres of land near Fort Fillmore.[36]

The inhabitants of Socorro County forwarded a petition to Floyd on behalf of Fort Craig. The post, they claimed, "from its geographical position is the key of the Rio Grande valley north of the jornada del Muerto." Not only did it protect the vital travel route; it made possible "all the Ranches and small farms lately reclaimed from the wilderness." If the post was not retained they would be deserted. Stock raising would be impossible in the valley "for a distance of more than one hundred miles" if the marauding Navajos were permitted to go unchecked. If the posts along the Rio Grande were abandoned the closest protection would be more than two hundred miles away, and the results would be "calamitous." The petitioners claimed, with some exaggeration, that they were not influenced by "pecuniary motives" because the Socorro region raised very little surplus grain for sale to the army and depended primarily on its herds and flocks for a livelihood. The petition carried more than one thousand signatures.[37]

The residents of Bernalillo County did not bother to address the Secretary of War. At a public meeting in Albuquerque on August 23, they decided to take their appeal directly to President James Buchanan. Their protest was against the abandonment of both Fort Craig and the Post of Albuquerque because it would leave an area "450 miles in length, and 300 miles in width, in which not a single soldier will be stationed to control the Indians, who roam at pleasure over this space." In a stirring plea, they contended that "our flocks can and will be driven off, our women and children carried into captivity, and the Indians safe in their mountain fastnesses, long ere notice can be sent to any military post giving them notice of such depredations." They were not permitted to protect themselves and, even if they were, they lacked the arms and ammunition, which, in any case, most of the people did not know how to use. Hence, they relied upon the government to fulfill its promises "to give them that protection granted to other parts of our common country."[38]

There was no criticism of the decision to relocate Fort Buchanan; indeed, the criticism had all been directed against its existing location, but there was concern now about the new site. The mining interests were dissatisfied with the protection thus far afforded to their operations. Charles D. Poston, mining promoter and leading advocate of separate territorial status for Arizona, informed Floyd that the mining companies had invested substantial sums of money in their enterprises, "relying upon the good faith of the Government for protection." But, he flatly stated, "adequate protection has not been given." Since the organization of the Sonora Exploring and Mining Company in 1856, more than one hundred of Poston's friends and acquaintances had been "murdered by Mexicans or Indians," and large quantities of property had been stolen or destroyed.[39] Edward A. Cross, the superintendent of the St. Louis Silver Mining Company and former editor of Arizona's first newspaper, the *Arizonian*, advocated three posts: a six-company post at the mouth of the Aravaipa; a three-company post at Calabasas Ranch; and a two-company post on the Arivaca Ranch, which was the property of the

Sonora Exploring and Mining Company. The three posts, he wrote, would be the least expensive and most effective means to protect the country, and "we hope for more security & better days."[40]

The civilian population was obviously concerned about some aspects of the departmental reorganization. In all of the communications emphasis was placed on the need for protection against Indian depredations. This differed from the appeals made in 1851, when most of the posts were moved away from centers of population. Then, the principal consideration had been the loss of revenue that the inhabitants of the towns anticipated. Of course, the economic factor was still present in 1860. Protection of flocks, fields, and mines, as well as of routes of commerce, was of major importance to the civilian economy.

The first post in the department to be abandoned was Cantonment Burgwin, evacuated on May 18, 1860. A month later a detachment of fifteen men under a noncommissioned officer reoccupied Burgwin to guard the public property still there. As soon as the property was removed the detachment was withdrawn, and the post was left to its already advanced state of decay. The Post of Los Lunas was next to go. On September 16 it was broken up and its one-company garrison moved to Albuquerque, with the rented property, including the buildings erected by the army, reverting to the owners.[41] Actually, these were the only posts abandoned as an immediate result of the reorganization of the department. This development arose not by intent, but because of the disruption brought about by the approach of the Civil War and, in the case of Fort Defiance, by an outbreak of hostilities with the Navajos.

When Captain Richard S. Ewell learned that six companies were to take post, as he put it, "near the silver mines of Arizonia," he told Fauntleroy that if a post of that size was to be maintained anywhere in the area, there was no better location for the protection of the mining districts than at the existing Fort Buchanan. The mining companies, he asserted, did not want the post moved to a new site. Indeed, a post in close proximity to the mines would actually hamper their production by using water and fuel essential to their operation.[42] Ewell was able to speak with authority on the desires of the mining interests, for he and several of his fellow officers had invested in the Patagonia Mines.[43] Admittedly, the location of Fort Buchanan was unhealthful—Ewell had often suffered from the effects of its fevers—but he believed that most of the sickness would be eliminated by an encampment during the summer months, presumably at a higher elevation and away from the swamps that surrounded the post on three sides.[44]

Early in May 1860 a company of Eighth Infantry under the command of Second Lieutenant John R. Cooke, son of Colonel Philip St. George Cooke, left Fort Buchanan to occupy the junction of the Aravaipa and San Pedro, the site designated to replace Fort Buchanan. Fauntleroy had already notified Surveyor General William Pelham that he had reserved an area ten-miles square, centered about the confluence of the two streams, and asked him to preserve it from private claims.[45] With a detachment of dragoons, Captain Ewell followed Cooke to lay out the reservation and to select the specific location for the post. Even before the troops were on the scene a number of men who had lived near Fort Buchanan, and who had apparently anticipated its early demise, arrived to take up farm land adjacent to the new post and to the market it would provide. Construction of the new post commenced before the end of May. Prior to its establishment it had been referred to simply as "new Fort Buchanan," but when Ewell selected the site he called it Fort Aravaipa. On August 6, 1860, it was officially designated Fort Breckinridge in honor of the vice-president. In the meantime, Fort Buchanan continued to be occupied.

Colonels Morrison and Reeve arrived in October, Morrison to take command of Fort Buchanan and Reeve of Fort Breckinridge. On October 8, Morrison set out to choose the site for the post to be established near the mines of Arizona. Referring to Morrison's post as the replacement for Fort Buchanan, which was contrary to the original orders, Fauntleroy now made a significant change in the reorganization plans. In reaching his decision, he was influenced by Captain Ewell. Both men were at Fort Bliss in October 1860, as witnesses in a court-martial, thus giving Ewell the opportunity to present his opinion of the proposed change more directly. There were, he said, five principal mining companies, and Fort Buchanan in its present position protected three of them better than any other available location. One or two companies stationed at Arivaca Ranch, in addition to Fort Buchanan, would be the best arrangement to protect all of the mines; but Arivaca, like Buchanan, was a sickly place. The only position that was reasonably healthful was near the Patagonia Mine, but it was poor from a strategic point of view. Fauntleroy concluded that Fort Buchanan should be left where it was.[46]

Criticized since its inception for its location and unhealthfulness, Fort Buchanan was saved largely because all other sites were rejected. The physical properties of Fort Buchanan had been described in many ways by army officers and civilians, but never favorably. The post was not to be moved, yet everyone agreed that it was not satisfactory where it was.

The answer was simple: Rebuild immediately to the northeast on the "high, dry, airy plain," as Surgeon Sloan had recommended. The work was commenced. Large numbers of adobes were made and carefully stored, thousands of which would be used in the construction of Camp Crittenden in 1868. The adobes and lumber for Forts Buchanan and Breckinridge were purchased under contract from William S. Grant; the timber was cut in the Santa Rita Mountains above Fort Buchanan and delivered at the posts. The lumber cost $132 per thousand feet, plus the cost of transportation.[47] Neither Fort Breckinridge nor the new Fort Buchanan was completed, in part because the full complement of men was never available to work on them. Most of the companies intended for the Arizona posts were detained to serve in a campaign against the Navajos, and by the time that conflict ended the Civil War was at hand. As a result, only five understrength companies were in southern Arizona to build the posts, to combat Indians, to provide escort service, and to engage in a variety of other duties.

Major Lynde got his post off to a slightly more auspicious start, largely because his two companies constituted half the number designated as the permanent garrison. Lynde arrived at the Mimbres River on September 16, 1860, and spent more than three weeks examining the area for an eligible position. He selected Apache Springs (Apache Tejo) for the usual reasons: adequate wood, water, and grass. The site was about fifteen miles south of the Santa Rita mines and twelve miles west of the point where the overland mail route crossed the Mimbres. The command immediately began putting up jacales to provide shelter until the following spring. Lynde posted a notice declaring a reserve of ten-miles square, centered about "a point, now occupied by the tent of the Commanding officer." He expected this reserve would secure the water and grass for the army "and prevent the Establishment of Liquor Shops nearer than Six or Seven miles, the nearest water."[48]

Major Lynde recommended that the post be called Fort Webster, thus perpetuating the name of the earlier post in the same vicinity. Colonel Fauntleroy, however, had already requested permission to call it Fort Floyd. Lynde objected on the reasonable ground that it would be confused with Camp Floyd in Utah Territory.[49] Neither name was adopted, and on January 18, 1861, the post was officially designated Fort McLane in honor of Captain George McLane of the Mounted Riflemen, who was killed in an engagement with Navajos at about the time that the fort was established.

In February 1861, when Colonel Morrison went on leave, Lynde be-

came the senior officer with the Seventh Infantry, and regimental headquarters and two more companies of the Seventh were transferred to Fort
McLane, which was still nothing more than the temporary housing that
had been erected during the previous fall.[50] There had been no difficulty
with the Apaches, nor would there be any in the few remaining months
of the post's existence. Scurvy was a greater menace to the troops than
were the Indians. The end of the post was foreshadowed in March, when
Lynde was instructed not to "make any contracts for lumber, adobies or
other building materials for the construction of Fort McLane."[51]

The significance of the new posts in Apache country was much less
than had been expected when the reorganization of the department was
ordered. Fort Breckinridge attracted a few settlers to its immediate vicinity, and there was some settlement where the overland mail route
crossed the Mimbres, but it was more the result of Sylvester Mowry's
promotional activities[52] than of the presence of Fort McLane. The posts
existed too briefly and the troops stationed at them were too few in
number to result in significant settlement, agriculture, or ranching.

The reorganization of the department moved quickly toward an unanticipated halt. Only two posts, Los Lunas and Cantonment Burgwin,
had been abandoned, and only one other, Fort Defiance, would be abandoned in accordance with the original orders. Three new posts had been
established, and the rebuilding of Fort Buchanan had commenced, but
on none of them had more than the preliminary work been accomplished.
The other five posts slated for abandonment continued to be occupied.
There would soon be further changes, but these changes would come as
a result of the civil conflict, which had in fact already begun.

8

ᒧᘺᕋᕼᕋᘺᕋᕼᕋᘺᕋᕼᕋ

The Approach of the Civil War

Throughout the decade of the fifties the army had concerned itself with the economical operation of the department, though never more overtly than during the command of Colonel Sumner. Military purchases of New Mexican products increased appreciably in quantity and variety during the later years of the decade, but prices remained high in comparison with those paid for similar goods in the East. Even though local production had grown in response to the expanded market, the great bulk of the stores required by the army were still freighted to New Mexico. The cost of transportation declined slightly in each successive contract, but it remained a significant item of expense.

Transportation was a major factor in the cost of maintaining the posts established in the territory acquired through the Gadsden Purchase. Agricultural development near Fort Buchanan, although limited, led to a decline in the price of a few articles, but the cost of most goods remained higher here than elsewhere in the department. The desire to reduce costs was probably a factor in the unusual decision made by Secretary of War Floyd in 1859, when he awarded Theodore W. Taliaferro of Alabama the privilege of furnishing all commissary and quartermaster's stores usually purchased in the "territory of Arizona"[1] for one year at prices not to exceed those previously paid by the army.[2] The arrangement was unique, for this was the first time that the business of internal supply had been removed from the determination of the department commander and his appropriate staff officers.[3]

Taliaferro arrived in New Mexico before notification of his concession had been received by the department headquarters. When he reached Fort Buchanan he found that the only contract available to him was for corn, and he arranged to furnish the quartermaster with 490,000 pounds at 4 cents per pound ($5.60 per fanega), a full cent less than had been paid previously at the post.[4] Dissatisfied with the very limited outcome of what he had expected to be a lucrative venture, Taliaferro returned to the Rio Grande where he encountered a train bound for Fort Buchanan with a load of flour milled by Simeon Hart. From Fort Fillmore, he complained that this was an infringement of his agreement with the War Department, and he asked Bonneville for an interpretation of his rights, including what redress he might expect to obtain in the matter of the flour.[5]

Hart did not hold a flour contract for Fort Buchanan in 1859, but Colonel Grayson had authorized him to delay deliveries under the 1858 contract and to make them "from time to time, instead of quarterly." This did not constitute an increase in quantity, but it did involve a shift in allocations of some of the flour intended for Forts Bliss and Fillmore, where the garrisons had been reduced, and for Fort Thorn, which had been abandoned. Second Lieutenant Horace Randal of the First Dragoons, the acting commissary at Fort Buchanan, was apparently unaware of Grayson's arrangement with Hart, and in view of Taliaferro's concession, Randal refused to accept a consignment of Hart's flour when it was presented for delivery. Hart appealed to Representative John S. Phelps of Missouri, who carried the complaint directly to Floyd. The Commissary General's Office recommended that "all contracts made for Fort Buchanan prior to the arrival of Mr. Taliafero [sic] at that post be carried out in good faith."[6] It was fairly obvious that communications between Washington, Santa Fe, and Fort Buchanan were neither swift nor efficient. In November, Lieutenant Randal made a contract with Taliaferro to deliver 82,000 pounds of flour during the coming year at 12 cents per pound, but the quantity was reduced by half at department headquarters because of existing commitments to Hart.[7]

In the spring of 1860 Taliaferro was joined in the business of purveyor for the army by William S. Grant of Maine. Early in March, Grant approached Floyd with the proposal that he, in partnership with Taliaferro, provide all quartermaster's and commissary supplies in "what is known as Arizona" for two years.[8] A few days later Floyd "authorized [them] to furnish all the supplies that may be needed at all the posts that may now or hereafter be established in that portion of the proposed territory of Arizona lying south of the parallel of 33° 36′ north latitude and west of the meridian 106° 35′ west longitude"—except horses, wagons, and harnesses. All items were to be furnished at 12 percent less than the price paid by the army for similar goods at the posts involved during the previous year. A "reasonable allowance" would be made to offset the cost of transportation. Included within the designated limits were Forts Buchanan and Fillmore and, after they were established, Forts Breckinridge and McLane.[9] Once again, it is not clear why Grant was especially favored, but he too came to the Southwest with the blessings of the War Department.

The concessions made to Taliaferro and Grant caused resentment at department headquarters in Santa Fe. The staff officers involved in making purchases, particularly Colonel Grayson, cooperated as little as possible with the recipients. Even the private citizens were less than enthusiastic. Grant later stated:

> When I arrived in the Territory, every trader and citizen was hostile to my contract, for under that I was obliged to buy at prices less than they persistently demanded, and tried by combinations, to force me to pay; but I always found the officers of the army on my side, and against such combinations, and they soon came to my prices, rather than have all the supplies come from Sonora.[10]

In May 1860 the *Missouri Republican* carried a report from its "Arizona correspondent," Thomas M. Turner, to the effect that instructions from the War Department had been received at Fort Buchanan to let all contracts "to certain party favorites *without advertising for bids.*" Turner went on to predict that Taliaferro and Grant—although he did not mention their names—would in a few months become "independent for life." In June they were given a contract, to run for twenty-one months, to provide beef cattle at $7^{92}/100$ cents per pound.[11] This was not particularly expensive beef, and the contract certainly was not intended to make the recipients independently wealthy.

In September 1860 Taliaferro sold his interests in the partnership to Grant for $8,000.[12] Immediately thereafter Grant received a commissary contract to run to March 26, 1862. It was more specific in its terms, calling for Grant to furnish fresh beef, bacon, bacon hams, flour, beans, candles, and soap to the Arizona posts. Quantities were not specified. Flour in sacks was to be provided at $10^{56}/100$ cents per pound. With one exception, this was the cheapest flour purchased under contract in the department in 1860. The commissary agreed to pay $6^{16}/100$ cents per pound for beans, which was not out of line with the price at other posts. Fresh beef carried the same price as in the contract made for Fort Buchanan in June. Grant acquired much of the wheat for his flour—as well as a large part of the beans and, apparently, all of the beef cattle—locally or in Sonora. None of the other items were available in the department, but were imported from California via Guaymas. Grant, who protested that he was to furnish "everything" required by the posts covered in the contract, also bound himself to establish a headquarters for his business in Tucson.[13]

A few days later the quartermaster signed a contract with Grant, this one also providing for delivery at all posts within the specified area. The items covered were forage (corn, hay, and topped forage), coal, lime, adobes, lumber, and wagon timbers. Prices were not stated, but the contract stipulated that all items would be furnished for 12 percent less than the army had paid for them during the past year.[14] Grant's price for corn, as well as for a small quantity of barley, was $3.06^{23}/100 per hundred pounds (approximately $4.29 per fanega), much less than was paid for corn elsewhere in the department at the time.[15] Most of the corn and all of the other quartermaster's stores except wagon timber, which was imported ash, were local products. Grant, at times, employed more than two hundred men in his various enterprises. He sold some goods to the army below his cost, and by his own deposition, he expected to make his profit from the transportation allowance.[16]

The difficulty and expense of getting supplies to the relatively isolated corner of the department were eased when Governor Ignacio Pesqueira of Sonora issued a decree permitting goods for Arizona to be landed at Guaymas and transported across Sonora, with the importer paying only one-tenth of the normal import duties. Grant immediately put wagon trains to work, hauling goods shipped from San Francisco.[17] In addition to handling his own goods, he offered to carry freight from Guaymas to the vicinity of Fort Buchanan for 3 cents per pound, or for 2 cents in the other direction. As the distance involved was more than three hundred miles, the rate was much cheaper than what the army paid for transportation under contract. Goods from San Francisco could be imported via Guaymas for only 5 cents per pound for the entire distance.[18] Grant, of course, was not alone in taking advantage of Pesqueira's decree. Mining companies imported quantities of their own supplies from San Francisco and exported their ore through Guaymas.[19] For the settlers and mining interests the reduction in transportation costs was a useful by-product of the army's presence.

Grant invested considerable sums of money in his various enterprises. He purchased the Rowlett gristmill for $5,500 and spent an additional $2,000 on improvements. He also imported machinery from California to erect a new gristmill, which he valued at $18,000. The latter was the only large, modern mill in the area, and was capable of grinding ten bushels of grain an hour.[20] Grant's milling facilities apparently were not sufficient to provide all of the flour required by the army under his contract; he continued to import flour from Sonora, keeping "a large number of wagons constantly running between the flour mills . . . near Hermosillo, and the military posts in Arizona."[21] His two lumber camps in the Santa Rita Mountains, opened to provide pine lumber for military construction, represented an investment of $6,150. Other real estate, erected or acquired in connection with his army business, included storehouses, corrals, and sundry buildings, and altogether it was valued by Grant at $5,850.[22] Grant also engaged in a variety of businesses that had nothing to do with his army contracts, such as a hotel in Tucson and a stage line.[23]

There were some complaints about the quality of the service provided by Grant, but they came more from departmental headquarters than from the posts he supplied. In November 1860, on the order of Colonel Grayson, a special contract was made with Simeon Hart to deliver flour at several posts. Included were ten thousand pounds for Fort Fillmore at 16 cents per pound, a rate more than a half-cent higher than Grant's delivered price.[24] When Grayson made his estimate of commissary stores required for the year 1861–62 he included all of the items in Grant's contract, "on the supposition that he will not be able to furnish them."[25] Early in 1861 Grant encountered difficulty in delivering some stores when a large shipment of his goods from the East Coast was seized in Texas, which was by this time in rebellion against the United States. The shortages were filled by drawing from posts supplied from the general depot, resulting in added expense and inconvenience to the army.[26] Grant's commissary contract contained the provision that if he could not furnish the required quantity or quality of any item, post commissaries would make up the shortage by individual purchases or special contracts. Grant was obligated to pay the difference, if any, in price. This could be accomplished without difficulty for Fort Fillmore, but for the other posts served by Grant their relative isolation rendered the solution impracticable.

In Washington the War Department considered it unwise to trust the supply of any post to a source that might be cut off by the Confederates. "Leaving out of consideration the peculiar character" of Floyd's arrangements with Taliaferro and Grant, the Commissary Department recommended that Grant's contracts be rescinded.[27] In April 1861 Secretary of War Simon Cameron expressed the opinion, without explanation, that the contract of September 9, 1860, was unauthorized and ordered that it and all subsequent contracts be revoked.[28] Grant's difficulties were not at an end. The failure of the Boston banking house on which he depended for funds led to the nonpayment of his drafts and seriously affected his credit in Sonora.[29] Actually, all this made little difference, for in July 1861 all troops were withdrawn from Forts Buchanan, Breckinridge, and McLane in the face of the impending Confederate invasion.

The Navajo conflict of 1860 delayed the abandonment of Fort Defiance and the construction of Fort Fauntleroy, but it also gave both posts an immediate importance. They served as bases of operations against the Indians, and additional companies were stationed at both forts as the campaign developed. In April 1861, following the close of hostilities, the troops were withdrawn from Fort Defiance, and the garrison of Fort Fauntleroy was reduced. Also in April, Colonel Chapman was informed that he must depend entirely on the labor of the troops to construct Fort Fauntleroy, but this was hardly an innovation, as troops had played a major part in building all of the forts in the department. Chapman was authorized to deviate as much as necessary from the approved plans in order to provide shelter for the troops and stores before the next winter.[30] Actually, construction of the post was not completed until after the Civil War, and never according to the original plans. Even the name was ephemeral. After Colonel Fauntleroy resigned to serve the Confederacy the post was renamed Fort Lyon in honor of Brigadier General Nathaniel Lyon, who was killed six weeks earlier in the Battle of Wilson's Creek in Missouri. In 1868 it became Fort Wingate.

Colonel Fauntleroy acted slowly to establish Fort Butler, in part because of its intended importance and in part because of his indecision in selecting a location. In April 1860, immediately after he received the order reorganizing the department, he visited the Pecos, Gallinas, and Canadian rivers, expecting to choose the site. Instead, he returned to Santa Fe convinced that neither the Canadian Valley nor the point where the Fort Smith road crossed the Gallinas had the necessary resources to support a large post and depot. The junction of Tecolote Creek and the Pecos River, although otherwise satisfactory, was too far west to serve a defensive purpose. Thus he recommended that the depot be placed at Tecolote or near the ruins of the old Pecos Pueblo church and that Hatch's Ranch be leased or purchased as the location for Fort Butler.[31]

Before undertaking his tour Fauntleroy had declared a ten-mile square reserve on the Canadian at its confluence with Ute Creek. After he returned, even though he rejected all sites on the Canadian, he retained the reservation but reduced it to eighteen sections.[32] A month later he added Hatch's Ranch to the list of unsuitable sites, because of its prohibitive cost and the impossibility of securing a clear title to it. The only reasonable location, Fauntleroy now believed, was at Tecolotito, three miles above Anton Chico on the Pecos River where the roads from Forts Smith and Union branched to Santa Fe, Albuquerque, and Fort Stanton, thereby "constituting the position one of great advantage for a general Depot." He expected that it might cost as much as $20,000 to acquire the land, but "there is no other place to be procured and [unless] this spot is purchased, the location of the declared post of Fort Butler will from necessity be postponed another season."[33] In two months Fauntleroy had succeeded in moving Fort Butler entirely out of Comanche country and so close to Albuquerque as to eliminate most of the expected reduction in transportation costs.

In June a contract was let to furnish the as-yet-unestablished post with 200 bushels of beans at the reasonable price of $3.50 per bushel. At about the same time a contract was made with Hart to provide 100,000 pounds of flour by October 1, delivered either at Fort Butler or at Hatch's Ranch, for 13 cents per pound. This was followed in September by a contract with Dr. Stephen Boice and Michele Desmarais of Las Vegas to deliver 246,000 pounds of flour at Fort Butler during the year 1860–61 at $7^{8}/10$ cents per pound.[34] There were more than the usual number of applicants for the position of sutler at Fort Butler; perhaps the fact that the post had a name gave it a greater reality. As the autumn of 1860 arrived, Fort Butler had a reserve (even though it was considered unsuitable); part of the garrison had been assigned; contracts had been let for some essential items of the ration; and a sutler had been appointed. All that was needed was a post to go with them.

In November, Fauntleroy instructed Captain and Brevet Lieutenant Colonel Benjamin S. Roberts of the Mounted Riflemen to examine the Canadian Valley "within about sixty miles of Hatch's Ranche," select a site, and prepare to establish Fort Butler. Roberts chose a point on the Canadian just below Mesa Rica as suitable for a post,[35] but he informed Fauntleroy that it was not a proper place for a depot. In such an exposed position the large number of draft animals necessary for the operation of a general depot would be an inevitable temptation to marauding Indians, and a large part of the garrison would constantly be occupied in protecting public property. He advised that Hatch's Ranch, already rejected, would be a much better location for the general depot.[36]

By this time the location of Butler had been in contention for eight months. All proposed sites had been examined and found wanting in some respect, yet the general orders remained to be carried out; and Fauntleroy, perhaps in desperation, accepted the site below Mesa Rica for both post and depot. He informed his superiors that part of the garrison was already en route to occupy the position and to establish the post. By the time supplies reached the department in the summer of 1861 he expected to have storehouses erected to receive them. He set aside a reserve, the third and largest declared for Fort Butler, of 120 square miles, roughly bisected by the Canadian River. Except for the Fort Stanton reserve it was the most extensive military reservation in the department. It was officially declared by the Secretary of War on March 22, 1861, and was retained by the government until July 1884.[37] On December 26, Fauntleroy ordered Second Lieutenant Lafayette Peck, Seventh Infantry, to procure from the general depot the supplies necessary "for the immediate establishment of Fort Butler."[38]

Despite the seeming finality of these decisions Fort Butler was still not established. Colonel Fauntleroy was frustrated by circumstances, which were compounded in turn by the communications gap between Washington and Santa Fe. First of all, Fauntleroy lost the companies previously assigned to garrison Fort Butler. As was true of many regiments, the Eighth Infantry was divided, with four of its companies in the Department of New Mexico and with six companies at western posts in the Department of Texas. In September 1860 Major Theophilus Hunter Holmes, the senior officer with the companies in New Mexico, complained about their distribution; they were, he said, "scattered over the Territory of New Mexico." The dispersal, he claimed, destroyed "that esprit de corps and harmony of action that is so necessary to the pride, spirit, self-respect and gallantry of any military organization." As the reorganization of the department called for three infantry companies at Fort Bliss, Holmes wanted all of them to be Eighth Infantry, with the fourth company stationed at Fort Fillmore until it was abandoned. This would place all four companies close to the Texas companies and would give the regiment a degree of unity.[39]

Holmes's request led General Winfield Scott to propose that Fort Bliss be transferred to the Department of Texas. At the time Fort Bliss was established it was about five hundred miles from the closest posts in the Department of Texas and nearly twice as far from the headquarters and general depot in San Antonio as it was from Albuquerque. In the intervening years a number of posts had been established in western Texas, the closest being Fort Quitman, some seventy miles east of Fort Bliss. Routes of travel had been improved, and regular mail and passenger service linked the El Paso district with other parts of Texas, including San Antonio. The reasons for attaching Fort Bliss to the Department of New Mexico no longer existed. The post was transferred to the Department of Texas on December 8, 1860. In the meantime, Fauntleroy was instructed, as soon as field operations permitted, to assign the Eighth Infantry companies to the "posts most contiguous" to the companies in Texas and insofar as possible to Fort Bliss. One company was transferred to Fort Bliss at once, and in January 1861 the three remaining companies were ordered to proceed there. As a result, all of the Eighth Infantry companies that had been in New Mexico were removed from the department and were placed at the same post in the Department of Texas.[40]

Not only was part of the garrison intended for Fort Butler gone, but there was grave concern that funds to construct the post were not available. The sum allocated to the quartermaster's department in New Mexico for the fiscal year 1860–61 was only $579,460.95, and Quartermaster General Joseph E. Johnston informed Major Donaldson that he must not exceed the amount appropriated. Almost 80 percent of the sum was designated for the purchase of feed, fuel, straw, and stationary, and only $8,777.36 for construction. Donaldson was convinced that the unusual expenses of the department required an additional appropriation of $230,000.[41] There was little that could be done to decrease quartermaster's expenses that would not also hamper the activities of the department. In a feeble effort to reduce soaring costs, Fauntleroy ordered that "all Subsistence stores . . . purchased in this Department for the use of U. S. Troops must be delivered by the vendor at the Post where required without charge to the Quarter Master's Department."[42] Most contracts already specified delivery, and subsequent bids continued to reflect transportation costs; therefore it is doubtful that the measure was particularly effective.

At the same time that Donaldson was instructed to remain within his allocation a circular from the Adjutant General's Office reached Fauntleroy's desk, "requiring" that the expenses of the Department of New Mexico not exceed the sum appropriated for the fiscal year. The two documents, coming to his attention at the same time, filled Fauntleroy with trepidation. "I am now," he wrote, "in the very *crisis* of a war with the Navajoes where the great body of the troops operating, have to be supplied at a distance of quite two hundred miles, requiring an almost incalculable amount of transportation, at costs perfectly frightful." All along the eastern frontier of the department the Kiowas and Comanches were "unsubdued & swearing vengeance against the settlements." Four new posts were under construction, all at a considerable distance from the general depot and all requiring an immediate expenditure of at least $200,000. With undoubted sincerity Fauntleroy admitted, "I know not what to do." The cost of the Indian campaigns alone would exceed the sum appropriated, leaving him with the "fearful alternative" of spending money that he had been instructed not to spend or of pulling the troops back and adopting a purely defensive posture. In the face of all this he still had to establish Fort Butler. He had planned, he said, to depart that very day for the Canadian River, to put Fort Butler "in the most active state of erection. . . . The cost however of the post must now compel me to pause—& to ask instructions."[43]

Most disturbing of the developments affecting the department were those associated with the approaching civil conflict. In Washington, Secretary of War Floyd, a Virginian, was caught up in the progress of secession. Under pressure, he withdrew from the cabinet on December 29, 1860, later to serve without particular distinction as a brigadier general in the Confederate army. In January 1861, he was succeeded for the remainder of President Buchanan's term by Joseph Holt, previously the Postmaster General. The rapid course of events close at hand left little time or concern in Washington for the problems of the Southwest. For those who were stationed in New Mexico, even as for their superiors in the East, attention was directed away from the department.

The Department of New Mexico had been plagued by a shortage of officers from the time the regular army took full control in the summer of 1848. They were absent for a variety of reasons: health, detached service, or simply because they were on leave of absence. In March 1860 all officers absent from New Mexico (including those belonging to the companies en route from Utah, but excluding those on special assignment other than the recruiting service) were ordered to the department to "join their respective post and companies."[44] For a time the number of officers in the department increased significantly, but the improvement was to be short-lived.

Few leaves of absence were authorized by Colonel Fauntleroy in September and October of 1860, fewer than were normally granted in the fall. However, beginning in November the number of leaves increased markedly, and among the officers receiving them were some who would fight on the side of the Confederacy. In February 1861, Brevet Second Lieutenant Benjamin F. Sloan, Second Dragoons, from South Carolina, became the first officer in the department to tender his resignation. In accordance with regulations he was permitted to go to his home to await the action of the War Department.[45] Additional resignations were soon submitted, but more officers preferred to take leaves and then resign after they had reached their destinations. Others took leaves only to offer their services to the Confederacy without bothering to resign.

No doubt Colonel Fauntleroy did a good bit of personal soul-searching during these months, but in the final analysis, he reached a decision only when his hand was forced. Colonel William Wing Loring,[46] Mounted Riflemen, arrived in Santa Fe on March 22, 1861, with orders to assume command of the department and with instructions for Fauntleroy to report to army headquarters in New York. Fauntleroy's moment of decision was at hand. On March 25 he wrote a letter offering his services to his natal state, Virginia, if war broke out.[47] Two days later he left with an escort to cross the plains to Fort Leavenworth, the first leg of the journey to headquarters. Instead of going to New York he chose to go to Richmond, Virginia, where, on May 13, 1861, he prepared his resignation from the army.

Like his predecessor, Loring was a southerner, a native of North Carolina. He first came to New Mexico when the Regiment of Mounted Riflemen was transferred to the department in 1856. In 1859 he was granted a leave of absence, and before he returned to New Mexico to supersede Colonel Fauntleroy, he was sent by the army on a tour of observation to Europe and the Near East. Even though the reorganization of the department initiated by Fauntleroy was far from complete, Loring had further changes to suggest, but he would remain in command too briefly to implement them.

On March 31, Fort Bliss was surrendered to the recently seceded state of Texas by order of Brigadier General David E. Twiggs, who commanded the Department of Texas, but who had already been dismissed from the service because of his traitorous acts. The acquisition of Fort Bliss brought the Confederacy to New Mexico's southern border and provided a strategic starting point for the invasion that would come a few months later. Forty miles to the north of Fort Bliss stood Fort Fillmore, now New Mexico's southern bastion of defense.

With the coming of the war it was no longer possible for the Butterfield Overland Mail to operate over the southern route; in March 1861, it was shifted to the central route, and so was no longer a concern of the Department of New Mexico. As a result, Loring recommended that Fort Breckinridge—"a most unhealthful, comfortless and expensive station"—

be abandoned. Insofar as the post was intended to protect the mail line the proposal was valid, but it was also designed to encourage the expansion of settlement and mining. Of course, the point was largely academic, because all federal troops would soon be withdrawn from Arizona.

Loring also noted that when the troops were removed from the Post of Albuquerque and from Fort Craig there would not be a garrison between Forts Fauntleroy and Fillmore (also scheduled for abandonment in Floyd's order of the previous year). Because Fort McLane rendered Fort Fillmore unnecessary, he asked permission to abandon Fort Fillmore and to retain Fort Craig. Yet the surrender of Fort Bliss, even though it was not occupied by Texas troops until the end of June 1861, and the pro-Confederate sympathies manifested throughout the Gadsden Purchase territory, most openly in Mesilla, cast some doubt on the wisdom of Loring's request. It must be said in fairness to Loring that he may have been unaware of the surrender. At the same time, the importance of Fort Union was, for a change, enhanced. Loring issued instructions to evacuate Hatch's Ranch and to transfer the garrison and all public property to Fort Union, which, "for the present," was to be the only garrisoned post in that part of New Mexico. However, Hatch's Ranch was not left without troops for long.

Finally, Loring reopened the matter of Fort Butler. He commended the location set aside by Fauntleroy, "on account of the influence it will give us over the Comanches whose favorite haunts are upon that [the Canadian] River and within striking distance of where Fort Butler is to be." As a depot neither the proposed site nor any other along the Canadian would do. Hence, he asked that he be given authority to choose as a location for the depot a place where all the necessary facilities for construction and maintenance would be available and from which it would be convenient to distribute military stores. Such a site, of course, had evaded his predecessors for the past several years. If all of Loring's recommendations were accepted there would be seven posts in the department—Forts Garland, Fauntleroy, Butler, Stanton, Craig, McLane, and Buchanan—"well placed for the general defence of the Territory"—and a general depot not associated with any of the forts. Presumably, department headquarters would remain in Santa Fe. Discipline and efficiency would be improved and expenses reduced, or so Loring professed to believe.[48]

After the suppression of the Taos uprising fourteen years earlier, the principal function of the army had been to exert control over the wild Indian tribes. Now, even though some of the tribes were openly hostile, the attention of the military was diverted. On May 13, 1861, the same day that Fauntleroy wrote out his resignation in Richmond, Virginia, Colonel Loring prepared his resignation in Santa Fe. After sending it off to army headquarters he stayed on in Santa Fe, apparently intending to remain until his successor was named. However, on June 11, he placed Colonel Edward R. S. Canby, Nineteenth Infantry, "in the general charge of the affairs of the Department and in the immediate command of the northern district." He did not formally relinquish his command, but he left for Fort Fillmore on the same day to await action on his resignation.[49]

The Civil War quickly brought changes in the disposition and composition of troops that were more far-reaching than those contemplated in the still incomplete reorganization. During the hectic weeks of June 1861 some measures were taken to restore a degree of order and to place New Mexico in a defensive position. On June 13, over Colonel Loring's signature, Canby issued the orders creating, under his own command, the northern military district, consisting of Forts Union, Garland, and Marcy, and including the adjacent country. Three days later, again over Loring's signature, Canby announced that the department south of 33° north latitude, comprising Forts Fillmore, McLane, Buchanan, and Breckinridge, would constitute the southern military district.[50] Pertaining to neither district for the time being were Forts Craig, Stanton, and Fauntleroy, and the Post of Albuquerque. Canby, convinced of Loring's treasonable intentions, took over the command of the department on June 22, issuing the first orders in his own name on that date.

On June 11, when for all practical purposes he began directing military affairs in New Mexico, Canby attempted to assess the situation in the department. The shift of emphasis is clearly seen in his complete lack of reference to the Indians. The political attitude of the New Mexican people, he believed, was "contingent upon the action of Missouri," so dependent were they on the Missouri trade. The unrest in the Gadsden Purchase territory affected only a small part of the population, but he expected Texas to attempt to take advantage of it. Hence, he planned to enlarge the garrison of Fort Fillmore to meet any threat from the south. He was perturbed by the great shortage of army mounts and draft animals, a consequence of the severe impact of two years of drought on all animals in the department. He reported also that his funds were insufficient to pay all of the troops in the department, some of whom had already gone unpaid for several months.[51]

Canby acted at once to strengthen the defensive capabilities of the department; and the results of his actions, augmented by the planned and unplanned changes soon brought about by the Civil War, bore little resemblance to the modifications proposed by either Fauntleroy or Loring. On June 14, 1861, following instructions from Washington, Canby directed all infantry units stationed in New Mexico (the Fifth and Seventh Infantry regiments and three companies of the Tenth) to march to Fort Leavenworth as soon as it was possible to do so.[52] This would require some time to accomplish: the infantry companies were scattered throughout the department, and the shortage of transportation facilities hampered the movement.

On the same day, Canby also ordered the abandonment of Fort Breckinridge, transferring the two dragoon companies constituting its garrison to Fort Buchanan, and thus relieved the two infantry companies at Buchanan to move to Fort Fillmore.[53] Two days later, pending arrangements for the departure of the regiments, Albuquerque became headquarters for the Fifth Infantry and Fort Fillmore headquarters for the Seventh Infantry. Major Lynde, with his headquarters staff and regimental band, left Fort McLane on June 30, and on July 3 the rest of the garrison evacuated the post and marched for Fort Fillmore.[54] Two mounted companies, one from Fort Craig and the other from Fort Stanton, were ordered to Fort Fillmore, thus further strengthening that post.

Fort Breckinridge was abandoned on July 10. The departing troops destroyed the stores for which no transportation could be provided, and before they left, they set fire to the post. On June 30 orders were issued for the immediate abandonment of Fort Buchanan. The garrison, which still included the two infantry companies from Breckinridge, was directed to proceed as rapidly as possible to Fort Fillmore.[55] When the troops withdrew on July 23, Fort Buchanan too was set afire and partly destroyed, as were large quantities of military stores.

William S. Grant was vitally affected by the abandonment of the Arizona posts, for the army was unwilling to leave behind anything of potential use to the Confederacy, and transportation for his goods was unavailable. All of his real estate in Tucson, including both gristmills, was put to the torch, and large stores of corn, bran, flour, lumber, tools, equipment, and other goods were destroyed. His property away from Tucson, primarily the two mountain lumber camps, was abandoned. Grant later placed the value of his losses at $61,418.44.[56] In addition he claimed that the army owed him more than $50,000 for goods delivered but not paid for, and he declared that he had amassed an indebtedness of more than $200,000.[57] With the departure of the troops, who were accompanied by Grant and some of his employees, southern Arizona was left without military protection, as the Apaches were well aware.

That the enlistment of volunteers would be required had been anticipated for some time. As soon as orders were received, transferring all regular infantry units from the department, Canby issued instructions to muster twelve companies of volunteers into the service of the United States.[58] Individuals who volunteered for the cavalry were required to provide their own horses and horse furnishings, for which they received "40 cents per day for their use and risk."[59] Additional companies were soon raised, and the volunteers were distributed among the existing posts and were also stationed at Taos, Hatch's Ranch, Gallinas, and Galisteo. Most of the regular troops, including the infantry companies, were still in New Mexico; and with the buildup of volunteers there were soon more men under arms than ever before in New Mexico.[60]

As a result of the rapid increase in troops, military stores of all kinds were required. Contracts were issued in 1861 for a larger quantity and a greater variety of New Mexico-produced commissary stores than in any previous year. Many of the contracts did not specify quantities but simply called for the delivery of the item or items at a particular post. In May, Colonel Grayson asked for proposals for contracts for flour, vinegar, beans, and beef cattle. He stated that he would accept no bids that were "too high or too low, so that the Government of the United States will not have justice done."[61] As the months passed other articles, as well as more of those already under contract, were added.

Table 9

Commissary Provisions Delivered under Contract
to New Mexico Military Posts, 1861[62]

Item	Quantity	Price range during year
flour	1,499,000 pounds	$.08–0.14 per pound
vinegar	5,000 gallons	.68³/₄–1.50 per gallon
beans	1,400 bushels	3.50–6.00 per bushel
beef cattle	1,098 head	.06⁷⁴/₁₀₀–0.11 per pound
sauerkraut	unspecified	1.12–3.00 per gallon
pickles	unspecified	2.00–3.00 per gallon
corn meal	unspecified	.05¹/₂–.09¹/₂ per pound
onions	unspecified	.05¹/₂–.10¹/₂ per pound
salt	unspecified	2.00–4.00 per bushel

The quartermaster's department made surprisingly few contracts. Only

1,600 fanegas of shelled corn were called for, and all of it for Fort Garland; it was provided in two contracts, one at $5.80 and the other at $6.94 per fanega. Both the commissary and quartermaster's departments made two contracts for hay, with the commissary contracting for the larger quantity:

Commissary Department	Fort Union	100 tons	$35.00 per ton
	Fort Craig	100	8.00
Quartermaster's Department	Fort Union	100	45.00
	Fort Craig	44	9.50

In addition to the contracts for corn and hay, the quartermaster's department made contracts for wood and horses. Wood, usually provided by the troops or purchased in individual transactions, was placed under contract for Forts Union and Craig, with hardwood to be delivered at $7.50 to $9.00 per cord and piñon at $3.75 per cord.[63] Horses had never before been purchased in large numbers in New Mexico, but in September 1861 contracts were made with Alexander Warfield for 600 head and with Oliver P. Hovey (one time publisher of the *Santa Fe Republican*) for 800 head at a price of $90 to $150 per head, to be paid for "when funds are received for the purpose."[64]

All contracts specified points of delivery, with by far the greatest quantities of subsistence stores going to Fort Union and to the general depot at Albuquerque. Delivery costs were again a significant part of the price paid to the contractors. Although the effects of the drought were still a factor and there was a greatly increased demand, all items for which a comparison is possible, except beans, were less expensive than in 1860. This is surprising, because in May the *Santa Fe Weekly Gazette* reported that "corn, beans and flour are at this time selling at almost fabulous prices [on the open market]—prices which place them beyond the reach of the poor."[65] The prices for most items rose as the year advanced, but only moderately. The number of individuals or partnerships holding army contracts increased markedly, and included among the contractors were many persons who had not sold goods to the army previously. It is clear that a large part, probably a majority, of the new purveyors were middlemen rather than producers.

Of the seven flour contractors in 1861, only three—St. Vrain, Otero, and John Dold, had previously provided flour to the army, and only they owned gristmills.[66] The largest contract, 700,000 pounds, was held by Henry M. Green, who earlier had been employed by St. Vrain. Oliver

P. Hovey contracted for a greater variety of items than did anyone else: flour, vinegar, beans, beef cattle, sauerkraut, hominy, pickles, and corn meal, in addition to horses. The Zeckendorf brothers, Santa Fe and Albuquerque merchants, held contracts for flour, vinegar, beans, sauerkraut, salt and onions. Maurice Schwarzkopf and Wendell Debus, long time residents of Santa Fe, provided flour, beans, hominy, and corn meal. There were several others who contracted to supply more than one item to the commissary department. The number of contractors for each category of supplies (including those items not a part of the prescribed ration) indicated a surprising availability or, perhaps, a willingness to gamble, because surety bonds were required.

Table 10
Supply Contractors, 1861

flour	seven contractors	sauerkraut	four contractors
vinegar	five "	pickles	two "
beans	eight "	hominy	six "
beef cattle	six "	corn meal	six "
salt	three "	onions	four "

To what extent the number of contractors implies competition is difficult to determine, as the contracts let after the middle of the year seem to have been special contracts that were negotiated individually rather than issued on the basis of bids.

In the south three posts had been abandoned by intent, and the troops were pulled back to the Rio Grande. Unplanned abandonments were about to take place. In July 1861, a Texan force under the command of Lieutenant Colonel John R. Baylor invaded New Mexico from Fort Bliss. Fort Fillmore was evacuated on July 27, and the troops departed from Fort Stanton on August 3. Both posts were set afire by the departing troops; although neither fort was entirely consumed, quantities of military stores were destroyed or abandoned. South of Albuquerque the only military post left in the department was Fort Craig.

Elsewhere the changes were less drastic. The garrison of Fort Defiance was withdrawn to Fort Fauntleroy in April 1861. When that occurred the regular army companies were moved to Albuquerque, leaving Fort Fauntleroy entirely in the hands of volunteers. On December 10, 1861, even the volunteer companies were pulled out, as Colonel Canby concentrated his defenses against a new Confederate threat developing in the south. A mail station was maintained at what was now officially Fort Lyon, but which was still commonly called Fort Fauntleroy, even in army correspondence, during the war years. Although troops were there temporarily from time to time, it was not again permanently occupied until 1868.

Fort Fauntleroy was the final post to be evacuated. Still active were Forts Union, Garland, Marcy, and Craig, as well as the Post of Albuquerque and an ever growing number of camps established to accommodate the increasing volunteer force. There was no further thought of abandoning Fort Marcy or Albuquerque, and Fort Union now assumed much of the importance that Colonel Sumner had intended it to have. Its garrison was greatly augmented, and the construction of the irregular eight-pointed earthwork, designed to turn it into the defensive position it had never been, was commenced in August 1861. Fort Union became the strong point in the north, and Fort Craig was built up as a bulwark in the south. In July 1861, Canby announced that Fort Union would be the general depot for the reception and distribution of all supplies coming into the department, except medical stores. Santa Fe remained the depot for medical stores, and Albuquerque was reduced to a subdepot to meet contingencies and to supply passing troops and trains.[67]

As the defensive periphery was drawn in, the Indians were not forgotten, but they were no longer of primary concern. Except for the Jicarilla Apaches, who had caused no particular trouble for several years, the Apaches were entirely without military control. After the evacuation of Fort Fauntleroy there were no troops in Navajo country, but the Navajos for the time being were relatively quiet, and in September 1861, they sent a delegation to Santa Fe to profess their desire for peace.[68] Fort Garland stood on the fringe of the Ute country, but it had never been called upon to suppress the normally inoffensive Utes.

The Apaches, already carrying on their depredations virtually unhampered, ravaged the Arizona countryside. The agricultural beginnings near Forts Buchanan and Breckinridge disappeared, mines were closed down, and all along the Santa Cruz Valley ranches and farms were deserted. Tubac was again depopulated, and Tucson remained the only center to afford a measure of protection to the inhabitants. When the Confederates sent a detachment to occupy Fort Stanton (which had suffered comparatively little from the attempt to burn it), the troops were constantly menaced by the Mescaleros. After a number of Texans had been killed by the Indians the invaders found it expedient to withdraw. Without military protection the work of the Indian superintendency was drastically curtailed.[69] Between abandoned farms and ranches, unrestrained Indians, and areas of production now in the hands of the Confederates, important sources of supply were lost to the army. Contractors were forced to go as far afield as eastern Kansas to obtain corn to fill their contracts, and flour was once again imported. For the time being, the supply situation was reminiscent of the occupation period.

The department had undergone extensive changes, both physically and in its functions. The events of 1861 effectively ended all contemplated changes, and some plans would never be revived. There were further changes during the war years that were even more far-reaching and lasting. On July 3, 1861, the Military Department of New Mexico was merged into the Western Military Department. It took some time for the merger to take effect, and not until September 21 did Colonel Canby write his last order as commander. The demise was premature, however, for the department was reconstituted on November 9, 1861, under Canby's command.[70] Also in 1861, Colorado Territory was created to encompass the northernmost part of what had been New Mexico Territory. Fort Garland lay within the boundaries of the new territory, but remained attached to the Department of New Mexico. In 1863 the western half of New Mexico was erected into Arizona Territory, but the limits of the department were not changed. The end came on June 27, 1865, when the Department of New Mexico was divided between the departments of California and Missouri and thus permanently laid to rest.[71]

9

⌒᪰ᴓ᪰⌒᪰ᴓ᪰⌒᪰ᴓ᪰

Conclusion

During the fifteen years between General Kearny's occupation of New Mexico in the summer of 1846 and the disruption caused by the outbreak of the Civil War, the Southwest experienced a period of unprecedented growth. To this growth the army contributed directly, as well as simply by its presence. Although precise figures are unavailable, it seems probable that in 1846 the population of the area embraced by the Department of New Mexico was about the same as it was in 1850.[1] The United States census of 1850 shows New Mexico with a population of 61,547, which included some of the Pueblo Indians but none of the so-called wild Indians.[2] In addition to New Mexico, the department took in the nascent settlement of Franklin (El Paso) and La Isla, Texas, with an estimated population of about 2,500.[3] The non-Indian population probably did not exceed 1,000 in that part of present-day Arizona which was then attached to Sonora but was later added to the department and to New Mexico after the limits of the Gadsden Purchase had been fixed. The Anglo portion of the population of the department numbered about 1,600, of whom just under 1,000 were army personnel.[4]

By 1860 the population of the area had increased by more than 50 percent. New Mexico Territory had attained a population of 93,516, a figure that again omitted wild Indians. Arizona County, created from all of the Gadsden Purchase west of a north-south line one mile east of Apache Pass, had a non-Indian population of 2,421. In addition to the Pueblo Indians, the 1860 census included the Pimas, Maricopas, at least some of the Papagos, and about 300 "tame" Apaches who resided on the outskirts of Tucson. In the department outside of New Mexico, Franklin had grown to 428, but the population of La Isla apparently had decreased slightly. The Anglo element in the department was approximately 6,300, a figure which included the military, who numbered just over 3,100 in 1860. This represented an increase of nearly 400 percent, greatly exceeding the growth rate of the general population.

The agricultural facet of the economy expanded markedly during the decade. Some entirely new areas were opened to production, such as the fertile valleys in the vicinity of Forts Stanton, Buchanan, and Breckinridge, and in the southern San Luis Valley. In many of the districts where agriculture already flourished additional land was brought under cultivation. The importance of the army in the spread of agriculture is clear, and not only because of its role as a consumer of various products. When troops were withdrawn from many of the military posts early in the Civil War, some of the recently opened farms and ranches were completely abandoned because the settlers could not remain once they no longer had military protection.

Agricultural production increased, particularly in those crops purchased regularly by the army.[5] The drought still prevailed in 1860. Throughout New Mexico the yield per acre of grain was reported to have fallen from 25 to 50 percent below that of a year of normal rainfall. Even so, corn production rose from 365,411 bushels in 1850 to 709,304 bushels in 1860.[6] Wheat production more than doubled, climbing from 196,516 bushels to 434,309. In Taos County almost four times as much wheat as corn was grown, and in San Miguel County and the newly-created Mora County there was about twice as much wheat as corn. These were the areas in which St. Vrain, the principal purveyor of the flour purchased by the army, had his three mills. Beans and peas (combined in the census reports) rose in output from 15,688 bushels to 38,514 bushels. None of the other products of agriculture purchased in quantity by the army were covered by the census reports. Of course, cornstalks, the chief item of fodder, were more abundant as the result of the expanded planting of corn.[7]

The number of cattle in New Mexico grew from 32,977 in 1850 to 88,729 in 1860.[8] Some cattle were still driven to the department for the use of the commissary, particularly at the southern posts, but most of the requirements for beef could be met locally. Military protection had encouraged the extension of grazing, notably in the general vicinity of Fort Union, the region where the army secured most of its beef cattle. In spite of the consistently large military consumption of pork, there was little increase during the decade in the number of swine, rising from 7,314 to only 10,813. Few individuals owned as many as a dozen animals, and St. Vrain's herd of 180 may have been the largest in the department. The army continued to depend on imported pork products. At the other extreme, sheep increased from 377,271 to 830,116. The army's occasional purchase of mutton was scarcely a factor in this increase, but the greater security afforded the flocks may have been significant.[9] The value of all livestock in New Mexico was estimated at just under $1,500,000 in 1850 and at almost $4,500,000 in 1860.[10] None of the figures for livestock includes the considerable number of animals in the possession of the wild Indians.

The only manufacturing that owed its rapid development specifically to army patronage was the flour milling industry. In 1850 there were three newly completed, large and modern flour mills, with a total annual capacity of 2,100,000 pounds of flour: St. Vrain's mills at Talpa and Mora, and the mill at Peralta that would soon become the property of Antonio José Otero. In 1860 there were nine large mills in the department, with a combined capacity of 6,055,400 pounds.[11] At one time or another, all of these mills furnished flour under contract to the army. During the years 1850–61 the army purchased 11,116,900 pounds of flour under contract; at least 2,000,000 pounds were purchased through contracts in which the quantities were not stated; and some flour was acquired without contract. The millers obtained most of their wheat, either by purchase or barter, from the farmers who raised it. In 1850 St. Vrain valued the wheat that he ground into flour at $1.00 per fanega. A decade later the price paid by the millers ran from $2.50 to about $4.50 per fanega. In 1860 the most expensive wheat was the grain purchased by William S. Grant for his Tucson mills.[12]

Saw milling, nonexistent before the American occupation, owed its inception to the army. The first sawmill to operate in New Mexico was set up by the troops in Santa Fe in 1847; but many additional sawmills, both military and privately owned, were soon erected in all parts of the settled Southwest. The army sometimes purchased "saw logs," but soldiers cut most of the timber and sawed most of the lumber utilized in military construction. The only major contract for lumber was signed with Grant in 1860, requiring him to provide lumber for Forts Buchanan, Breckinridge, McLane, and Fillmore for $132 per thousand feet, plus an allowance for transportation.[13] The army sometimes obtained lumber in individual transactions, usually in small amounts, at prices ranging from as little as $30 to as much as $180 per thousand feet.

Production statistics are not available for vinegar, pickles, and salt, which were processed items purchased with some regularity by the commissary department. Not until 1861 were corn meal (a permissible substitute for flour in the ration) and hominy (to be issued in lieu of rice) purchased in quantity.[14] Comparatively small amounts of other goods manufactured or processed in New Mexico were purchased at times. Commercial breweries did not exist in New Mexico before the Mexican War, and distilleries had been most numerous in the Taos area. By 1861 both were found in many parts of the territory. Although the army per se did not purchase the products of breweries and distilleries, there is ample evidence that the troops contributed to their prosperity, sometimes excessively.

Merchants of all kinds benefited from the presence of the army. Those merchants whose places of business were in towns readily accessible to the troops profited the most from casual purchases. To fill shortages of stores normally imported by the army itself, the commissary and quartermaster's departments usually dealt with the large merchandising firms, those whose businesses were at least partly wholesale. Undoubtedly, the greatest profits were made by individuals who received army contracts; but they, in turn, purchased much of what they sold to the army from the farmers who produced it. The army frequently paid more for goods acquired under contract than the same goods cost on the open market. About 15 percent of the contractors were Spanish Americans, while another 15 percent were Anglos who had resided in the area before the Mexican War. More than two-thirds of all contractors were persons who arrived in the Southwest during or after the war.

In Santa Fe, where hotels had proliferated in the first few years following the occupation, only the well-established Exchange Hotel continued to offer its services to the public in 1861. Now that more adequate quarters were available at Fort Marcy, the Exchange no longer hosted many visiting army men, but it was often the scene of dinners or parties given by officers. Elsewhere in the department, hotels, at least in name, were to be found in most towns by the eve of the Civil War. In southern New Mexico, for example, the neighboring towns of Doña Ana, Las Cruces, Mesilla, and Picacho each had its own hostelry, and there were two hotels in the not too distant Franklin, Texas. Tucson could boast of three hotels and Tubac of one. Many of the hotels were converted private homes, but some provided a wide range of facilities for the comfort and amusement of their guests. Public entertainment varied surprisingly little from that available in the late Mexican period, but the number of establishments providing it had increased. Gambling, drinking, and fandangos remained the most popular pastimes, and ample opportunity existed for all three diversions. After most of the troops were stationed at posts away from centers of population there were, of course, fewer occasions for the men to spend their pay in the towns.

Mining, even though it was not of major importance in the years be-tween the wars, attracted periodic interest. The number of persons who listed their occupation as miner rose from 9 in 1850 to 917 in 1860, and most of these were residents of Doña Ana and Arizona counties. The mines in the Ortiz Mountains, immediately south of Santa Fe, were not ham-pered by Indian depredations. However, in other parts of the territory military protection was essential for the uninterrupted operation of the mines. When General Garland threatened to withdraw the garrison from Fort Fillmore in 1858, miners in the Organ Mountains immediately an-nounced that they would be forced to suspend their work.[15] Activity in the Santa Rita and Pinos Altos districts was frequently brought to a halt by difficulties with the Indians, and work could only be carried on in rel-ative safety when troops were stationed in the vicinity.[16] The southern Arizona mines were virtually deserted at the time United States troops arrived in 1856, and mining again came to a standstill when they were withdrawn in 1861. In both Arizona and New Mexico mining entered upon a period of major growth during the Civil War as a result of new mineral discoveries and the establishment of posts located where they could offer some protection to the mining districts.

The growth of the economy, given impetus by military patronage and protection, created additional jobs. The number of persons employed in the territory (including the self-employed but not the military), grew from about 17,000 to 29,000 during the course of the 1850s, a growth in line with that of the general population.[17] The army itself was the single largest employer of civilian personnel. The number of persons regularly hired at the various posts fluctuated from month to month, but in 1860 civilian employees averaged about 250. The monthly payroll approached $8,000. Additional civilians were temporarily employed in various capacities, and the greatest number worked at the general depot in Albuquerque. The army was also indirectly responsible for a number of jobs, such as the men hired by the post sutlers and by army contractors. John M. Francisco, for example, employed three clerks and a laborer in his sutler's store at Fort Garland. William S. Grant, admittedly not typical of the contractors, employed at times nearly a hundred men in his various enterprises.

The cost of freighting goods to the department had been a cause for serious concern in the immediate postwar years and a major inducement for the army to obtain more of its supplies in New Mexico. The price paid for freighting under contract declined over the years, but the decrease was more than offset by the growing number of troops in the department and by the wider dispersion of posts. However, after Sumner's departure in

1853 the cost of transportation was no longer viewed as a particular problem. Within the department contractors were usually required to deliver directly to the posts, but their added expense was reflected in the bids they submitted or it was covered by a separate allowance. The movement of goods from the general depot or between posts was normally handled by the quartermaster's department. Yet, despite the large number of teamsters regularly employed by the army, it was often necessary to hire additional civilian transportation on a temporary basis. The cost of private transportation at the general depot in 1860 averaged more than $1,500 per month, while the total cost of transportation within the department as a whole exceeded $80,000 for the fiscal year.

The expense of renting facilities in towns had been one of the several reasons advanced by the army for erecting its own posts. Rental costs were never entirely eliminated, although they were reduced. Before the Post of Los Lunas was broken up in September 1860, rents in the department came to $772 per month. The largest sum paid at any post was $335 for the buildings occupied in Albuquerque. As noted previously, a number of the posts were built on private land, which was leased for that purpose. For the use of the land the army made only token payments, except in the case of the Fort Union reserve, for which it paid $1,200 per year.[18]

The amount of money spent by the army in the Southwest is only partly determinable, because not all of the records for the period have been preserved. During the years 1846–48, when the occupying force consisted largely of volunteers, there was frequent movement of troops into and out of the department, and the accounts of sums spent within the department are scant. With the departure of the volunteers at the close of the war and the arrival of additional regular troops, the situation became more stable and more records are available, although they are still far from complete. From slightly more than 200, early in the fall of 1848, the number of officers and men in the department grew to some 3,100 by the beginning of 1861. Military expenditures increased from 1848 to 1851, declined modestly during the Sumner years, and then again increased, reaching a pre–Civil War peak in the fiscal year 1860–61.

In the fiscal year 1860–61 the amount of pay earned by officers and men serving in the department exceeded three-quarters of a million dollars. Payments were in arrears at some of the posts, notably those in Arizona, and when Colonel Canby assumed command in June 1861 he reported that his paymasters did not have sufficient funds to pay all of the troops.[19] The purchasing power of the individual soldier was small. The base pay for cavalry and infantry privates, who constituted the great majority of the enlisted men, was $13 per month. However, $2 of the pay of each enlisted man was retained each month until he was discharged, and he was taxed 12½ cents per month for the support of the United States Soldiers' Home. By the time he settled his indebtedness to the post sutler and to the company laundresses, his ability to contribute to the civilian economy was further reduced.[20]

The commissary department issued contracts providing for an expenditure of $264,990.63 in the fiscal year 1860–61. In addition, there were a number of contracts, including Grant's extensive commitment, in which quantities were not specified. These may represent an additional commissary expense of as much as $100,000, and perhaps even more.[21] In the spring of 1861, when Colonel Grayson requested bids for commissary stores for the year 1861–62, he specified quantities consistent with those purchased during the previous year. However, as volunteers were called up, beginning in July, additional bids were solicited for a variety and quantity of goods much greater than had previously been obtained in the department.[22] The commissary soon found itself without funds and was forced to make purchases on credit.

The appropriation for the quartermaster's department for the fiscal year 1860–61 was $579,460.95, plus a small sum allocated for additions and repairs to Fort Stanton. Contracts for feed and fuel amounting to a total of only $46,818 have been located, and this was little more than one-tenth the sum provided for those items; but, here again, not all of the contracts specified quantities. On the other hand, purchases of corn and fodder from individuals rose considerably at most posts. The high cost of corn in 1860 and the unusual demand for transportation created by the establishment of so many new posts led to a shortage of quartermaster funds before the year was out.

When the army first occupied New Mexico it purchased whatever was available to meet its requirements, but it was often faced by shortages. By the eve of the Civil War it had achieved a system of procurement that assured an adequate supply of those goods that the territory could furnish. In the process the army annually expended significant sums of money in the department, exceeding one and three-quarters million dollars in the fiscal year 1860–61.[23] The money spent by the army per se and by military personnel stimulated the growth of the economy and directly or indirectly benefited all segments of the settled population. In addition, the army furnished a degree of protection against the menace of hostile Indians and was available to maintain order, thus providing a climate more conducive to economic expansion.

List of Abbreviations

AAG   Assistant Adjutant General
ACS   Assistant Commissary of Subsistence
CGS   Records of the Office of the Commissary General of Subsistence
Cons. Corres. File   Consolidated Correspondence File
DNM   Department of New Mexico
HEH   The Henry E. Huntington Library
HQ   Headquarters
LR   Letters Received
LS   Letters Sent
MNM   Museum of New Mexico
NMHR   *New Mexico Historical Review*
NMS   New Mexico Superintendency
NMSA   New Mexico State Records Center and Archives
OAG   Records of the Office of the Adjutant General
OIA   Office of Indian Affairs
QMG   Records of the Office of the Quartermaster General
QM L and Rpts R   Quartermaster Letters and Reports Received
RG   Record Group
Reg. Cont.   Register of Contracts
USACC   Records of United States Army Continental Commands, 1821–
           1920

Notes

Chapter 1

1. Donaciano Vigil, speech presented to the Legislative Assembly, May 16, 1846, Ritch Collection, No. 231, HEH. Donaciano Vigil, born in Santa Fe in 1802, held the rank of captain in the Mexican army, had served the governor as military secretary, and twice had been elected to the departmental assembly.

2. A census taken in 1840 gave New Mexico a population of 55,403, excluding wild Indians. H. Bailey Carroll and J. Villasana Haggard, eds. and trans., *Three New Mexico Chronicles* (Albuquerque, 1942), pp. 88–89. The final census of the Mexican period (1844) gave a population of 100,064, but it was at least partly an estimate and included wild Indians. James W. Abert, *Abert's New Mexico Report, 1846–47* (Albuquerque, 1962), pp. 477–79.

3. Kearny, who had been a colonel in the First Regiment of Dragoons, became a brigadier general as soon as he commenced his march to New Mexico, although the commission did not catch up with him until the evening before he entered Las Vegas.

4. The organization of the Army of the West is discussed by John T. Hughes, *Doniphan's Expedition* (Chicago, 1962), pp. 26–27.

5. O. No. 35, October 13, 1848, RG 94, OAG, Orders, Army of the West.

6. Doniphan, born in Kentucky in 1808, was a lawyer by profession. He commanded the First Regiment of Missouri Mounted Volunteers.

7. Price had served in the Missouri state legislature and represented Missouri in the National Congress when the Mexican War began. He resigned his seat to organize the Second Regiment of Missouri Mounted Volunteers and was rewarded by being elected colonel.

8. The valuation was generous. The cost of a ration at Fort Leavenworth, 1849–1854, ranged between 10.10 and 12.95 cents. RG 192, CGS, Reg. Cont.

9. *Revised Regulations for the Army of the United States* (Philadelphia, 1861), pp. 179–80, 243, 246; Bernard E. Bee to Gouverneur Morris, June 15, 1852, RG 393, USACC, DNM, LR. Until 1852 the fresh beef ration was $1\frac{1}{2}$ pounds per day. By 1861 desiccated potatoes and mixed vegetables were permissible substitutes for beans, and occasional issues (extra) of molasses were authorized.

10. George A. McCall to Roger Jones, December 26, 1850, RG 94,

OAG, LR; Amos B. Eaton to George Gibson, January 8, 1850, RG 92, QMG, Cons. Corres. File. Colonel and Brevet Major General Gibson was Commissary General of the Army, 1818–61.

11. Robert W. Frazer, ed., *Mansfield on the Condition of the Western Forts, 1853–54* (Norman, 1963), p. 61.

12. *Revised Regulations*, p. 277.

13. Ibid., pp. 241–42.

14. McCall to William G. Freeman, September 3, 1850, RG 94, OAG, LR.

15. William J. Sloan to William A. Nichols, December 12, 1859; Theophilus H. Holmes to Nichols, May 31, 1856, RG 393, USACC, DNM, LR.

16. Hughes, *Doniphan's Expedition*, p. 81

17. Philip St. George Cooke, *The Conquest of New Mexico and California in 1846–1848* (New York, 1878), p. 39.

18. Most contemporary accounts mention the meeting, but only Lieutenant Emory referred to Town (he called him Towle), who "reported himself just escaped from Taos" and said nothing about the flour. William H. Emory, *Lieutenant Emory Reports*, ed. Ross Calvin (Albuquerque, 1951), p. 42. Charles Town, a native of St. Louis, was a permanent resident of Taos by 1841. Following the meeting with Doniphan he returned to Taos. He was killed in a fight with Jicarilla Apaches in 1848. Janet Lecompte, "Charles Town," *The Mountain Men and the Fur Trade of the Far West*, ed. LeRoy R. Hafen (Glendale, Calif., 1965), I, 391–93. William C. Kennerly, who was a corporal in the battalion of light artil-

lery which was behind Doniphan's regiment, said that a group of Mexicans met them at Raton Pass with cheese, chickens, and fresh vegetables to sell. Kennerly, *Persimmon Hill, a Narrative of Old St. Louis and the Far West* (Norman, 1949), p. 187.

19. Emory, *Reports*, pp. 46–47; George R. Gibson, *Journal of a Soldier under Kearny and Doniphan, 1846–1847*, ed. Ralph P. Bieber (Glendale, Calif., 1935), pp. 191–92; *The Original Journals of Henry Smith Turner with Stephen Watts Kearny to New Mexico and California, 1846* (Norman, 1966), ed. Dwight L. Clarke, p. 71. Turner referred to the man who provided the beef as an Englishman named Bonney. James Bonney (or Boney) was killed by insurrectionists from Mora during the uprising of January 1847.

20. Ralph P. Bieber, ed., *Marching with the Army of the West* (Glendale, Calif., 1936), p. 153. Private Jacob S. Robinson wrote: "the Mexicans brought cheese, bread, mutton, onions, &c., which they sold us at very high prices." Jacob S. Robinson, *A Journal of the Santa Fe Expedition under Colonel Doniphan* (Princeton, N.J., 1932), p. 23.

21. Emory, *Reports*, p. 50.

22. Gibson, *Journal*, p. 194n; Bieber, ed., *Marching with the Army of the West*, p. 153.

23. Gibson, *Journal*, pp. 206, 212.

24. Bieber, ed., *Marching with the Army of the West*, p. 167.

25. Cooke, *Conquest of New Mexico and California*, p. 51.

26. Bieber, ed., *Marching with the Army of the West*, p. 170.

27. William H. H. Gist to John L. Gist, February 2, 1867, in Vivian K.

McLarty, ed., "Letters of William H. H. Gist, a Volunteer from Weston, Missouri, in the War with Mexico," *Missouri Historical Review,* XLVIII (April 1954): 240–41.

28. *General Regulations of the Army of the United States* (Washington, D.C., 1847), pp. 50, 53; *Revised Regulations,* p. 248. The post fund was derived from a tax on the sutler and from the savings in the flour ration that was realized by baking bread in a post bakery. The company fund consisted of the "savings arising from the economical use of the ration," other than flour. For most companies the fund was small or nonexistent. Later, extra duty pay was increased to 18 and then to 25 cents per day for laborers and teamsters, and to 40 cents per day for skilled workers.

29. The pay scale, in effect since 1838, was $8 per month for privates and musicians, $9 for corporals, $13 for sergeants, and $17 for master sergeants.

30. Emory, *Reports,* p. 59.

31. Ralph P. Bieber, "The Papers of James J. Webb, Santa Fé Merchant, 1844–1861," *Washington University Studies,* XI, *Humanistic Series,* No. 2, (1924), p. 276; Frank S. Edwards, *A Campaign in New Mexico with Colonel Doniphan* (New York, 1966), pp. 60–61.

32. Gibson, *Journal,* pp. 223ff.

33. Gibson described the wheat growing in Santa Fe as "all spring wheat, large, plump, [and] white." Ibid., p. 235.

34. Originally the *fanega* was an imprecise bulk measure. The army soon specified that it was 2¹/₂ bushels; then,

in 1852, it was fixed at 140 pounds for grain.

35. James W. Abert, *Western America in 1846–47* (San Francisco, 1866), p. 40.

36. Carroll and Haggard, eds. and trans., *Three New Mexico Chronicles,* p. 43.

37. William H. Grier with W. S. Smith, September 21, 1846; Grier with Hubert Gosselin, September 28, 1846, RG 192, CGS, Reg. Fresh Beef Cont., 1820–56.

38. Abert, *New Mexico Report,* p. 65.

39. Gibson, *Journal,* p. 262.

40. Edwards, *A Campaign in New Mexico,* p. 81

41. James H. Carleton to Samuel G. Sturgis, December 2, 1852, RG 393, USACC, DNM, LR.

42. Cooke, *Conquest of New Mexico and California,* pp. 99, 102.

43. Hughes, *Doniphan's Expedition,* pp. 258, 274; Gibson, *Journal,* pp. 312–14, 323.

44. Collins, born in Kentucky ca. 1800, moved to Missouri as a young man and participated in the Santa Fe and Chihuahua trade for more than a decade and a half. Now a resident of Santa Fe, he played a prominent role in the early history of the territory. He was for a time owner and publisher of the *Santa Fe Weekly Gazette,* and he held a variety of appointive offices. He was murdered in Santa Fe in 1869.

45. James L. Collins to Manuel Alvarez, February 4, 1847, Benjamin M. Read Collection, NMSA.

46. Emory, *Reports,* p. 61. Emory probably referred to the price of wheat.

47. Cooke, *Conquest of New Mexico and California*, p. 59.

48. Gibson, *Journal*, p. 261.

49. Ibid., pp. 259ff; Emory, *Reports*, p. 60.

50. Jeremy F. Gilmer to Joseph G. Totten, December 7, 1846, RG 77, Records of the Chief of Engineers, LR. Lieutenant Gilmer said that lumber could not be secured in sufficient quantity to meet the "most essential" needs of the army, even at $60 to $70 per thousand feet.

51. Juan Sena, a native of Old Mexico, was in the mercantile business in Santa Fe as late as 1856. Ralph E. Twitchell, *The Leading Facts of New Mexican History*, 5 vols. (Cedar Rapids, Iowa, 1911–17), II, p. 288n.

52. James J. Webb, *Adventures in the Santa Fé Trade, 1844–1847*, ed. Ralph P. Bieber (Glendale, Calif., 1931), p. 93. Webb, describing Santa Fe in 1844, believed this to be the "only plank floor in New Mexico, except a store in Taos built by Mr —— Branch, and I think, perhaps Mr Turley at Turley's Mill, had one or two rooms floored with plank."

53. Gibson, *Journal*, pp. 230, 233, 245, 263, 272. Manuel Alvarez, a native of Spain, became a United States citizen in 1842. He entered the Santa Fe trade in 1824 and settled in Santa Fe in possibly the same year. He was appointed United States consul in 1839, and he was named United States commercial agent at Santa Fe in March 1846. Read Collection, NMSA. For many years he maintained a store in his home on the plaza.

54. The fort was named for Secretary of War William L. Marcy, Initially the name was applied only to the earthwork. In 1851 it was extended to the entire post in Santa Fe. The earthwork had deteriorated badly by the time of the Civil War.

55. Bieber, ed., *Marching with the Army of the West*, p. 212; Cooke, *Conquest of New Mexico and California*, pp. 88, 96.

56. Lee was not a member of the battalion but he came with it to receive part of its pay, money that was badly needed to help finance the Mormon exodus from Illinois to Utah.

57. John D. Lee, "Diary of the Mormon Battalion Mission," ed. Juanita Brooks, *NMHR*, XLII (October 1967), p. 301.

58. Susan Shelby Magoffin, *Down the Spanish Trail and into Mexico*, ed. Stella M. Drumm, pp. 112, 132. Samuel Magoffin was one of three brothers, all natives of Kentucky and all engaged in the Santa Fe trade. He entered the trade perhaps as early as 1830 and dropped out in 1847. James W. Magoffin, the best known of the three, entered the trade in 1825, and in 1830 he married a Chihuahua girl, the cousin of Governor Manuel Armijo. Ibid., pp. xvii–xviii.

59. Mr. Dodge [owed] to Sutler A. G. Wilson, Ritch Collection, No. 247, HEH. Wilson came to Santa Fe with Colonel Price's regiment. He died early in 1847 of an unspecified illness.

60. Cooke, *Conquest of New Mexico and California*, p. 51.

61. Gibson, *Journal*, pp. 238, 245–46.

62. See Abert, *New Mexico Report*, pp. 66, 96. Abert wrote: "Mexicans generally do not like to receive anything but 'plata blanca.'"

63. Bieber, ed., *Marching with the Army of the West*, pp. 169–70, 211; William B. McGrorty, ed., "William H. Richardson's Journal of Doniphan's Expedition," *Missouri Historical Review*, XXII (January 1928): 235.

64. Edwards, *A Campaign in New Mexico*, p. 52.

65. Cooke, *Conquest of New Mexico and California*, pp. 83, 91.

66. Gibson, *Journal*, p. 250n.; Abert, *New Mexico Report*, pp. 64–65; Kennerly, *Persimmon Hill*, pp. 191–92.

67. The Narbona census of 1827, which is more detailed than others of the Mexican period, gave Santa Fe a population of 5,160. Carroll and Haggard, eds. and trans., *Three New Mexico Chronicles*, p. 88. However, the United States census of 1850 recorded only 4,846, including army personnel.

68. S. O. No. 4, RG 94, OAG, Special Orders, Army of the West.

69. Ralph E. Twitchell, *The Story of New Mexico's Ancient Capital, Old Santa Fe* (Chicago, 1963), p. 236n.; Cooke, *Conquest of New Mexico and California*, p. 43. One of the best contemporary (1844) descriptions of the plaza is in Webb, *Adventures in the Santa Fé Trade*, pp. 92–95.

70. The spelling varies in Spanish records, but the United States used the form "San Elizario" as does the present town. The former island is now part of the left bank of the Rio Grande.

71. Map: Reconnaisance of Santa Fé and Its Environs made by order of Brig. Genl. Kearny by Lt. W. H. Emory, Corps Topl. Engrs. & Lt. J. F. Gilmer, Corps of Engineers, Aug. 19h 1846, Manuscript, MNM.

72. Hughes, *Doniphan's Expedition*, pp. 138–39; Kennerly, *Persimmon Hill*, p. 193.

Chapter 2

1. O. No. 231, August 13, 1847; O. No. 232, August 14, 1847; O. No. 1, August 29, 1847, RG 94, OAG, Orders, 9th Mil. Dept.

2. Raphael P. Thian, *Notes Illustrating the Military Geography of the United States* (Washington, D.C., 1881), p. 49.

3. James Conklin, a French Canadian, first came to Santa Fe as a trader in the 1820s. He settled in Santa Fe, became a Mexican citizen, and married a Spanish American girl.

4. Ralph P. Bieber, ed., *Marching with the Army of the West* (Glendale, Calif., 1936), p. 320. A Missouri Mounted Volunteer private was detailed to work with the press, which he did for two weeks until his company was ordered to El Paso del Norte. Ibid., p. 322.

5. The reference may be to a hotel opened by Benjamin Pruett of Jackson County, Missouri, in the summer of 1846. Pruett was killed at Mora in the uprising of 1847. James W. Goodrich, "Revolt at Mora, 1847," *NMHR*, XLVI (January 1972): 51. Gibson said that Pruett had the only "real" hotel in Santa Fe and that he set a "respectable table." George R. Gibson, *Journal of a Soldier under Kearny and Doniphan, 1846–1847*, ed. Ralph P. Bieber (Glendale, Calif., 1935), p. 215 and n.

6. The present Fonda, certainly a modern-day landmark, is at the southeast corner of the plaza. Ralph E.

Twitchell placed the old inn at the southwest corner and described what was left of the building ca. 1910 in his *Leading Facts of New Mexican History,* 5 vols. (Cedar Rapids, Iowa, 1911–17), II, p. 138.

7. The collected sketches have been published as *Matt Field on the Santa Fe Trail,* ed. John E. Sunder (Norman, 1960).

8. James J. Webb, a native of Connecticut, was engaged in the Santa Fe trade throughout the period 1846–61. His firm maintained a retail and wholesale business in Santa Fe. Webb's *Adventures in the Santa Fé Trade, 1844–1847,* ed. Ralph P. Bieber (Glendale, Calif., 1931) provides a good picture of commercial activity during the first year of the occupation.

9. Benjamin F. Taylor, *Short Ravelings from a Long Yarn, or Camp Marches on the Santa Fe Trail* (Santa Ana, Calif., 1936), p. 143. A native New Mexican reminisced many years later that the inns in Santa Fe in the 1830s were all of a very primitive nature, but the rates were reasonable and the accommodations good. W. H. H. Allison, "Santa Fe as It Appeared during the Winter of the Years 1837 and 1838," *Old Santa Fe,* II (October 1914): 178–79.

10. The census of 1850 listed Abell as 30 years of age, his birthplace unknown. Nicolás Pino was a member of one of Santa Fe's most prominent families. He was one of the original conspirators in what became the Taos uprising of January 1847. After the plot was disclosed in December 1846, he took no more part in the movement and served in the volunteer company that was raised in Santa Fe to aid in putting down the uprising.

11. Amos and Mrs. de Habiles (mentioned below) had left Santa Fe by 1850 and have not been identified.

12. Preston Beck, Jr., and Francis Redman may have been the proprietors of the Beck and Redman Hotel, but this is conjectural. Redman, who died in Santa Fe in 1863, was a barkeeper as late as 1861. Beck, a native of Indiana, was a Santa Fe merchant. In 1853 and 1854 he acquired the San Juan Bautista del Ojito del Rio de las Gallinas (Preston Beck) Grant on the Pecos River. He died in April 1858, as a result of a stab wound. Frank Springer, *Territorial Statutes and Land Claim Reports,* 2 vols. (History Library, MNM), I, 71–72; *Santa Fe Weekly Gazette,* April 10, 1858.

13. George D. Brewerton, *Incidents of Travel in New Mexico* (Ashland, Calif., 1969), pp. 37–38; Lansing B. Bloom, ed., "From Lewisburg (Pa.) to California in 1849. (Notes from the Diary of William H. Chamberlin)," *NMHR,* XX (January 1945): 54.

14. Alex (Alexander) Duval, who was born in Baltimore, Maryland, later acted as agent for the army and as sutler at a number of military posts. He was also at times a merchant, and he owned property in what was then Santa Ana County.

15. Moody did not take out a dramshop license in 1849 and does not appear in the 1850 census.

16. *Santa Fe Weekly Gazette,* September 18, 1852. Dorrence, a native of France, engaged in a great many business enterprises in the 1840s and

1850s, but none apparently with success. In 1860 he was a butcher.

17. The original proprietors of the Exchange Hotel were Charles S. Rumly, William O. Ardinger, and Reuben F. Green. Rumly, a native of Ireland, had been chief clerk in the commissary department. Green of Missouri and Ardinger of Virginia were listed as hotel keepers in 1850. Ardinger and Rumly held a dramshop license in 1850 and a gambling license in 1851. The newly opened Exchange Hotel was mortgaged for more than $5,000, at 12 percent per annum interest, to Francis A. Cunningham, Major Paymaster United States Army. Deed Records, Santa Fe County, New Mexico, Book A, 23–26, Santa Fe County Court House. By 1853 the Exchange was apparently the only hotel in Santa Fe. William W. H. Davis, *El Gringo; or New Mexico and Her People* (New York, 1857), p. 167.

18. Unfortunately, the Sheriff and Collectors Record—Licenses, 1847–1867, and the Santa Fe County Licenses, 1851–1878, both NMSA, do not distinguish between kinds of merchants. Fees were based on the value of the goods, and most of the Spanish Americans would be classified as small merchants.

19. Max Moorhead gives an extensive list of goods in the prewar trade, based on invoices and manifests. Moorhead, *New Mexico's Royal Road: Trade and Travel on the Chihuahua Trail* (Norman, 1958), p. 81.

20. The firm ceased operation in 1850. By that date John Hartley, an Irishman by birth, had moved to Socorro where he opened a store. John Powers apparently had left New Mex-

ico. Henry J. Cuniff, a native of Ireland, opened a store in Las Cruces in 1850, and in 1859 he moved to Franklin (El Paso), Texas.

21. Ralph P. Bieber compiled a long list of goods in describing "The Papers of James J. Webb, Santa Fé Merchant, 1844–1861," *Washington University Studies*, XI, Humanistic Series, No. 2 (1924): 301–3. The advertisements in the *Santa Fe Republican* also give an excellent idea of the variety of goods offered for sale.

22. Robert Carey was a native of Delaware. Quinn, who listed his profession as lawyer, was born in Maryland. He came to New Mexico with the Army of the West and was active in the business and political life of the territory until his death in December 1856, at the age of thirty-nine. *Santa Fe Weekly Gazette*, January 10, 1857.

23. Dunn's school lapsed for several years, but reopened in 1856, offering a wider range of subjects at slightly higher tuition. Ibid., November 15, 1856. In the interim, he served as clerk in the paymaster's department and as interpreter in the Indian department. He was a native of Ohio.

24. Gertrudis Barceló, according to the census of 1850, was born in Old Mexico and was thirty-nine years old. Unverified accounts hold that she loaned (or gave) several thousand dollars to the army during the early months of the occupation, when money was in short supply. She is also credited with disclosing the plotting for an uprising in December 1846. She died in 1852.

25. Thomas B. Hall, *Medicine on the Santa Fe Trail* (Dayton, Ohio, 1971), pp. 71, 118. See also John P. Bloom,

"New Mexico Viewed by Anglo Americans, 1846–1849," *NMHR, XXXIV* (July 1959): 165–98.

26. *Santa Fe Republican*, November 15, 1848.

27. Doctor Robinson also took part of the census for Valencia County, but he is not himself listed in the census. He was appointed coroner for Santa Fe County in 1851. Seventh Census, 1850, NMSA; April 5, 1851, RG 59, Records of the State Department, Territorial Papers, New Mexico.

28. Bieber, ed., *Marching with the Army of the West*, p. 321.

29. O. No. 10, February 5, 1848, RG 94, OAG, Orders, 9th Mil. Dept.; Sheriff and Collectors Record of Revenues, NMSA.

30. John T. Hughes, *Doniphan's Expedition* (Chicago, 1962), p. 406. Hughes was a member of Doniphan's command and accompanied Doniphan when he left New Mexico; hence, his information in this matter was secondhand.

31. George R. Gibson, *Over the Chihuahua and Santa Fe Trails, 1847–1848*, ed. Robert W. Frazer (Albuquerque, 1981), p. 39.

32. *Santa Fe Republican*, October 1, 1847; November 20, 1847.

33. *Santa Fe Republican*, May 15, 1848.

34. James White had operated a large general store in Warsaw, Missouri, before he and his brother Charles entered the Santa Fe trade and opened a store in Santa Fe, probably in 1848. James White was killed by Jicarilla Apaches and Utes in October 1849.

35. Francis J. Thomas to George Gibson, October 25, 1848, RG 393, USACC, ACS, DNM, LS.

36. *Santa Fe Republican*, September 17, 1847. The same advice was repeated in later issues.

37. *Santa Fe Weekly Gazette*, July 29, 1854.

38. Eighth Census, 1860, NMSA.

39. Edward W. B. Newby to Roger Jones, September 18, 1847, RG 94, OAG, LR.

40. W. H. H. Allison, "Santa Fe in 1846," *Old Santa Fe*, II (April 1915): 396.

41. Richard M. Hamilton with Charles Holmes and David Spaulding, April 1, 1848, RG 92, QMG, Reg. Cont.

42. *Santa Fe Republican*, June 17, 1848.

43. The *Missouri Republican*, December 10, 1849, reported receiving a *Santa Fe Republican* extra dated October 20, 1849, the first issue published since the extra of August.

44. The first page carried the date November 24 and pages two and three November 28. Oliver La Farge made a good case for the correctness of the latter. La Farge, *Santa Fe, the Autobiography of a Southwestern Town* (Norman, 1959), p. 3. According to Porter A. Stratton, the *New Mexican* was published intermittently in the years 1849–50. Stratton, *The Territorial Press of New Mexico, 1834–1912* (Albuquerque, 1969), p. 3. Only two issues are known to exist. The later *New Mexican*, which first appeared in January 1863 and is still published, had no connection with the earlier newspaper of the same name.

45. Smith was a native of Kentucky who came to New Mexico as a private

in Doniphan's regiment. He was a lawyer by profession and was attorney general of New Mexico when he died of
apoplexy in 1859. *Santa Fe Weekly Gazette*, September 24, 1859.

46. Johnson, a native of Pennsylvania, had been a first lieutenant in
the Eighth Infantry, before he was
cashiered in 1845 for "embezzlement
and misapplication of public funds" belonging to the commissary department. G. O. No. 22, May 30, 1845,
in *Speech of the Hon. Richard H. Weightman of New Mexico Delivered in the House
of Representatives, March 15, 1852*
(Washington, D.C., 1852), pp. 22–
23. In New Mexico, despite his record,
he was employed as a clerk in the quartermaster's department. In 1850 he
owned real estate valued at $30,000.

47. Reynolds replaced Captain
Thomas L. Brent as chief quartermaster on April 1, 1850, when Brent was
relieved from duty in the department.
O. No. 11, April 1, 1850, RG 94,
OAG, Orders, 9th Mil. Dept. Reynolds left New Mexico in 1851 and was
dismissed from the service in 1855, but
he was reinstated in 1858. In 1850 he
owned real estate in New Mexico valued at $32,500; his wife owned real
estate valued at $35,000; and his seven-
year-old son owned real estate valued
at $4,200.

48. Weightman came to New Mexico with the Army of the West, as captain of a Missouri volunteer artillery
company, and was retained as additional paymaster in New Mexico until
May 1849. He went to Washington in
1852 as New Mexico's territorial
representative.

49. O. No. 4, February 19, 1850;

O. No. 10, March 19, 1850, RG 94,
OAG, Orders, 9th Mil. Dept.;
Weightman, *Speech*, pp. 20–21. There
is no complete file of the *Gazette*, but
it began publication sometime in 1850.

Chapter 3

1. O. No. 55, August 31, 1848, RG
94, OAG, Orders, 9th Mil. Dept.

2. Washington, a native of Virginia, was a distant cousin of the nation's first president and a graduate of
the United States Military Academy.
He had served in the artillery since the
age of twenty.

3. John Macrae Washington to Roger
Jones, October 13, 1848, RG 94, OAG,
LR. On November 7, 1848, the command of Departments No. 8 (Texas)
and No. 9 were consolidated with
headquarters in San Antonio, Texas.
They were again divided on April 3,
1849. Colonel Washington did not learn
of the consolidation until March 6,
1849, and it had little effect in New
Mexico. Raphael P. Thian, *Notes Illustrating the Military Geography of the
United States* (Washington, D.C.,
1881), p. 49.

4. Washington to William L. Marcy,
November 8, 1848, RG 94, OAG, LR.

5. Lansing B. Bloom, ed., "From
Lewisburg (Pa.) to California in 1849.
(Notes from the Diary of William H.
Chamberlin)," *NMHR*, XX (January
1945): 54; Walker Wyman, "Freight-
ing: A Big Business on the Santa Fe
Trail," *Kansas Historical Quarterly*, I
(November 1931): 19; *Missouri Repub-
lican*, August 25, 1849. Messervy, a na-
tive of Salem, Massachusetts, entered

the Santa Fe trade in 1839. He was appointed territorial secretary by President Pierce in 1853 and served for a time as acting governor.

6. Thomas L. Brent to Thomas S. Jesup, October 9, 1850, 31st Cong., 2d Sess., Sen. Exec. Doc. 1, II, p. 292.

7. Grant Foreman, *Marcy & the Goldseekers* (Norman, 1939), p. 266ff; Lorenzo D. Aldrich, *A Journal of the Overland Route to California & the Gold Mines* (Los Angeles, 1950), p. 21; Charles Edward Pancoast, *A Quaker Forty-Niner,* ed. Anna Paschall Hannum (Philadelphia, 1930), p. 220.

8. Robert Eccleston, *Overland to California on the Southwestern Trail, 1849,* eds. George P. Hammond and Edward H. House (Berkeley and Los Angeles, 1950), pp. 128–40, 161.

9. Mabelle E. Martin, ed., "From Texas to California in 1849," *Southwestern Historical Quarterly,* XXIX (October 1925): 133.

10. This was not the first use of the route, which had been traversed in whole or in part by both military and civilian parties. Josiah Gregg made the first trip in 1839, down the north side of the Canadian with wheeled vehicles from Van Buren, Arkansas, to Santa Fe. He described the trip in his *Commerce of the Prairies,* ed. Max L. Moorhead (Norman, 1954), pp. 225–62.

11. Foreman, *Marcy and the Gold Seekers,* pp. 148–51, 152–59, 195–205, 211–14, 215–33, 235–50, 339–403, includes Marcy's instructions and reports; James H. Simpson, *Report and Map of the Route from Fort Smith, Arkansas, to Santa Fe New Mexico* (1850), 31st Cong., 1st sess., Sen. Exec. Doc. 12.

12. *Reports of the Secretary of War with Reconnaissances of Routes from San Antonio to El Paso* (1850), 31st Cong., 1st sess., Sen. Exec. Doc. 64.

13. *Memorial* of the Legislative Assembly of the Territory of New Mexico to the Senate and House of Representatives of the United States [1851], RG 59, State Department, Territorial Papers, New Mexico.

14. Blumner, Prussian by birth, probably entered the Santa Fe trade in 1839 and took up residence in Santa Fe in 1840. He was appointed treasurer by General Kearny.

15. Sterling Price to Roger Jones, February 6, 1848, and encl. O. No. 10, February 5, 1848, RG 94, OAG, LR.

16. William E. Prince to William S. Messervy, Thomas L. Brent, et al., August 19, 1848, ibid.; *Santa Fe Republican,* August 16, 1848.

17. O. No. 57, September 25, 1848; O. No. 6, April 3, 1849, RG 94, OAG, Orders, 9th Mil. Dept.; Washington to Marcy, November 8, 1848, ibid., LR.

18. Report of Charles Blumner, December 28, 1850, Ritch Collection, No. 414, HEH. The report left $110 unaccounted for.

19. Washington with J. M. Whitlock, November 17, 1848, RG 393, USACC, DNM, LR. Dr. John M. Whitlock was a native of Kentucky and a resident of Las Vegas. The 1850 census listed him as a physician and farmer, and the 1860 census listed him as a merchant. After the outbreak of the Civil War he was appointed Surgeon, First Regiment, New Mexico Volunteers. S. O. No. 118, August 14, 1861,

ibid., Special Orders, DNM. He was killed in a quarrel with a fellow officer in 1862.

20. Lewis A. Edwards to John H. Dickerson, June 5, 1849, ibid., LR; Washington to Jones, June 5, 1849, RG 94, OAG, LR.

21. Dickerson to Francis J. Thomas, June 5, 1849, RG 393, USACC, DNM, LR.

22. Thomas to George Gibson, October 25, 1848 and February 6, 1849, RG 393, USACC, DNM, LR; Thomas to Richard B. Lee, November 17, 1848, and Brent to John Adams, May 14, 1849, ibid., ACS, LS.

23. Thomas to Joseph N. G. Whistler, September 28, 1850, ibid.

24. Thomas to Andrew J. Smith, July 30, 1850, ibid.

25. See Richard H. Coolidge, comp., *Statistical Report on the Sickness and Mortality in the Army . . . January, 1839, to January, 1855*, pp. 432–35.

26. Thomas to George Gibson, October 25, 1848, and February 26, 1849, RG 393, USACC, ACS, DNM, LS.

27. Alexander W. Reynolds to Joseph H. Whittlesey, February 15, 1850, ibid.

28. Edwards to Dickerson, October 27, 1848; July 25, 1849; September 13, 1849, ibid., DNM, LR.

29. Coons, a Missourian, obtained the ranch in June 1849. He was engaged in the Santa Fe and Chihuahua trade until his bankruptcy in 1850.

30. Washington to Jones, July 30, 1849; Jefferson Van Horne to [Dickerson], September 10, 1849, RG 94, OAG, LR.

31. John Munroe, a native of Scotland, graduated from the Military

Academy in 1814. He replaced Washington as commander of the department on October 23, 1849. He was the last military governor of New Mexico, holding the office until March 3, 1851.

32. John Munroe to William G. Freeman, October 30, 1849, RG 94, OAG, LR.

33. Robert W. Frazer, ed., *New Mexico in 1850: A Military View* (Norman, 1968), p. 184. If the companies had been at full strength there would have been 1,603 officers and men, not counting headquarters staff and medical officers.

34. Maxwell, a native of Illinois, had a residence in Taos as well as a home on the Rayado. He was married to the daughter of Charles Beaubien, and he was later the owner of the famed Maxwell Grant.

35. Henry Pickering Walker, *The Wagonmasters* (Norman, 1966), p. 230.

36. Langdon C. Easton with James Brown, May 17, 1848; May 18, 1848; June 25, 1848; Simeon Hart with Jabez Smith and Co., August 28, 1848, RG 92, QMG, Reg. Cont.

37. Thomas Swords with John S. Jones and William Russell, February 17, 1851; Swords with Joseph Clymer, April 18, 1851; Edmund A. Ogden with Jones and Russell, May 15, 1851, ibid.

38. Edwin B. Babbitt with Lewis and Groesbeck and Benjamin F. Coons, April 13, 1850, ibid.; Van Horne to Lafayette McLaws, October 1, 1850 and November 2, 1850, RG 393, USACC, DNM, LR; Rex W. Strickland, "Six Who Came to El Paso, Pioneers of the 1840's," *Southwestern Studies*, I (Fall, 1963): 15–17.

39. Thomas to Gibson, November 8, 1848, RG 393, USACC, ACS, DNM, LS. Thomas blamed the deterioration of stores on the poor construction of the buildings where they were stored and on a year of unusually wet weather. Thomas to George Deas, March 28, 1849, ibid.

40. Thomas to Gibson, December 20, 1848 and February 6, 1849, ibid.

41. West moved from Kentucky to New Mexico in 1847, settling in Albuquerque. A lawyer by training, he served as New Mexico's attorney general during the years 1848–52, and as United States attorney from 1851 to 1853.

42. Thomas to Elias P. West, September 7, 1849, RG 393, USACC, ACS, DNM, LS. Thomas later entered into a contract with West to run the mill.

43. Thomas to McLaws, June 14, 1850, ibid.; Thomas to Gibson, June 1, 1850, ibid.

44. Winslow, a native of Georgia, resided in Albuquerque where he was a merchant. He served as agent for the army throughout the period before the Civil War, and he was also sutler at the Post of Albuquerque. For a time in the 1850s he was alcalde for Bernalillo County.

45. Marshall S. Howe to McLaws, May 25, 1850; Thomas to McLaws, July 14, 1850, ibid.; Charles B. Brower to Thomas, July 18, 1850, RG 393, USACC, DNM, LR; John C. McFerran to Henry Winslow, December 11, 1851, ibid., LS.

46. Thomas L. Brent, Memorandum for the information of Col. Munroe, collected . . . during the months

of November & December 1849, n.d., ibid., LR.

47. Robert W. Frazer, "Purveyors of Flour to the Army: Department of New Mexico, 1849–1861," NMHR, XLVII (July 1972): 216–18.

48. Thomas to Gibson, August 5, 1849, RG 393, USACC, DNM, LS.

49. Ceran St. Vrain, born in 1801 in what was later Missouri, entered the Santa Fe trade in 1824 and became a citizen in 1831. He was associated with the Bent brothers in the trading empire of Bent, St. Vrain and Co. until 1848. Isaac McCarty, a native of Missouri, was associated with St. Vrain in various enterprises in 1849. He died in 1850 at the age of thirty-eight.

50. Thomas with Ceran St. Vrain and Isaac McCarty, RG 192, CGS, Reg. Cont.

51. Janet Lecompte, "Ceran St. Vrain's Stone Mill at Mora," Cultural Properties Review Committee, State Planning Office, Santa Fe, pp. 1–2.

52. Frazer, ed., New Mexico in 1850, p. 97.

53. Frazer, "Purveyors of Flour to the Army," p. 220.

54. Andrew W. Bowman with Hart, March 28, 1850, RG 192, Reg. Cont.; Articles of Agreement, Bowman with Hart, December 20, 1850, RG 92, Cons. Corres. File. At this time flour sold on the market in El Paso area for 10 to 12$\frac{1}{2}$ cents per pound. John Russell Bartlett, Personal Narrative of Exploration and Incidents in Texas, New Mexico, California, Sonora, and Chihuahua 2 vols. (New York, 1856), I, p. 191.

55. Dixon S. Miles to Don Carlos

Buell, September 18, 1851, RG 393, USACC, DNM, LR.

56. Gibson to ———, October 12, 1850, RG 94, OAG, LR; Isaac Bowen to Edwin Vose Sumner, July 25, 1852, RG 393, USACC, DNM, LR.

57. Proceedings of a Board of Survey, September 26, 1850, RG 94, OAG, LR.

58. Robert W. Frazer, ed., *Mansfield on the Condition of the Western Forts, 1853–54* (Norman, 1963), p. 62.

59. In 1850 St. Vrain employed twelve men at his two mills, and William Skinner employed fourteen at his mill in Peralta. Seventh Census, 1850, NMSA.

60. Whittlesey to William N. Grier, September 12, 1850, RG 393, USACC, DNM, LR.

61. Oliver H. P. Taylor to Brent, March 29, 1849, ibid.; Henry P. Judd to Dickerson, July 31, 1849, ibid.; Brent to Jesup, October 9, 1850, 31st Cong., 2d Sess., Sen. Exec. Doc. 1, II, p. 292.

62. Memorandum for the information of Colonel Munroe, n.d., RG 393, USACC, DNM, LR.

63. Bartlett, *Personal Narrative*, II, pp. 386–87.

64. William B. Johns to McLaws, November 14, 1850, RG 393, USACC, DNM, LR.

65. Brent to Jesup, October 9, 1850, 31st Cong., 2d Sess., Sen. Exec. Doc. 1, II, p. 291; Table Showing Expected Corn Purchases by Districts, ibid., p. 301. One bushel of corn would feed one horse for less than five days if the full ration of twelve pounds (often expressed as eight quarts) was issued. The ration for a mule was nine pounds. Both horses and mules received fourteen pounds of hay per day.

66. Frazer, ed., *New Mexico in 1850*, pp. 134, 140, 149.

67. [John Greiner] to ———, July 29, 1851, in Tod B. Galloway, ed., "Private Letters of a Government Official in the Southwest," *Journal of American History*, III (No. 4, 1909), pp. 544–45; Samuel Ellison to Easton, July 4, 1851, 32d Cong., 1st Sess., House Exec. Doc. 2, pp. 252–53.

68. Daniel T. Chandler to McLaws, September 11, 1850, RG 393, USACC, DNM, LR.

69. Dodge, whose father and brother were United States senators, worked for the army in various capacities. He was appointed agent for the Navajos and the western Pueblo Indians in 1853. William Carr Lane to George W. Manypenny, June 30, 1853, RG 75, OIA, LR, NMS. Dodge was killed by Apache Indians in the autumn of 1856.

70. Henry L. Dodge to Munroe, May 12, 1851; Chandler to McLaws, July 24, 1851, RG 393, USACC, DNM, LR. Neither Dodge nor Chandler said what quantity constituted a bag.

71. John Fox Hammond, *A Surgeon's Report on Socorro, New Mexico, 1852* (Santa Fe, 1966), p. 41.

72. John T. Fitzwater, the forage-master, was a longtime resident of Old Mexico. He was hired by the quarter-master's department during the Mexican War and continued to work for it until his death in 1856. *Santa Fe Weekly Gazette*, May 17, 1856.

73. Charles A. May to McLaws, June 1, 1850, RG 393, USACC, DNM, LR.

74. Judd to Dickerson, June 1, 1849, ibid.; Swords to Jesup, October 25,

1851, 32d Cong., 1st Sess., House Exec. Doc. 2, pp. 235-37.

75. Easton with Philip Shoaff, March 7, 1851, RG 92, QMG, Reg. Cont. In the 1850 census Shoaff, a native of Maryland, was listed as a clerk residing in Santa Fe. At the time the contract was made hay delivered at Forts Smith and Washita, Indian Territory, under contract, for $4 to $6 per ton.

76. Whistler with Edward Ownby, May 15, 1851, ibid. Previously, Ownby had been employed as a wagon master in Santa Fe.

77. Ownby to ———, July 16, 1851, RG 393, USACC, DNM, LR; Chandler to McLaws, July 24, 1851, ibid.; Ownby to Munroe, July 16, 1851, RG 94, OAG, LR.

78. The contract has not been located. Nesbitt, a native of New York, was employed as a foragemaster in the quartermaster's department in Santa Fe He also had a dramshop license in Santa Fe. Parker, a twenty-five-year-old native of North Carolina, had no regular occupation, but he did own real estate in Santa Fe that was valued at $4,000 in 1850.

79. Robert Nesbitt with Hiram R. Parker to Munroe, n.d.; Beverly H. Robertson to McLaws, July 17, 1851, RG 94, OAG, LR.

80. Reynolds with Tomás Ortiz and Domingo Baca, June 25, 1851, RG 92, QMG, Reg. Cont. An arroba was approximately 25^1/$_3$ pounds.

81. Sumner, a native of Massachusetts, did not attend the Military Academy. In 1819, he entered the regular army as a second lieutenant in the infantry, and when the regiment was formed in 1833, he became a captain in the First Dragoons.

82. Sumner to Jesup, January 17, 1852, RG 393, USACC, DNM, LS.

83. S. O. No. 54, July 22, 1851; S. O. No. 74, October 14, 1851, ibid., Special Orders, 9th Mil. Dept.; Lucien B. Maxwell to Richard S. Ewell, July 30, 1851, ibid., DNM, LR; Ebenezer S. Sibley, Statement of forage paid for at Fort Union during the fiscal year ending the 30th of June 1852, RG 92, QMG, Cons. Corres. File.

84. Read was a native of Maryland and a resident of Santa Fe. He committed suicide in 1857.

85. Samuel Hackelton with Benjamin F. Read, June 18, 1848; Whittlesey with Maxwell and James H. Quinn, April 1, 1849; John C. McFerran with Duvall and Co., June 10, 1851, RG 192, CGS, Reg. of Fresh Beef Cont.

86. Thomas to Thomas Biggs, January 21, 1850, RG 393, USACC, ACS, DNM, LR.

87. [McFerran] to Ewell, March 31, 1852; Sumner to Sibley, May 3, 1852, ibid., DNM, LS.

88. Thomas to Gibson, February 6, 1849 and June 1, 1850, ibid., ACS, DNM, LS.

89. William T. Sherman with T. C. Gordon, May 20, 1852; George G. Waggaman with J. C. Irvin, May 18, 1853, RG 192, CGS, Reg. Fresh Beef Cont.

90. [Citizens of Taos, Petition,] June 25, 1854, RG 393, USACC, DNM, LR.

91. Easton to Jesup, August 2, 1854, RG 92, QMG, Cons. Corres. File; S.

O. No. 56, September 6, 1854, RG 393, USACC, Special Orders, DNM.

92. White, whose background is not known, erected a trading house at Frontera in 1848. Strickland, "Six Who Came to El Paso," pp. 11–12. Frontera was located on the Rio Grande about eight miles above El Paso.

93. Van Horne to McLaws, November 14, 1850, RG 393, USACC, DNM, LR. The White contract has not been located.

94. McLaws to Van Horne, December 5, 1850, ibid., LS; Washington L. Elliott to Benjamin L. E. Bonneville, June 10, 1859, ibid., LR.

95. Thomas to McLaws, June 7, 1850, ibid.

96. William Z. Angney to Manuel Alvarez, March 13, 1854, Alvarez Papers, NMSA.

97. Thomas with George Reed, November 6, 1848, RG 192, CGS, Reg. Cont. At this time salt delivered at Fort Leavenworth for 80 cents to $1 per bushel and vinegar for $12^{1}/_{2}$ to 33 cents per gallon.

98. *New Mexican*, December 8, 1849.

99. Thomas to Charles H. Humber, November 22, 1849; Thomas to William C. Skinner, November 30, 1849; Thomas to Humber, April 30, 1850; Thomas to McLaws, August 3, 1850, RG 393, USACC, ACS, DNM, LS. The actual contracts have not been located. In 1849 tallow candles were purchased under contract at Fort Leavenworth for 12 cents per pound.

100. Thomas to A. B. Eaton, January 30, 1850, ibid.

101. Samuel Ellison, a native of Kentucky and a resident of Santa Fe, was employed at one time or another by the army during the 1850s as an interpreter, as quartermaster's clerk, and as purchasing agent. He was also at various times secretary to the governor, acting governor, and a member of the territorial legislature. William J. Davy, a native of Ireland, resided in Rio Arriba County and listed his profession as a trader.

102. McFerran with Ellison and Davy, April 5, 1851, RG 192, CGS, Reg. Cont.; Frazer, ed., *New Mexico in 1850*, p. 169.

103. This was broken down into 643,860 rations for the troops; 219,000 for government employees; 5,000 for detachments "coming and going"; and 60,000 for the boundary commission.

104. Estimate of Subsistence for the use of Troops and Government Employees in the 9th Military Department; McFerran to Sherman, February 11, 1851, RG 92, QMG, Cons. Corres. File.

105. Petition signed by Merrill Ashurst, et al., n.d., RG 393, USACC, DNM, LR.

106. Calhoun, a native of Georgia, was the first Indian agent sent to New Mexico, arriving in Santa Fe in July 1849. He was inaugurated as New Mexico's first territorial governor on March 3, 1851. By the summer of 1852 he was gravely ill and died on the plains en route to Missouri.

107. Statement of buildings rented, Santa Fe, 32d Cong., 1st Sess., House Exec. Doc. 2, p. 242.

108. The figures for 1849 are from Memorandum for the information of Colonel Munroe, n.d., RG 393, USACC, DNM, LR. Those figures for

1850, except Santa Fe, are from McCall's inspection reports in Frazer, ed., *New Mexico in 1850*. Most of those for 1851 are from 32d Cong., 1st Sess., House Exec. Doc. 2, pp. 235ff.

109. Report of Persons [employed] at Santa Fe, July 1851, 32d Cong., 1st Sess., House Exec. Doc. 2, p. 243.

110. Thomas to Gibson, June 4, 1849, RG 393, USACC, ACS, DNM, LS.

111. January 8, 1851, 32d Cong., 1st Sess., House Exec. Doc. 2, pp. 164–65.

112. Edmund A. Ogden to Jesup, October 4, 1851, ibid., p. 292.

113. Jesup report, December 22, 1847, and Gibson endorsement, December 23, 1847, RG 94, OAG, LR.

114. See p. 63.

115. Munroe to Jones, March 30, 1851, RG 94, OAG, LR. The report did not reach Washington until May 6, more than a month after Conrad had issued his instructions to Munroe's successor.

116. McLaws to John G. Parke, March 12, 1851; Parke to McLaws, April 14, 1851; Easton to McLaws, April 21, 1851; Easton to Parke and McLaws, April 21, 1851, ibid.

Chapter 4

1. Charles M. Conrad to Edwin Vose Sumner, April 1, 1851, 32d Cong., 1st Sess., Sen. Exec. Doc. 1, pp. 125–26.

2. Sumner to Roger Jones, October 28, 1851, RG 393, USACC, DNM, LS.

3. O. No. 17, July 19, 1851, ibid., Orders, 9th Mil. Dept.; Swords to Je-

sup, October 25, 1851, 32d Cong., 1st Sess., House Exec. Doc. 2, p. 239.

4. Sumner to Jones, October 24, 1851, RG 393, USACC, DNM, LS.

5. When Cebolleta was broken up a portion of its garrison was stationed for several months at Laguna, directly on the road to the newly established Fort Defiance. S. O. No. 71, October 1, 1851, ibid., Special Orders, 9th Mil. Dept.

6. Sumner to Jones, October 24, 1851, ibid., LS.

7. George P. Hammond, *The Adventures of Alexander Barclay, Mountain Man* (Denver, 1976), p. 66 n. 38. The Scolly Grant, made in 1846 to John Scolly and five others, was eventually confirmed as 108,507.64 acres. Scolly Grant Papers, NMSA; L. C. White, Sumner S. Koch, et al., *Land Title Study* (Santa Fe, 1971), p. 222. Scolly, who settled in New Mexico in the 1830s and became a Mexican citizen, died in 1847.

8. Hammond, *Alexander Barclay*, pp. 165–76; *Santa Fe Weekly Gazette*, February 19, 1853.

9. Justice of the Peace Record Book No. 1, 1856–1868, County Records, Mora County, p. 98, NMSA.

10. [Lease] Territory of New Mexico, County of Santa Fe, July, 1851, RG 393, USACC, DNM, Unentered LR. The Mora Grant was made in 1835 to seventy-six persons. It was eventually confirmed by Congress as 827,621.01 acres.

11. O. No. 30, May 11, 1852, ibid., Orders, 9th Mil. Dept.

12. United States District Court, County of Taos, Book A, 1851–1857,

pp. 45, 90–91, 96–97, 119, 121–22, NMSA.

13. Indenture, Barclay and Doyle with Daniel H. Rucker, March 22, 1854, RG 92, QMG, Reg. Cont.

14. Scolly Grant Papers, NMSA.

15. Pedro Ascue de Armendáriz, one-time first lieutenant in the garrison of the Presidio of San Elizario, was given two adjoining grants, sometimes known as the Valverde and San Cristóbal tracts, in 1819 and 1820. As eventually confirmed, the two grants contained a total of 447,535.18 acres. Armendáriz attempted to occupy the land, but he gave up in the face of repeated Indian hostilities. He died in Chihuahua in 1853. Smith and Biggs purchased a portion of the Armendáriz Grant. Petition to William Pelham, July 22, 1854, 36th Cong., 1st Sess., House Exec. Doc. 14, pp. 193–95; James Josiah Webb, *Adventures in the Santa Fé Trade 1844–1847*, ed. Ralph P. Bieber (Glendale, Calif., 1931), pp. 283–84.

16. Sumner to Gouverneur Morris, August 17, 1851, RG 393, USACC, DNM, LS.

17. Morris to Sumner, August 27, 1851; Benjamin F. Coons to Sumner, August 26, 1851, ibid., LR.

18. Morris to Don Carlos Buell, August 27, 1851, ibid.

19. Electus Backus to Lafayette McLaws, July 13, 1851, ibid.

20. Morris to Buell, September 18, 1851, ibid. Fort Fillmore was on the Brazito Grant, 14,808.07 acres, given to Juan Antonio García y Noriega of El Paso, retired dragoon lieutenant, in 1823. Hugh Stephenson, a Kentuckian who had engaged in the Santa Fe trade as early as 1824, purchased two-thirds of the grant from García's heirs. 35th Cong., 1st Sess., House Report 457, pp. 24–25, 28; José M. Flores, et al., vs. the United States, RG 123, U.S. Court of Claims General Jurisdiction Case No. 9521, Filed July 8, 1874.

21. Sumner to James W. Magoffin, August 17, 1851, RG 393, USACC, DNM, LS.

22. Dixon S. Miles to John C. McFerran, June 17, 1852; July 17, 1852; Miles to Sumner, September 9, 1852, ibid., LR.

23. A portion of the old fort, built with four-feet-thick walls, stood into the twentieth century before it was engulfed by the expansion of open pit mining. See "Journal of Captain A. R. Johnston," 30th Cong., 1st Sess., House Exec. Doc. 41, p. 578.

24. O. No. 44, December 2, 1851, RG 393, USACC, Orders, 9th Mil. Dept.; Sumner to Morris, September 5, 1851, ibid., DNM, LS.

25. Morris to McFerran, March 16, 1852, ibid., LR.

26. Morris to McFerran, April 13, 1852, ibid.

27. Morris to McFerran, May 31, 1852, ibid.

28. Andrew W. Bowman, Statement . . . Transportation of Stores to the A.A.G. at Fort Webster, N. M., July 9, 1852, ibid., Unentered LR.

29. O. No. 56, November 18, 1852, ibid., Orders, 9th Mil. Dept.

30. Enoch Steen to Sumner, December 13, 1852, ibid., DNM, LR.

31. Samuel G. Sturgis to Steen, January 26, 1853, ibid., LS.

32. O. No. 41, August 7, 1852, ibid., Orders, 9th Mil. Dept.

33. George A. H. Blake to Sumner, June 23, 1852, ibid., DNM, LR.

34. Sturgis to Blake, January 26, 1853, ibid., LS.

35. Cantonment Burgwin was named for Captain John H. K. Burgwin, First Dragoons, who was killed in the Taos uprising. Most western military posts were named in honor of military men, but this was the only post established by Sumner that was so named.

36. Sumner to Robert Ransom, August 11, 1852, RG 393, USACC, DNM, LS.

37. The grant, which encompassed more than 91,800 acres, was not confirmed by the United States until 1872. 42d Cong., 2d Sess., House Exec. Doc. 181, p. 85; White, Koch, et al., *Land Title Study*, p. 225.

38. Memorial and petition to the Honorable House of Representatives, and Members of the Legislative Senate of the Territory of New Mexico, December 12, 1852; Ransom to Sturgis, January 21, 1853, RG 393, USACC, DNM, LR.

39. Sumner to Jones, January 1, 1852, ibid., LS.

40. McFerran to Henry Winslow, December 20, 1851, ibid.; Winslow to Sumner, December 23, 1851, ibid., LR.

41. Sumner with A. J. Pillings, agent for A. W. Reynolds and W. McGrorty, December 28, 1851, RG 92, QMG, Reg. Cont. The lease was later extended by seventeen months. Articles of agreement, Major D. H. Rucker with William McGrorty and Martha Ann Thomas, April 2, 1853, ibid. Mrs. Thomas was the wife of Lieutenant Francis J. Thomas, who resigned from the army in June 1852 and left New Mexico in 1853.

42. Sumner to Rucker, May 3, 1852, RG 393, USACC, DNM, LS.

43. S. O. No. 92, December 15, 1851, ibid., Special Orders, 9th Mil. Dept.; McFerran to Richard S. Ewell, December 16, 1851, ibid., DNM, LS; O. H. P. Taylor to Sumner, February 9, 1852, ibid., LR. By mid-1852 the total cost of rentals at Los Lunas was $50 per month.

44. Ewell to McFerran, May 7, 1852, ibid.

45. Ewell to Ben [Ewell], July 21, 1852, in Percy Gatling Hamlin, ed., *The Making of a Soldier: Letters of General R. S. Ewell* (Richmond, Va., 1935), p. 75.

46. Sumner to Miles, March 30, 1852, RG 393, USACC, DNM, LS.

47. O. No. 6, January 9, 1852, ibid., Orders, 9th Mil. Dept.

48. For a more extensive discussion of the agricultural program see Robert W. Frazer, "Army Agriculture in New Mexico, 1852–53," *NMHR*, L (October 1975): 313–34.

49. Alvarez's property, the 69,440 acre Ocate Grant, was given to him by Governor Manuel Armijo in 1837. His title to the land had not been confirmed by the United States when he died in 1856. In 1885 the Surveyor General of the United States recommended that it be rejectd because, among other things, Alvarez had not fulfilled the terms of the grant. The claim was rejected. The army gave up the farm land in 1854, but continued to pay Alvarez a small sum annually for the privilege of cutting grass on his land.

50. Blake to Samuel Cooper, October 1, 1853, RG 393, USACC, DNM, LR.

51. Backus to Jones, July 1, 1852, ibid., Unentered LR.

52. Henry L. Kendrick to Jones, October 1, 1852, ibid.; Kendrick to Sumner, September 10, 1852, ibid., LR.

53. Robert W. Frazer, ed., *Mansfield on the Condition of the Western Forts, 1853–1854* (Norman, 1963), p. 48.

54. Report of the General in Chief, November 22, 1852, 32d Cong., 2d Sess., House Exec. Doc. 1, II, p. 35.

55. Frazer, ed., *Mansfield*, pp. 62–64.

56. Philip St. George Cooke to William A. Nichols, January 20, 1854, RG 393, USAC, DNM, LR.

57. Cooper to Jefferson Davis, January 26, 1854, and Davis endorsement, February 7, 1854, RG 94, OAG, LR; G. O. No. 3, February 9, 1854, ibid., General Orders, HQ Army; Statement of Expenditures on account of Farm Culture since May 1st 1851, n.d., RG 393, USACC, DNM, Unentered LR.

58. Richard H. Coolidge, comp., *Statistical Report on the Sickness and Mortality in the Army of the United States, 1839–1855* (Washington, D.C., 1860), p. 429.

59. Blake to Cooper, October 1, 1853, RG 393, USACC, DNM, LR.

60. Kendrick to Jones, October 1, 1853, ibid., Unentered LR.

61. Henry L. Dodge to George W. Manypenny, August 2, 1855; Dodge to David Meriwether, May 16, 1856, RG 75, OIA, NMS, LR.

62. Sumner to George G. Wagga-man, December 15, 1852, RG 393, USACC, DNM, LS.

63. Lane, a resident of Missouri, had served in the regular army, 1814–18. See Calvin Horn, *New Mexico's Troubled Years* (Albuquerque, 1963), pp. 37–38.

64. Ralph E. Twitchell, "Historical Sketch of Governor William Carr Lane, Together with Diary of His Journey from St. Louis, Mo., to Santa Fe, N. M., July 31st, to September 9th, 1852," *Historical Society of New Mexico, Papers*, No. 20 (November 1, 1917), pp. 47–48.

65. Backus to Jones, July 1, 1852, RG 393, USACC, DNM, Unentered LR.

66. *Santa Fe Weekly Gazette*, March 15, 1856.

67. Sumner to Miles, September 22, 1852, RG 393, USACC, DNM, LS.

68. Major Ogden was assistant quartermaster at Fort Leavenworth.

69. Sumner to Thomas Swords, October 25, 1851; Sumner to Jones, October 24, 1851, RG 393, USACC, DNM, LS.

70. Sumner to Swords, October 25, 1852, ibid.

71. McFerran to Bowman, November 30, 1851, ibid.; Sumner to James H. Carleton, March 4, 1852, ibid.

72. Sibley to Sumner, February 28, 1852; August 26, 1852; October 15, 1852, ibid., LR; Sumner to Sibley, July 17, 1852, ibid., LS. Moore, a native of New York, was a farmer and merchant. In 1860 his personal property was valued at $150,000. Rees, who was from Missouri, was associated with Moore in various contracts throughout the 1850s.

73. S. O. No. 46, July 20, 1852, ibid., Special Orders, 9th Mil. Dept.; Sumner to Sibley, July 17, 1852, ibid., LS.

74. Charles Griffin to McFerran, May 26, 1852, ibid., LR.

75. Blake to Sumner, November 24, 1852, ibid.

76. Bernard E. Bee to Morris, June 16, 1852, ibid.

77. Miles to McFerran, March 30, 1852, ibid.

78. Miles to McFerran, May 19, 1852, ibid.

79. Ebenezer S. Sibley to Thomas S. Jesup, September 1, 1852 and December 6, 1853, RG 92, QMG, Cons. Corres. File; Sumner to Sibley, August 23, 1852; Sumner to Jones, August 24, 1852, RG 393, USACC, DNM, LS.

80. Sumner to Jones, October 24, 1851, RG 393, USACC, DNM, LS.

81. Sumner to Ewell, February 13, 1852; McFerran to Rucker, May 30, 1852, ibid.

82. Sumner to Jesup, February 27, 1852, ibid.

83. Sumner to Samuel Ellison, October 16, 1851, ibid.; Sibley with John J. Lease and Charles W. Kitchen, November 1, 1851, RG 92, QMG, Reg. Cont. Both Lease and Kitchen were native Virginians. The 1850 census listed Lease as a merchant and Kitchen and his brother John as merchants and farmers.

84. Horace Brooks to McFerran, March 30, 1852, RG 393, USACC, DNM, LR.

85. Miles to McFerran, March 30, 1852; Bee to Morris, June 16, 1852, ibid. Major Bernard E. Bee explained the shortage of corn south of the Jor-nada as the result of "the continuous drain to supply the deficiency to a starving population in the state of Chihuahua."

86. Ransom to McFerran, March 3, 1852; Rucker to McFerran, May 29, 1852 and July 5, 1852, ibid.; Sumner to Rucker, July 23, 1852, ibid., LS.

87. Mitchell was a merchant. The 1850 census listed his birthplace as unknown.

88. Sibley to Sumner, October 12, 1852, RG 393, USACC, DNM, LR; Sumner to Sibley, October 29, 1852, ibid., LS.

89. Russell has not been identified.

90. George R. Gibson, *Journal of a Soldier under Kearny and Doniphan, 1846–1847*, ed. Ralph P. Bieber (Glendale, Calif., 1935), p. 276.

91. Sibley to Sumner, October 21, 1852, RG 393, USACC, DNM, LR. The contracts are in RG 92, QMG, Reg. Cont.

92. John Garland to Cooper, October 28, 1853, RG 393, USACC, DNM, LS.

93. *Santa Fe Weekly Gazette*, November 6, 1852.

94. Sumner established Camp Vigilance when it was rumored that the Spanish Americans were planning an uprising. Albuquerque, he wrote, was the "central point in the territory from which to repress the insurrectional spirit in the people." The camp was broken up in August 1852. Sumner to Jones, April 28, 1852, RG 393, USACC, DNM, LS; O. No. 27, April 28, 1852, ibid., Orders, 9th Mil. Dept.

95. Antonio José Otero was a large land holder, sheep owner, and merchant. General Kearny appointed him

one of the justices of New Mexico's first Superior Court, an office he held until March 1, 1852. In 1860 his mill represented an investment of $15,000. Eighth Census, 1860, NMSA; James W. Abert, *Abert's New Mexico Report, 1846–47* (Albuquerque, 1962), p. 100; Adolph Wislezenus, *Memoir of a Tour to Northern Mexico, 1846–1847* (Albuquerque, 1969), p. 41.

96. Sumner to Isaac Bowen, April 19, 1852; Sumner to Ceran St. Vrain, April 10, 1852, RG 393, USACC, DNM, LS.

97. Seventh Census, 1850, NMSA. Skinner, who resided in Peralta in 1850, came to New Mexico in the Army of the West. He was a native of Connecticut and a lawyer by profession. He was killed in Albuquerque in March 1851. *Speech of the Hon. Richard H. Weightman of New Mexico, Delivered in the House of Representatives, March 15, 1862* (Washington, D.C., 1862), pp. 23–26.

98. Sumner to Bowen, November 7, 1852, RG 393, USACC, DNM, LS.

99. *Santa Fe Weekly Gazette*, December 25, 1852. The same notice appeared in each issue of the *Gazette* for about two months.

100. Hersch, a native of Poland, came to the United States in 1837 and lived in New York state for a decade before moving to New Mexico. He became a prominent merchant in Santa Fe, and at one time he was considered the wealthiest resident of the territory. He died in Santa Fe in 1901. *Santa Fe New Mexican*, August 26, 1901.

101. Deed Record, Santa Fe County, New Mexico, Book A, pp. 113–15. The contracts are in RG 192, CGS, Reg. Cont.

102. O. No. 17, July 19, 1851, RG 393, USACC, Orders, 9th Mil. Dept.; Sumner to Swords, October 25, 1851, ibid., DNM, LS.

103. O. No. 5, January 9, 1852, ibid., Orders, 9th Mil. Dept.; Lawrence P. Graham to Sumner, March 29, 1852, ibid., DNM, LR.

104. Kendrick to Sumner, September 9, 1852; Kendrick to Bowen, July 5, 1853, ibid.

105. McFerran to Bee, September 9, 1852; Rucker to Sumner, August 25, 1852, ibid.

106. Ewell to McFerran, February 24, 1852, ibid.

107. Miles to Sturgis, April 24, 1853, ibid.

108. Jones to Newman S. Clarke, June 9, 1852, ibid.; Bowman with Levin Mitchell, November 1, 1852, RG 192, CGS, Reg. Cont.

109. Sumner to Miles, September 22, 1852, RG 393, USACC, DNM, LS.

110. O. No. 17, July 19, 1851; O. No. 25, August 8, 1851, ibid., Orders, 9th Mil. Dept. The base pay of a second lieutenant in the infantry, was $45 per month. If by emoluments Sumner meant the commutation value of rations and a servant, the total was $103.50, more than any clerk received at the time.

111. G. O. No. 43, July 22, 1851, RG 94, OAG, LR.

112. Swords to Jesup, October 25, 1851, 32d Cong., 1st Sess., House Exec. Doc. 2, pp. 235ff.

113. Sibley, Statement of the amount of money paid to citizens hired

at the depot of Fort Union, during the fiscal year ending June 30th 1852, n.d., RG 92, QMG, Cons. Corres. File.

114. McFerran to Commanding Officer, Taos, January 27, 1852, RG 393, USACC, DNM, LS.

115. McFerran to Post Commanders, October 24, 1851, ibid.

116. McFerran to Horace Brooks, March 3, 1852, ibid. Rafael Carabajal was a native of San Ysidro. Little is known of his background, but he had an intimate knowledge of much of the Navajo country, gained in expeditions in which he had participated prior to the American period. Frank McNitt, *The Navajo Wars* (Albuquerque, 1972), pp. 140–41.

117. Sibley to Sturgis, July 20, 1853, RG 393, USACC, DNM, QM L and Rpts R.

118. Sumner to [Cooper], September 24, 1852, ibid., LS.

119. Garland, a Virginian, was not a graduate of the Military Academy. He entered the army as a first lieutenant in 1813 and became colonel of the Eighth Infantry in 1849.

Chapter 5

1. Meriwether, a native of Kentucky, was appointed by President Pierce.

2. G. O. No. 25, October 31, 1853, RG 94, OAG, General Orders, War Dept.; Raphael P. Thian, *Notes Illustrating the Military Geography of the United States* (Washington, D.C., 1881), p. 79.

3. Yuma, originally Colorado City, was laid out in 1854.

4. John Garland to Lorenzo Thomas, October 29, 1853; November 27, 1853, RG 393, USACC, DNM, LS.

5. William S. Messervy to James J. Webb, October 27, 1853, in Bieber, "The Papers of James J. Webb, Santa Fé Merchant, 1844–1861," Washington University Studies, XI, *Humanistic Series*, No. 2 (1924), p. 294.

6. Garland to Samuel Cooper, July 30, 1854, RG 393, USACC, DNM, LS; O. No. 27, September 6, 1854, ibid., Orders. In Santa Fe Garland purchased a five-room adobe house for $317. In 1855 he sold it to Colonel Horace Brooks for $400. Deed Record, Santa Fe County, Book B, pp. 40–41, 126–27.

7. Indenture, Barclay and Doyle with Daniel H. Rucker, March 22, 1854, RG 92, QMG, Reg. Cont.

8. Langdon C. Easton to Thomas S. Jesup, August 2, 1854, ibid., Cons. Corres. File; Garland to Cooper, April 27, 1856, RG 393, USACC, DNM, LS; S. O. No. 27, April 1, 1856, ibid., Special Orders.

9. Garland to Cooper, October 28, 1853, USACC, DNM, LS.

10. Ebenezer S. Sibley to Jesup, September 21, 1852, RG 92, QMG, Cons. Corres. File.

11. Garland to Thomas, October 29, 1853; Garland to Electus Backus, November 7, 1853, RG 393, USACC, DNM, LS; O. No. 48, November 7, 1853, ibid., Orders; Robert W. Frazer, ed., *Mansfield on the Condition of the Western Forts, 1853–54* (Norman, 1963), pp. 25–26.

12. Garland to Cooper, January 27, 1854, RG 94, OAG, LR; Israel B. Richardson to William A. Nichols,

January 11, 1854 and June 27, 1854, RG 393, USACC, DNM, LR. The post was named for First Lieutenant Herman Thorn, First Infantry, who drowned in the Colorado River in 1849.

13. Sibley to Jesup, September 1, 1852, RG 92, QMG, Cons. Corres. File; Garland to Daniel T. Chandler, November 7, 1853, RG 393, USACC, Fort Conrad, LR; Chandler to Nichols, November 15, 1853, ibid., DNM, LR; Frazer, ed., *Mansfield*, pp. 24, 51. Valverde was a camping spot, not a settlement.

14. Garland to Thomas, October 29, 1853, RG 393, USACC, DNM, LS; Indenture, Juan N. Zuberán with Garland, May 28, 1854, RG 92, QMG, Reg. Cont. The post was named for Captain and Brevet Lieutenant Colonel Louis S. Craig, Third Infantry, murdered by deserters in 1852. It remained active until 1885.

15. Frazer, ed., *Mansfield*, pp. 19, 41.

16. See Morris F. Taylor, "Campaigns Against the Jicarilla Apaches, 1854," *NMHR*, XLIV (October 1969): 269–91.

17. Garland to Thomas, October 29, 1853; July 30, 1854; June 30, 1856, RG 393, USACC, DNM, LS; S. O. No. 15, March 12, 1854, ibid., Special Orders.

18. Garland to Thomas, October 29, 1853, ibid., LS; Joseph E. Johnston to AAG, HQ Army, September 12, 1859, RG 94, OAG, LR; Frazer, ed., *Mansfield*, p. 56.

19. Johnston to AAG, HQ Army, August 27, 1859, RG 94, OAG, LR; Frazer, ed., *Mansfield*, p. 22.

20. Johnston to AAG, HQ Army, August 25, 1859, RG 94, OAG, LR. Fort Defiance was reoccupied under the name Fort Canby, 1863–64, during Kit Carson's Navajo campaign.

21. Benjamin S. Roberts to Nichols, September 28, 1856 and February 12, 1857, RG 393, USACC, DNM, LR.

22. Easton to Jesup, August 2, 1854, RG 92, QMG, Cons. Corres. File.

23. Corpus Christi de Ysleta, sometimes called Isleta del Sur.

24. Frazer, eds., *Mansfield*, pp. 28–29.

25. Garland to James Gadsden, December 27, 1853, RG 393, USACC, DNM, Unentered LR.

26. The post was named for Captain William W. S. Bliss, Zachary Taylor's son-in-law.

27. Easton to Jesup, August 2, 1854, RG 92, QMG, Cons. Corres. File; J. F. Crosby to Garland, May 17, 1855, and Cooper endorsement, RG 94, OAG, LR; Report of Persons and Articles employed at Fort Bliss, January, 1858, RG 393, USACC, QM L and Rpts R.

28. Report of Subsistence Stores remaining on hand at the Dépôt, Fort Union, New Mexico on the 31st day of July 1853, RG 393, USACC, DNM, Unentered LR; Sibley to Edwin Vose Sumner, June 20, 1853; Sibley to Dixon S. Miles, July 14, 1853, ibid., LR; Garland to Thomas, October 29, 1853, ibid., LS.

29. Joseph H. Whittlesey with Russell, Waddell & Co., September 15, 1853; Whittlesey with Alexander Majors, September 16, 1853; Whittlesey with James B. Yager, September 15, 1853; James Belger with William T.

Smith, December 13, 1853, RG 92, QMG, Reg. Cont.

30. David H. Vinton with Jones Creech and Armistead Dawson, May 2, 1854; Vinton with Russell and Majors, April 25, 1854; Vinton with Willam S. McKnight, April 28, 1854, ibid. There are two contracts of this date with McKnight.

31. Russell, Majors, and Waddell signed their partnership agreement on December 28, 1854. The contract noted, "trading under the firm and styles of Majors and Russell."

32. Sibley with Majors, Russell, and Waddell, March 27, 1855; Belger with George H. Giddings and J. K. Jefferson, May 29, 1855, RG 92, QMG, Reg. Cont.

33. Stewart Van Vliet with Irwin, Jackman and Co., March 30, 1861, ibid.

34. Jesup with Russell, Majors, and Waddell, January 16, 1858, ibid.

35. E. S. Sibley, Estimate of Funds required, August 12, 1852, RG 393, USACC, DNM, QM L and Rpts R. The estimate is for the quartermaster's department.

36. The higher sum was paid to James Russell, who had been employed as wagon master since 1852. The figures are compiled from Reports of Persons and Articles employed and hired at the various posts, ibid.

37. The expressmen were employed at Fort Buchanan to carry dispatches between that post and Fort Thorn.

38. Wheelwrights and blacksmiths were paid $55 at Fort Fillmore. A millwright was paid $85 while setting up and supervising a sawmill for the construction of Fort Garland.

39. One herder at Albuquerque received $25.

40. Beginning in 1855 the army maintained ferries on the Rio Grande at Albuquerque and at the San Diego crossing. The higher wage was paid at the latter.

41. In December 1859 Lucero was appointed sheriff of Bernalillo County. RG 59, State Department, Ter. Papers, NM. He continued to hold his position with the army as well.

42. S. O. No. 43, March 28, 1857; S. O. No. 103, August 23, 1860, RG 393, USACC, Special Orders, DNM.

43. Francis A. Cunningham to Adam D. Steuart, September 27, 1851, RG 92, QMG, Cons. Corres. File.

44. Easton to Jesup, August 2, 1854, ibid.

45. Garland to Chandler, November 7, 1854; Garland to Backus, November 7, 1853, RG 393, USACC, DNM, LS.

46. The contracts are in RG 92, QMG, Reg. Cont. At about the same time corn sold on the open market in Taos for $2 and in Santa Fe for $3.

47. Sumner to Backus, January 30, 1852, RG 393, USACC, DNM, LS.

48. Chandler to AAG, HQ Army, April 15, 1853, ibid., Unentered LR. Major Kendrick considered the cost of corn at Zuñi excessive at this time, even referring to the "annoying rapacity" of the Zuñis. Henry L. Kendrick to Cooper, May 15, 1853, ibid.

49. Kendrick to David Meriwether, February 6, 1854, ibid., LR; Backus to Henry B. Schroeder, March 24, 1852, ibid., Unentered LR; Kendrick to Meriwether, June 12, 1856, RG 75, OIA, LR, NMS.

50. George L. Willard to Timothy McGowan, RG 92, QMG, Reg. Cont.; Willard with Charles W. Beach, RG 192, CGS, Reg. Cont.

51. Horace Brooks to [Nichols], October 8, 1853, RG 393, USACC, DNM, LR.

52. Easton, Circular, February 4, 1856, RG 92, QMG, Cons. Corres. File. In making feed contracts the army distinguished between corn, hay, and fodder.

53. Dr. Connelly, a medical doctor by training, was born in Virginia in 1880. He had long engaged in the Santa Fe trade and before the Mexican War had made his home in Chihuahua. He owned property in various parts of New Mexico and engaged in a variety of business enterprises. In 1861 President Lincoln appointed him territorial governor of New Mexico, an office he held until 1866. He died in Santa Fe in August 1866, less than a month after leaving office. Calvin Horn, *New Mexico's Troubled Years* (Albuquerque, 1963), pp. 93–110.

54. He was Vicente Romero of La Cueva, Mora County. At least two of the others had Spanish American mothers.

55. Samuel Magoffin was the son of James W. Magoffin. He was born in 1835, probably in Chihuahua.

56. Francisco, a native of Virginia who had been active in the Santa Fe trade, served as sutler at various posts and had been agent for the army at Abiquiu.

57. Richard S. Ewell to Easton, November 10, 1853, RG 393, USACC, DNM, QM L and Rpts R. Machebeuf came to New Mexico with Jean B.

Lamy, the first bishop and later archbishop of New Mexico. A *costal* was a sack that, theoretically, held half a fanega. It was a common measure for cob corn.

58. Rafael Armijo Business Papers, NMSA.

59. Abstract of Purchases, RG 393, USACC, DNM, QM L and Rpts R. The Moore and Rees contracts are in RG 92, QMG, Reg. Cont.

60. Abstract of Purchases . . . in the Quarter ending 31st of December, 1858, RG 393, USACC, DNM, QM L and Rpts R. It was noted in 1858 that only recently had barley been raised in New Mexico. Baldwin Möllhausen, *Diary of a Journey from the Mississippi to the Coast of the Pacific with a United States Government Expedition*, 2 vols. (London, 1858), II, p. 16.

61. In the fall of 1858 the commissary at Fort Stanton purchased from individuals 100 tons of fodder at $20.00 per ton and 1,400 fanegas of corn at prices of $2.75 and $3.00, this to feed the post's beef cattle herd.

62. Monthly reports of forage issued at Fort Massachusetts, March, 1858, RG 393, USACC, DNM, QM L and Rpts R.

63. Abstract of Purchases . . . during the quarter ending March 31st 1858, ibid.

64. The figures are from Abstracts of Purchases at various posts, RG 393, USACC, DNM, QM L and Rpts R. The figures here are approximate. In the abstracts they are given in pounds.

65. Jerga was a coarse, woolen cloth woven by the Spanish Americans and used for everything from clothing to carpeting.

66. John B. Grayson with James A. Donavant, February 25, 1857; Horace Randal with Theodore W. Taliaferro, November 20, 1859, RG 192, CGS, Reg. Cont. Donavant, a Kentuckian by birth and a millwright by profession, later owned a gristmill on the Santa Fe River, but there is no record that he owned one at this time. Taliaferro's activities are discussed in chap. 8.

67. In 1856 Hart stated that he could manufacture 800,000 pounds of flour at his El Paso mill and 1 million pounds at his Santa Cruz mill in a one-year period. Simeon Hart to Grayson, February 20, 1856, RG 92, QMG, Cons. Corres. File. Actually, a much greater part of Hart's production was at the Santa Cruz mill, particularly after a flood swept away his mill dam at El Paso later in 1856.

68. The figures are from contracts recorded in RG 192, CGS, Reg. Cont. Hart did not have a contract for the Department of New Mexico in 1859, but he did hold one that year to deliver 400,000 pounds of flour at Fort Davis, Texas, for 11 cents per pound.

69. *Santa Fe Weekly Gazette*, October 2, 1858. According to the 1860 census, Hersch's two mills represented an investment of $20,000 and were capable of producing annually 650,000 pounds of flour, 270,000 pounds of shorts, and 270,000 pounds of bran, with a total value of $61,500.

70. Johnston to AAG, HQ Army, August 18, 1859; John B. Floyd endorsement, January 11, 1860. RG 94, OAG, LR.

71. The contracts are in RG 192, CGS, Reg. Cont. No herding contract was registered for 1853. Michael Glea-

son, a native of Ireland, resided at Algodones, where he maintained a tavern. He died in February 1858. *Santa Fe Weekly Gazette*, February 27, 1858.

72. Ibid., August 8, 1857.

73. Taylor, born in Ohio, resided on Taylor's Ranch, part of the Antonio Ortiz Grant, near Anton Chico.

74. Skillman, originally from Kentucky, came to the Southwest at an early but undetermined date. He held the first mail contract for the San Antonio-Santa Fe mail route. He was killed in April 1864, while acting as a scout for the Confederates in Texas. Roscoe P. and Margaret B. Conkling, *The Butterfield Overland Mail, 1857–1869*, 3 vols. (Glendale, Calif., 1947), I, pp. 90–94, 375n.

75. John W. Davidson to [Nichols], May 1, 1854, RG 393, USACC, DNM, LR. Peter Joseph, a native of Mont-Saint-Michel, France, established a store in Taos in 1840 and engaged in merchandising and ranching.

76. Circular, June 1, 1859, RG 192, CGS.

77. Grayson to John D. Wilkins, April 6, 1859 and April 7, 1859; Milton Cogswell to Grayson, April 6, 1859, RG 393, USACC, DNM, LR; S. O. No. 54, April 9,1859, ibid., Special Orders. Dr. Boice, a medical doctor, was a native of Canada. He owned a store in Las Vegas. Connelly and Boice dissolved their partnership in April 1861. John Dold and his brother Andres were natives of Württemberg who settled in Las Vegas in the early 1850s. They became prosperous merchants, each having a store on the plaza, and engaged in banking, freighting, flour milling, and other ventures. Eighth

Census, 1860, NMSA; Milton W. Callon, *Las Vegas, New Mexico, the Town That Wouldn't Gamble* (Las Vegas, N.M., 1962), pp. 27, 38.

78. James Cumming has not been identified.

79. Bids were asked on 1,050 bushels of "superfine quality" salt to be delivered at four posts. *Santa Fe Weekly Gazette*, January 28, 1854. Only the contract for delivery at Albuquerque has been located. All contracts are in RG 192, CGS, Reg. Cont.

80. The Zeckendorf brothers, Aaron, Louis, and William, came from their native Hanover to New Mexico in the 1850s. They operated stores in Santa Fe and Albuquerque. Floyd S. Fierman, "Peddlers and Merchants—the Jewish Businessman on the Southwest Frontier: 1850–1880," *Password*, VIII (Summer 1963): 54n.

81. *Santa Fe Weekly Gazette*, February 26, 1859.

82. Grayson to George Gibson, March 27, 1856, RG 92, QMG, Cons. Corres. File.

83. Henry M. Lazelle with Hart, September 16, 1856, RG 192, CGS, Reg. Cont.; O. No. 10, November 5, 1858, RG 393, USACC, Orders, DNM.

84. Franz Huning was born in Hamburg in 1827 and came to New Mexico in 1849. For a time he worked in San Miguel, then clerked for Joseph Hersch in Santa Fe before opening his own store in Albuquerque in 1857. Huning, *Trader on the Santa Fe Trail* (Albuquerque, 1973), p. 64.

85. The contracts are in RG 192, CGS, Reg. Cont.

86. John P. Hatch with Tomás C.

de Baca and P. and F. Delgado, July 21, 1861, ibid.

87. Manuel A. Otero of Valencia was a landowner, merchant, and one of the wealthiest men in New Mexico. He served as New Mexico's territorial delegate in the 34th, 35th, and 36th United States Congresses.

88. The contracts are in RG 192, CGS, Reg. Cont. The *Santa Fe Weekly Gazette*, December 6, 1856, stated that 10,000 gallons of vinegar, "produced from grapes of the Territory," were under contract by the army, but no vinegar contracts issued in 1856 have been located.

89. Clever, a native of Prussia, came across the plains to New Mexico with Franz Huning in 1849. He was a merchant and later held a variety of political offices. William J. Parish, "The German Jew and the Commercial Revolution in Territorial New Mexico, 1850–1900," *NMHR*, XXXV (January 1960): 11.

90. Kessler has not been positively identified. A Herman Kessler, born in Germany, was a private in the Third Infantry, serving in New Mexico in the early years of the decade, and in 1858 H. Kessler took out a license to sell wine. Santa Fe County Licenses, 1851–1878, NMSA.

91. Peter Deus was a native of Prussia and John May a native of Bavaria. They arrived in Santa Fe prior to 1850.

92. Thomas H. Logan has not been identified.

93. Davenport, a Missouri attorney, was appointed by President Pierce. He held office from 1853 to 1858.

94. Grayson to Nichols, March 5, 1857, and William J. Sloan endorse-

ment, RG 393, USACC, DNM, LR.
Troops in the field sometimes ate wild
plants as an antiscorbutic. In 1857 an
officer wrote that his dinner consisted
of "bacon, bread, with sometimes, when
I can get it, a dish of antiscorbutics,
in the shape of a green plant which
goes by the refreshing name of 'Lamb's
quarter.'" Henry M. Lazelle, "Puritan
and Apache, A Diary," ed. Frank D.
Reeve, *NMHR*, XXIV (January 1949):
35.

95. Grayson with Charles E. Whilden, November 3, 1857, RG 192, CGS,
Reg. Cont. The contract stipulated that
the rate of transportation would be that
in effect for the months when Whilden
made deliveries. Whilden, a native of
South Carolina, came from Fort Leavenworth to New Mexico in 1855 to
work as clerk in the commissary
department.

96. *Santa Fe Weekly Gazette*, February 26, 1895.

97. Solomon Houck to Manuel Alvarez, January 25, 1854, Alvarez Papers, NMSA.

98. Grayson to Jesup, September 28,
1855, RG 92, QMG, Cons. Corres.
File.

99. Grayson to Gibson, August 28,
1855, ibid.

100. Extract from John R. Hagner
to Steuart, December 23, 1852, ibid.

101. Garland to Thomas, August 1,
1857, RG 393, USACC, DNM, LS.
A Mexican law of January 31, 1856,
imposed an export tax of 3½ percent
on coined silver. The tax was increased
to 6 percent on February 18, 1857.
Matías Romero, *Memoria de Hacienda
y Crédito Público, Correspondiente al*

Cuadragésimoquinto Año Económico
(Mexico, D. F., 1870), p. 469.

102. Hart to Grayson, February 20,
1856, RG 92, QMG, Cons. Corres.
File.

103. John Pope to Sumner, May 19,
1853, RG 393, USACC, DNM,
Unentered LR.

104. Wylly C. Adams to George
Sykes, September 8, 1853, ibid., LR;
Joseph K. F. Mansfield to Cooper, September 19, 1853, RG 94, OAG, LR.

105. Kendrick to Cooper, May 15,
1853; Chandler to AAG, HQ Army,
April 15, 1853, RG 393, USACC,
DNM, Unentered LR.

106. Jefferson Davis to Eliakim P.
Scammon, November 28, 1854, RG
94, OAG, LR.

107. Garland to Thomas, November 1, 1855; Charges and Specifications preferred against Captain Eliakim
P. Scammon, n.d., ibid.; S. O. No.
25, March 27, 1856, RG 393, USACC,
Special Orders, DNM; *Santa Fe Weekly
Gazette*, April 12, 1856. Scammon
served in the Union Army during the
Civil War as a brigadier general in the
volunteers

108. Rencher, a North Carolinian,
was appointed by President Buchanan
to succeed Meriwether. He had long
been prominent in the politics of his
native state and had served as United
States minister to Portugal. He held
the territorial governorship from November 12, 1857, to September 4, 1861.
Horn, *New Mexico's Troubled Years*, pp.
73–79.

109. *Santa Fe Weekly Gazette*, March
27, 1858 and December 4, 1858; Abraham Rencher, *The Annual Message of
Governor Rencher Delivered before the*

Legislative Assembly, Territory of New Mexico, December 8th 1858 (Santa Fe, 1858); W. Turrentine Jackson, *Wagon Roads West* (New Haven, Conn., 1965), pp. 112–17.

110. *Santa Fe Weekly Gazette,* December 11, 1858.

Chapter 6

1. David Meriwether to George W. Manypenny, September 15, 1855, RG 75, OIA, LR, NMS; John Garland to Lorenzo Thomas, September 30, 1855, RG 94, OAG, LR.

2. Eagle Springs is in eastern Hudspeth County, Texas.

3. Garland to Samuel Cooper, October 28, 1853, RG 393, USACC, DNM, LS.

4. William A. Nichols to Daniel T. Chandler, December 11, 1853, RG 94, OAG, LR.

5. Chandler to Nichols, January 24, 1854, and encl., ibid.

6. Garland to Thomas, January 31, 1855, ibid.

7. O. No. 3, March 14, 1855, RG 393, USACC, Orders, DNM; Gouverneur Morris to [Cooper], March 30, 1855, RG 94, OAG, LR; *Santa Fe Weekly Gazette,* March 17, 1855.

8. Dr. Michael Steck, a native of Pennsylvania, was appointed Indian agent in 1852 and arrived in New Mexico at the end of the year. In 1855 he was agent for all the Apaches in New Mexico, except the Jicarilla. He was later Superintendent of Indian Affairs in New Mexico and continued to reside in the territory until his death in 1881.

9. O. No. 8, May 11, 1855, RG 393, USACC, Orders, DNM; Garland to Thomas, May 31, 1855, RG 94, OAG, LR. The post was named for Captain Henry W. Stanton, First Dragoons, killed by Apaches in January 1855. It remained active until 1896.

10. Joseph E. Johnston to AAG, HQ Army, September 21, 1859, RG 94, OAG, LR.

11. Isaac V. D. Reeve to John D. Wilkins, November 17, 1858, RG 393, USACC, DNM, LR. No records have been seen of the purchase of oats in the department.

12. Johnston to AAG, HQ Army, September 21, 1859; Benjamin L. E. Bonneville to Thomas, July 15, 1859, RG 94, OAG, LR.

13. This was modified on February 1, 1860, when Arizona County was created from the western portion of Doña Ana County.

14. See William H. Goetzmann, *Army Exploration in the American West, 1803–1863* (New Haven, Conn., 1959), p. 197.

15. Dixon S. Miles to Nichols, October 12, 1854, RG 393, USACC, DNM, LR.

16. O. No. 34, ibid., Orders; Meriwether discusses the events in his book, *My Life in the Mountains and on the Plains,* ed. Robert A. Griffen (Norman, 1965), pp. 233–38.

17. Raphael P. Thian, *Notes Illustrating the Military Geography of the United States* (Washington, D.C., 1881), pp. 79, 86.

18. Edward E. Dunbar to John E. Wool, March 26, 1855, and Jefferson Davis endorsement, May 19, 1855, RG 94, OAG, LR.

19. William H. Emory to Robert McClelland, May 13, 1855, ibid.

20. Emory to Garland, August 11, 1855, ibid.

21. [Petition] September 10, 1855; Frederick Goerlitz to Garland, September 21, 1855, ibid. Goerlitz, a native of Germany, was a naturalized United States citizen and a merchant in Tucson.

22. Emory to McClelland, May 13, 1855, RG 94, OAG, LR.

23. John M. Pinkston to Garland, September 20, 1855, and endorsement, ibid.

24. Samuel Cooper to Garland, March 23, 1856, RG 393, USACC, DNM, LR.

25. O. No. 7, July 28, 1856, ibid., Orders.

26. Nichols to Enoch Steen, August 31, 1856, ibid., LS.

27. Richard S. Ewell to Isaiah N. Moore, March 2, 1857, ibid., LR.

28. Calabasas was originally a rancho for the support of the nearby Jesuit mission of Guebabi and a *visita* of the mission.

29. Steen to Nichols, November 30, 1856, RG 393, USACC, DNM, LR. There are two pertinent letters of this date. Gándara had acquired the ranch in 1844.

30. Camp Moore was probably named for Major Steen's fellow Kentuckian, Captain Benjamin D. Moore of the First Dragoons, who was killed on December 6, 1846, in the Battle of San Pascual, California.

31. Steen to Nichols, January 31, 1857, RG 393, USACC, DNM, LR.

32. Bonneville was born near Paris, France, in 1796 and came to the United States while he was a child. He graduated from the Military Academy in 1815 and in 1855 became colonel of the Third Infantry, which had been stationed in New Mexico since 1849.

33. Nichols to Steen, December 26, 1856, RG 393, USACC, DNM, LS.

34. Steen to Nichols, March 3, 1857; William T. Carr to Steen, March 4, 1857, RG 94, OAG, LR.

35. Ewell to Moore, March 2, 1857, RG 393, USACC, DNM, LR.

36. Steen to Nichols, March 3, 1857, ibid.

37. Copy of a petition from the citizens of Tucson and vicinity to Garland, n.d., ibid.

38. O. No. 3, February 11, 1857, ibid., Orders; Benjamin Sacks, "The Origins of Fort Buchanan, Myth and Fact," *Arizona and the West*, VII (Autumn 1965): 222–23.

39. William J. Sloan to Wilkins, July 17, 1859, RG 94, OAG, LR; Bonneville to Thomas, July 15, 1859, ibid.

40. Steen to Nichols, August 23, 1857, and Garland endorsement, September 12, 1857; David H. Hastings to Langdon C. Easton, July 30, 1857; Richard S. C. Lord to Easton, April 27, 1858, RG 393, USACC, Fort Buchanan, LS, Box 38. The original intention was to make "7 or 8 hundred thousand" adobes.

41. Steen to Nichols, January 3, 1858, ibid.

42. Reeve to Wilkins, April 21, 1859, ibid., DNM, LR.

43. Johnston to Thomas, October 4, 1859, RG 94, OAG, LR.

44. Richard H. Coolidge, comp., *Statistical Report on the Sickness and Mortality in the United States Army, 1855–*

1860 (Washington, D.C., 1860), pp. 210–11.

45. Sloan to Wilkins, July 17, 1859, RG 94, OAG, LR.

46. Brevoort, who came to New Mexico in 1850, went with the army in 1856 as sutler, first at Camp Moore and then at Fort Buchanan. He acquired property in New Mexico and became a great extoller of the virtues of the Southwest. See, for example, his *New Mexico, Her Natural Resources and Attractions* (Santa Fe, 1874).

47. S. O. No. 135, October 11, 1856; S. O. No. 6, January 16, 1857, RG 393, USACC, Special Orders, DNM.

48. Steen to Nichols, November 30, 1856, ibid., LR. A small quantity of flour was purchased at the post for 6 cents per pound. *Santa Fe Weekly Gazette*, December 20, 1856.

49. David H. Hastings, Estimate for Subsistence stores . . . from March 1st to December 31st 1857, December 31, 1856; Estimate of funds required . . . during the quarter ending the 31st of March 1857, November 30, 1856, RG 94, OAG, LR.

50. Aguilar was Gándara's predecessor as governor of Sonora and had been driven out of office by him.

51. Steen to Nichols, January 1, 1857, RG 393, USACC, DNM, LR.

52. Steen to Nichols, March 3, 1857, ibid.

53. Nichols to Steen, March 25, 1857, RG 94, OAG, LR.

54. John B. Grayson to Nichols, April 14, 1857; Simeon Hart to Bonneville, April 26, 1857, RG 393, USACC, DNM, LR.

55. *Santa Fe Weekly Gazette*, February 14, 1857.

56. Hastings to Easton, January 3, 1857; February 3, 1857; March 22, 1857, RG 393, USACC, Fort Buchanan, LS, Box 38.

57. O. No. 3, April 3, 1858, ibid., Orders, DNM.

58. Ewell to Nichols, October 12, 1858, ibid., LR; Gilbert J. Pedersen, "A Yankee in Arizona: the Misfortunes of William S. Grant, 1860–1861," *Journal of Arizona History*, XVI (Summer 1975): 130. Ewell noted that "with encouragement" bacon could be produced locally. As at Los Lunas, Ewell had a good garden where he raised "all kinds of vegetables except Irish potatoes, and they have never been raised in the territory." James H. Tevis, *Arizona in the '50's* (Albuquerque, 1954), pp. 62–63.

59. Henry M. Lazelle with Hart, May 15, 1858, RG 192, CGS, Reg. Cont.

60. Wilkins to Ewell, November 2, 1858, RG 393, USACC, DNM, LS.

61. Hastings to Easton, March 30, 1858, ibid., Fort Buchanan, LS, Box 38; Report of Persons and Articles employed and hired at Fort Buchanan, 1858, ibid., QM L and Rpts R.

62. Bonneville to Thomas, July 15, 1858, RG 94, OAG, LR.

63. Ewell to Nichols, October 12, 1858, RG 393, USACC, DNM, LR.

64. Abstract of purchases during the quarter ending March 31st 1858, ibid., QM L and Rpts R.

65. Monthly reports of the quartermaster, Fort Buchanan, ibid.

66. S. O. No. 107, October 11, 1857, ibid., Special Orders, DNM. Fort Garland was located at the present town

of Fort Garland, Colorado, about eighteen miles in a direct line east of the closest point on the Rio Grande. Although it was never much involved in suppressing Indian activities, it remained active until November 30, 1883. It is now a state historical monument.

67. Francisco's contract was later revoked over an argument as to whether he was to deliver the adobes or whether the army was to receive them where they were made. The distance involved was 800 yards. Edward R. S. Canby to [James L. Donaldson], August 13, 1860, RG 393, USACC, Fort Garland, LS.

68. Johnston to AAG, HQ Army, August 8, 1859, RG 94, OAG, LR.

69. Pelham, a native of Kentucky and former surveyor general of Arkansas, was the first surveyor general of New Mexico. He was appointed by President Pierce. He arrived in New Mexico in December 1854 and held office until 1860.

70. Garland to Thomas, August 8, 1858, RG 94, OAG, LR. The contract for the mail route was awarded to Thomas F. Bowler of Santa Fe on May 27, 1858. Morris F. Taylor, *First Mail West, Stagecoach Lines on the Santa Fe Trail* (Albuquerque, 1971), pp. 54–55.

71. John W. Davidson to Steen, March 20, 1858, and Steen endorsement, RG 94, OAG, LR.

72. Garland to Thomas, May 1, 1858, ibid.

73. Sloan to Wilkins, July 17, 1859, ibid.

74. James L. Collins to C. E. Mix, December 5, 1858, RG 75, OIA, LR, NMS.

75. O. No. 6, September 15, 1858; O. No. 7, September 15, 1858, RG 393, USACC, Orders, DNM. Garland remained in poor health and died on June 5, 1861.

76. Bonneville to Thomas, July 15, 1859, RG 94, OAG, LR.

77. Collins to J. W. Denver, February 22, 1859, RG 75, OIA, LR, NMS.

78. S. O. ———, June 12, 1859, RG 393, USACC, Special Orders, DNM. The special orders issued by Bonneville during a tour of the southern posts were not numbered.

79. William H. Gordon to Wilkins, July 28, 1859; George E. Cooper to Gordon, July 25, 1859, RG 94, OAG, LR. Lee Myers discusses the location of the camp in "Military Establishments in Southwestern New Mexico: Stepping Stones to Settlement," *NMHR*, XLIII (January 1968): 14–16.

80. George W. Howland to [Wilkins], August 16, 1859, RG 393, USACC, DNM, LR; S. O. No. 117, September 19, 1859, ibid., Special Orders.

81. Bonneville to Thomas, July 15, 1859, RG 94, OAG, LR.

82. Sloan to Wilkins, July 17, 1859, ibid. Sloan's report was published in Coolidge, comp., *Statistical Report, 1855–1860*, pp. 218–20.

83. Collins to A. B. Greenwood, July 10, 1859, RG 75, OIA, LR, NMS; Victor Westphall, *The Public Domain in New Mexico, 1854–1891* (Albuquerque, 1965), pp. 8–9; Bonneville to Thomas, July 10, 1859, RG 94, OAG, LR.

84. *Santa Fe Weekly Gazette*, November 20, 1858; Taylor, *First Mail West*,

pp. 56–57. The mail began its unsuccessful operation in October 1858.

85. Collins to Bonneville, July 11, 1859, RG 75, OIA, LR, NMS.

86. S. O. No. 55, April 11, 1859, RG 393, USACC, Special Orders, DNM; [Bonneville] to [Thomas], April 23, 1859, ibid., Unentered LR; Stewart Van Vliet to Thomas S. Jesup, September 16, 1859, RG 92, QMG, Cons. Corres. File.

87. Henry L. Scott to Johnston, May 25, 1859, RG 393, USACC, DNM, Unentered LR.

88. Johnston to AAG, HQ Army, July 11, 1859, RG 94, OAG, LR.

89. Hatch's Ranch, the property of Alexander Hatch, a native of New York, was located on the Antonio Ortiz Grant, a short distance above the junction of the Pecos and Gallinas rivers. Troops were often stationed on the ranch, sometimes for extended periods. San Miguel County Deed Book No. 1, pp. 103–106, Office of the San Miguel County Clerk, Las Vegas, N.M.

90. Bonneville to Thomas, August 6, 1859, RG 94, OAG, LR; Collins to Alfred B. Greenwood, August 4, 1859, RG 75, OIA, LR, NMS.

91. Johnston to AAG, HQ Army, July 11, 1859, RG 94, OAG, LR. The inspection reports are in ibid. Johnston did not inspect the temporary posts.

Chapter 7

1. O. No. 4, October 25, 1859, RG 393, USACC, Orders, DNM. Fauntleroy, a Virginian, did not attend the Military Academy. He was appointed major, Second Dragoons, when the regiment was organized in 1836, and became lieutenant colonel in 1846. He was promoted to colonel, First Dragoons, in 1850.

2. Thomas T. Fauntleroy to Samuel Cooper, November 30, 1853; Irvin McDowell to Fauntleroy, January 4, 1854, RG 94, OAG, LR.

3. Fauntleroy to Lorenzo Thomas, November 8, 1859, and enclosure, ibid.

4. Beale was a native of the District of Columbia and a graduate of the United States Naval Academy. Beale's expeditions are discussed in W. Turrentine Jackson, *Wagon Roads West* (New Haven, Conn., 1965), pp. 245–56.

5. See Frank McNitt, *The Navajo Wars* (Albuquerque, 1972), p. 361.

6. William J. Sloan to John D. Wilkins, December 12, 1859, RG 94, OAG, LR.

7. Fauntleroy to Cooper, December 6, 1859, ibid.

8. Winfield Townley Scott endorsement on *supra*, January 7, 1860.

9. See Norman F. Furniss, *The Mormon Conflict, 1850–1859* (New Haven, Conn., 1966), pp. 205, 229.

10. The post was first named in honor of Governor Henry A. Wise of Virginia. When Virginia seceded from the Union it was designated Fort Lyon for Brigadier General Nathaniel Lyon, killed in the Battle of Wilson's Creek, Missouri.

11. Sangre de Cristo Pass is between the headwaters of Gunnison Creek, an affluent of the Huerfano River, and the headwaters of Sangre de Cristo Creek.

12. G. O. No. 6, March 12, 1860,

RG 94, OAG, General Orders, HQ Army.

13. Charles F. Smith to AAG, HQ Army, April 13, 1860; Edward R. S. Canby to AAG, HQ Army, June 24, 1860, ibid.; William J. L. Nicodemus to Donald C. Stith, June 24, 1860, ibid., LR.

14. Stith to Dabney H. Maury, September 1, 1860, RG 393, USACC, DNM, Unentered LR.

15. G. O. No. 6, March 12, 1860, RG 94, General Orders, HQ Army.

16. S. O. No. 52, April 29, 1860, RG 393, USACC, Special Orders, DNM; Benjamin L. E. Bonneville to Cooper, July 29, 1860, RG 94, OAG, LR; William H. Wood with Fernando Lucero, and Wood with Ronaldo Sesenero, both June 5, 1860, RG 92, QMG, Reg. Cont.

17. Stewart Van Vliet with Russell, Waddell, and Majors, April 11, 1860, RG 92, QMG, Reg. Cont. (There are two contracts of this date.) Russell, Majors, and Waddell, faced with bankruptcy, were unable to fulfill the contracts and in 1861 were replaced by Irwin, Jackman, and Co. and a contract more favorable to the army. March 30, 1861, ibid. See also Raymond W. and Mary Lund Settle, *War Drums and Wagon Wheels, the Story of Russell, Majors and Waddell* (Lincoln, Nebr., 1966), pp. 127–30.

18. Fauntleroy to Thomas, December 1, 1860, RG 393, USACC, DNM, LS.

19. Thomas K. Jackson with Joseph Magoffin, October 24, 1860, RG 92, QMG, Reg. Cont. Joseph Magoffin, born in Chihuahua in 1847, was the son of James W. Magoffin. The contract price for corn delivered at Fort Bliss in 1859 had been $3.15 per fanega.

20. James L. Donaldson to Fauntleroy, November 13, 1860, RG 94, OAG, LR.

21. James L. Collins to Alfred B. Greenwood, October 20, 1860; November 26, 1860; January 27, 1861, RG 75, OIA, LR, NMS.

22. The quartermaster's contracts are in RG 92, QMG, Reg. Cont., and the commissary contracts in RG 192, CGS, Reg. Cont. The lateness of the season was probably a factor in the high price in the García contract.

23. *Santa Fe Weekly Gazette*, October 20, 1860.

24. The flour contracts are in RG 192, CGS, Reg. Cont.

25. The contracts are in ibid.

26. Canby to [Donaldson], August 27, 1860, RG 393, USACC, Fort Garland, LR.

27. Canby to [John B. Grayson], August 5, 1860; August 16, 1860, ibid.

28. S. O. No. 157, November 17, 1860, ibid., Special Orders, DNM.

29. Canby to [Donaldson], August 21, 1860; C. Grover to [Donaldson], November 3, 1860, ibid., Fort Garland, LS.

30. S. O. No. 42 and S. O. No. 43, both April 10, 1860, ibid., Special Orders, DNM.

31. Fauntleroy to Thomas, June 16, 1860, and John B. Floyd endorsement, July 21, 1860, RG 94, OAG, LR.

32. S. O. No. 95, August 10, 1860; S. O. No. 98, August 17, 1860, RG 393, USACC, Special Orders, DNM.

33. Collins to Greenwood, April 8, 1860, RG 75, OIA, LR, NMS.

34. [Citizens of Doña Ana County] to Floyd, n.d., RG 94, OAG, LR.

35. John T. Sprague to Floyd, April 27, 1860, ibid.

36. Darlis A. Miller, "Carleton's California Column: A Chapter in New Mexico's Mining History," *NMHR*, LIII (January 1978): 23, 36n 60.

37. [Citizens of Socorro County] to Floyd, n.d., RG 94, OAG, LR.

38. Petition to James Buchanan, encl. in Henry Winslow to Manuel A. Otero, April 25, 1860, ibid.

39. Charles D. Poston to Floyd, n.d., ibid. Poston, a Kentuckian, was a director of the Sonora Exploring and Mining Company; he is sometimes referred to as the "father of Arizona."

40. Edward A. Cross to Floyd, April 20, 1860, ibid. The Arivaca Ranch (La Arivac) was a grant to Tomás and Ignacio Ortiz, residents of Tubac, with the final title awarded on July 2, 1833. In 1854 it was described as a deserted ranch set in hills rich in minerals. It was purchased by the mining company in 1856 for $10,000 in gold. It was located in the present Pima County. Will Barnes, *Arizona Place Names* (Tucson, 1960), p. 259.

41. Thomas Duncan to Cooper, May 18, 1860; Gabriel R. Paul to Cooper, September 8, 1860, RG 94, USACC, OAG, LR.

42. Richard S. Ewell to John D. Wilkins, April 15, 1860, RG 393, USACC, DNM, LR.

43. See B. Sacks, *Be It Enacted: the Creation of the Territory of Arizona* (Phoenix, 1964), p. 42.

44. Ewell to Wilkins, April 15, 1860, RG 393, USACC, DNM, LR.

45. ——— to William Pelham, April 4, 1860, RG 393, USACC, DNM, Unentered LR.

46. Ewell to Fauntleroy, October 29, 1860, RG 94, OAG, LR; Fauntleroy to Floyd, October 29, 1860, ibid.

47. Constance Wynn Altshuler, ed., *Latest from Arizona* (Tucson, 1969), p. 217; Statement exhibiting prices paid Grant, and Statement of William S. Grant, February 4, 1862, RG 123, U.S. Court of Claims, General Jurisdiction Case 1883, William S. Grant vs. the United States (1863).

48. Isaac Lynde to AAG, HQ Army, October 9, 1860; Lynde to Cooper, October 18, 1860, and enclosure, RG 94, OAG, LR. See also Lee Myers, "Military Establishments in Southwestern New Mexico: Stepping Stones to Settlement," *NMHR*, XLIII (January 1968): 16–18. The reservation was never officially declared.

49. Fauntleroy to Thomas, August 26, 1860; Lynde to Cooper, December 2, 1860, RG 94, OAG, LR.

50. S. O. No. 17, February 24, 1861, RG 393, USACC, Special Orders, DNM.

51. Dabney H. Maury to Lynde, March 10, 1861, ibid., LS.

52. Mowry, a graduate of the Military Academy, resigned his commission in 1858 to engage in mining promotion and to work for separate status for Arizona.

Chapter 8

1. Arizona Territory did not yet exist but was under discussion. At this time it was thought that it might be formed from all of southern New Mex-

ico. See B. Sacks, *Be It Enacted: the Creation of the Territory of Arizona* (Phoenix, 1964), pp. 24–30.

2. John B. Floyd to Thomas S. Jesup and George Gibson, March 26, 1859, RG 123, U.S. Court of Claims.

3. This was not Floyd's only interference in departmental affairs. When the War Department appointed a sutler for Fort Fillmore without seeking the recommendation of the post's council of administration, as was customary, the sutler found the position untenable and resigned less than two months after his arrival. G. W. Gillespie to Floyd, November 12, 1860, Fort Fillmore, RG 94, OAG, LR; S. O. No. 34, December 3, 1860, ibid.

4. John R. Cooke with Theodore W. Taliaferro, September 12, 1859, RG 92, QMG, Reg. Cont.

5. Taliaferro to Benjamin L. E. Bonneville, September 25, 1859, RG 393, USACC, DNM, LR.

6. John S. Phelps to Floyd, December 14, 1859; Joseph P. Taylor to Floyd, December 16, 1859, RG 92, QMG, Cons. Corres. File. Taliaferro's name frequently appears with one r but he himself used two rs in at least some of his correspondence.

7. Horace Randal with Taliaferro, November 20, 1859, RG 192, CGS, Reg. Cont.

8. William S. Grant to Floyd, March 5, 1860, RG 123, U.S. Court of Claims.

9. Floyd to Jesup and Gibson, March 9, 1860, ibid.

10. Statement of William S. Grant, February 4, 1862, ibid. Presumably the officers to whom he referred were at the posts served by Grant.

11. Randal with Taliaferro and Grant, June 12, 1860, RG 192, CGS, Reg. Cont.; Constance Wynn Altshuler, ed., *Latest from Arizona* (Tucson, 1969), pp. 77–78.

12. Statement of William S. Grant, February 4, 1862, RG 123, U.S. Court of Claims.

13. Randal with Grant, September 9, 1860, ibid.

14. Randal with Grant, September 20, 1860, ibid.

15. Statement exhibiting prices . . . paid Grant . . . during the years 1860 and 1861, ibid.

16. Statement of William S. Grant, ibid.

17. *Daily Alta California* (San Francisco), January 5, 1861.

18. *Los Angeles Star*, February 2, 1861.

19. *San Francisco Herald*, August 16, 1861.

20. Statement of Mark H. Dunnell, attorney for Grant, RG 123, U.S. Court of Claims; Gilbert J. Pedersen, "A Yankee in Arizona: the Misfortunes of William S. Grant, 1860–1861," *Journal of Arizona History*, XVI (Summer 1975): 129–30.

21. *San Francisco Herald*, February 7, 1861.

22. Statement of property destroyed and abandoned, RG 123, U.S. Court of Claims.

23. Pedersen, "A Yankee in Arizona," p. 133.

24. Thomas K. Jackson with Simeon Hart, November 3, 1860, RG 192, CGS, Reg. Cont. Grant's price included a transportation allowance of $4.93^{24}/100 per hundred pounds for delivery at Fort Fillmore.

25. John B. Grayson to Gibson,

January 25, 1861, RG 92, QMG, Cons. Corres. File.

26. W. W. Loring to Lorenzo Thomas, April 7, 1861, RG 393, USACC, DNM, LS; Pedersen, "A Yankee in Arizona," p. 134.

27. J. P. Taylor to Simon Cameron, April 3, 1861, RG 123, U.S. Court of Claims.

28. Taylor to Mark E. Dunnell, August 26, 1863, ibid.

29. *San Francisco Herald*, August 16, 1861.

30. Thomas T. Fauntleroy to Samuel Cooper, May 22, 1860, RG 94, OAG, LR; Dabney H. Maury to William Chapman, April 11, 1861, RG 393, USACC, DNM, LS.

31. Fauntleroy to Cooper, April 29, 1860, RG 393, USAC, Records Relating to Indian Affairs, DNM, Box 39. See also Robert W. Frazer, "Fort Butler: the Fort That Almost Was," *NMHR*, XLIII (October 1968): 253–70.

32. —— to William Pelham, April 4, 1860; —— to Register and Receiver of Land Office [W. A. Davidson], May 1, 1860, RG 393, USACC, DNM, Unentered LR.

33. [Fauntleroy to Cooper], June 10, 1860, ibid.

34. Grayson with Tomás C. de Baca, June 12, 1860; Jackson with Hart, June 28, 1860; Grayson with Stephen Boice and Michele Desmarais, September 22, 1860, RG 192, CGS, Reg. Cont. Desmarais, a native of Canada, maintained a store in Las Vegas.

35. Mesa Rica extends for several miles along the right bank of the Canadian River, which is bordered on the left bank by a series of lower mesas. The site selected was below the point where the river emerges from the canyon between the mesas.

36. Maury to Benjamin S. Roberts, November 11, 1860, RG 393, USACC, DNM, LS; Roberts to Maury, December 8, 1860, ibid., LR.

37. Fauntleroy to Cooper, December 16, 1860, ibid., LS; Victor Westphall, *The Public Domain in New Mexico, 1854–1891* (Albuquerque, 1965), p. 146. The reservation was entirely on the Pablo Montoya Grant, a tract of 655,468.07 acres.

38. S. O. No. 184, December 26, 1860, RG 393, USACC, Special Orders, DNM.

39. Theophilus Hunter Holmes to Thomas, September 10, 1860, RG 94, OAG, LR.

40. Thomas to Cooper, September 12, 1860, ibid.; Thomas to Fauntleroy, September 12, 1860, ibid.; S. O. No. 5, January 25, 1861, RG 393, USACC, Special Orders, DNM; Rapahel P. Thian, *Notes Illustrating the Military Geography of the United States* (Washington, D.C., 1881), p. 79.

41. Joseph E. Johnston to James L. Donaldson, October 2, 1860, RG 393, USACC, QM L and Rpts R; Donaldson to Fauntleroy, November 13, 1860, RG 94, OAG, LR.

42. O. No. 10, December 2, 1860, RG 393, USACC, Orders, DNM.

43. Fauntleroy to Cooper, November 12, 1860, ibid., LS.

44. G. O. No. 7, March 20, 1860, RG 94, OAG, General Orders, HQ Army.

45. S. O. No. 9, February 2, 1861, RG 393, USACC, Special Orders, DNM. Sloan rose to the rank of major in the Confederate army.

46. Loring did not attend the Military Academy. His first military service was as a volunteer, fighting the Seminole Indians in Florida. He entered the regular army as a captain in the Mounted Riflemen, when the regiment was organized in 1846. His advancement was unusually rapid. He became a major in 1847, a lieutenant colonel in 1848, and a colonel in December 1856.

47. O. No. 9, March 22, 1861, RG 393, USACC, Orders, DNM; William A. Keleher, *Turmoil in New Mexico, 1846–1868* (Santa Fe, 1952), p. 138n.

48. William Wing Loring to Thomas, April 7, 1861, RG 393, USACC, DNM, LS; Maury to Commanding Officer, Hatch's Ranch, March 23, 1861; Maury to Thomas Duncan, April 13, 1861, ibid., Fort Union, LS.

49. Edward R. S. Canby to AAG, HQ Army, June 11, 1861, ibid., DNM, LS. Canby, a native of Kentucky and a graduate of the Military Academy, was appointed colonel in the Nineteenth Infantry on May 14, 1861. The commission had not reached him at this time. He retained command of the department until September 18, 1862.

50. S. O. No. 84, June 13, 1861; S. O. No. 89, June 16, 1861, ibid., Special Orders. In August the southern district was expanded to include Albuquerque and the country to the south, and the district placed under the command of Colonel Benjamin S. Roberts. O. No. 27, August 8, 1861, ibid., Orders.

51. Canby to AAG, HQ Army, June 11, 1861, ibid., LS.

52. O. No. 12, June 14, 1861, ibid., Orders. The orders were issued in Loring's name.

53. S. O. No. 85, June 14, 1861, ibid., Special Orders.

54. S. O. No. 89, June 16, 1861, ibid.; Lee Myers, "Military Establishments in Southwestern New Mexico: Stepping Stones to Settlement," *NMHR*, XLIII (January 1968): 18.

55. Because Fort Fillmore was evacuated while they were en route, the troops went to Fort Craig.

56. RG 123, U.S. Court of Claims. The court awarded Grant damages of $41,530. Grant also claimed $84,370 for the goods seized by the rebels in Texas. In 1898 Congress passed an act authorizing the payment of an additional $78,989.38.

57. Statement of William S. Grant, RG 123, U.S. Court of Claims.

58. *Santa Fe Weekly Gazette*, June 15, 1861; O. No. 15, June 27, 1861, RG 393, USACC, Orders, DNM.

59. O. No. 16, June 27, 1861, RG 393, USACC, Orders, DNM. Volunteers also received a clothing allowance of $3.50 per month.

60. Annual returns of officers and men, present and absent, 1861, gave a total of 3,690. 37th Cong., 2d Sess., Sen. Exec. Doc. 1, II, pp. 16–19.

61. *Santa Fe Weekly Gazette*, May 25, 1861.

62. The contracts are in RG 192, CGS, Reg. Cont.

63. Only at Fort Bliss had fuel been purchased regularly under contract. There the wood was mesquite roots, for which the quartermaster paid from $4.25 per cord in 1856 to 14.87\frac{1}{2}$ in 1859.

64. All contracts are in RG 92,

QMG, Reg. Cont., and RG 192, CGS, Reg. Cont. Warfield, born in New Orleans, had from his youth participated in the Rocky Mountain fur trade, for a time in association with Bent and St. Vrain. Nicholas P. Hardeman, "Charles A. Warfield," in *The Mountain Men and the Fur Trade of the Far West*, ed. LeRoy R. Hafen, VII, pp. 353–69.

65. *Santa Fe Weekly Gazette*, May 25, 1861.

66. By 1860 St. Vrain owned three large gristmills. There were at least four large gristmills owned by non-contractors, including Hersch's two mills. See Eighth Census, 1860, NMSA.

67. Canby to Chapman, July 15, 1861, RG 393, USACC, Fort Union, LR; O. No. 22, July 20, 1861, ibid., Orders, DNM.

68. James L. Collins to William F. Dole, September 7, 1861, RG 75, OIA, LR, NMS.

69. Collins to Dole, August 11, 1861, ibid.

70. Canby was replaced in September 1862 by James H. Carleton, Brigadier General, Volunteers, who commanded the department until it was dissolved.

71. Thian, *Military Geography*, pp. 79–80.

Chapter 9

1. See John P. Bloom, "Notes on the Population of New Mexico, 1846–1849," *NMHR*, XXXIV (July 1959): 200.

2. Some of the Pueblos refused to be counted, and no attempt was made to take the census of the Hopi villages.

3. William S. Henry to Lafayette McLaws, February 20, 1850, RG 393, USACC, DNM, LR.

4. The figures include the posts of El Paso and San Elizario, the only posts outside the limits of New Mexico. Some of the officers and men stationed in New Mexico were not enumerated, thus the total for Anglos should probably be a little higher. See Richard R. Green, "Origins of the Foreign-Born Population of New Mexico During the Territorial Period," *NMHR*, XVII (October 1942): 282–83.

5. The following production figures are derived from the Seventh and Eighth United States Census reports, neither of which are fully accurate for New Mexico, and do not include El Paso district.

6. This is the equivalent of 146,164 and 283,721 fanegas.

7. Production of crops for which the army was not a particular market also increased but, according to the census, were of minor value. The value of garden produce, for example, grew from $6,679 to $17,664.

8. The census divides cattle into cows: 10,635 (1850), 34,369 (1860); oxen: 12,257, 25,266; other cattle: 10,085, 29,094.

9. There were some charges that the Indians stole more livestock after the United States occupation than before. See John S. Watts, *Indian Depredations in New Mexico and Arizona* (Tucson, 1964). Watts was a judge of the territorial supreme court, 1851–54, and continued to practice law in Santa Fe until 1875.

10. The value of stock slaughtered in the department rose from $82,125

in 1850 to $347,105 in 1860, presumably including meat animals slaughtered for the use of the commissary.

11. The census gives mill capacity but does not always give actual production. A tenth large mill (at Socorro) was completed in 1860 but had not gone into production. There were also several modern, medium-sized mills and a large number of small, primitive mills.

12. The costs of wheat are derived from the census reports.

13. Horace Randal with William S. Grant, September 20, 1860; Statement exhibiting prices, RG 123, U.S. Court of Claims.

14. *Revised United States Army Regulations, of 1861, with an Appendix Containing the Changes and Laws Affecting Army Regulations and Articles of War to June 25, 1863* (Washington, D.C., 1863), p. 244.

15. The same warning was issued in 1860 when Colonel Fauntleroy proposed the abandonment of Fort Fillmore. John T. Sprague to John B. Floyd, April 27, 1860, RG 94, OAG, LR.

16. Even the presence of troops was not always sufficient. In the spring of 1861, when the miners of the Pinos Altos district precipitated hostilities with the Apaches, the Indians ran off most of the public animals at Fort McLane and forced the abandonment of the district. See Pinckney R. Tully to James L. Collins, June 2, 1861, RG 75, OIA, NMS, LR.

17. The greatest increase was in laborers, from 6,100 to 13,800. According to census the number of farmers declined by almost 2,000 to 5,900. The only other category with as many as a thousand persons was servants.

18. In 1878, when the government contemplated purchasing the Fort Union reserve, Secretary of War George W. McCrary stated that "no compensation has been made by this Department for the use and occupation of said reservations to any party or parties claiming title thereto." By this time it was known that the reserve was entirely on the Mora Grant. George W. McCrary to George E. Spencer, October 21, 1878, in *The Mora Grant of New Mexico* (Washington, D.C., n.d.), p. 23.

19. Edward R. S. Canby to AAG, New York, June 11, 1861, RG 94, OAG, LR.

20. By regulation, the sutler had a lien on up to one-sixth of a soldier's pay. The right was abolished on December 24, 1861. *Revised United States Army Regulations, of 1861*, pp. 528, 531, 546.

21. The contracts are in RG 192, CGS, Reg. Cont. In an eighteen-month period Grant delivered goods valued at $37,488.87 to Fort Fillmore alone. Statement of William S. Grant, RG 123, U.S. Court of Claims.

22. See the *Santa Fe Weekly Gazette*, May 27, 1861; September 7, 1861; and October 12, 1861.

23. In comparison, the territorial treasury collected a total of $9,954.75 and expended $10,007.99 during the same fiscal year. *El Diario de la Cámara de la Asamblea del Nuevo Méjico* [1861] (Santa Fe, 1862), p. 40.

Bibliography

Manuscript Material

The Henry E. Huntington Library, San Marino, California.
    William G. Ritch Collection.
The National Archives of the United States, Washington, D.C.
    RG 29. Records of the Bureau of the Census. Seventh Census, 1850, New Mexico; Eighth Census, 1860, New Mexico.
    RG 59. Records of the Department of State. Territorial Papers, New Mexico.
    RG 75. Records of the Bureau of Indian Affairs. New Mexico Superintendency, Letters Received.
    RG 77. Records of the Office of the Chief of Engineers, Letters Received.
    RG 92. Records of the Office of the Quartermaster General.
    RG 94. Records of the Office of the Adjutant General, Letters Received.
    RG 123. U.S. Court of Claims. General Jurisdiction Cases.
    RG 192. Records of the Office of the Commissary General of Subsistence.
    RG 393. Records of United States Army Continental Commands, 1821–1920. Department of New Mexico.
New Mexico State Records Center and Archives, Santa Fe, New Mexico.
    Alvarez Papers.
    Antonio Ortiz Grant Papers.
    Benjamin M. Read Collection.
    Eighth Census, 1860, New Mexico.
    Justice of the Peace Record Book No. 1, 1856–1868, County Records, Mora County (microfilm).
    Ocaté Grant Papers.
    Rafael Armijo Business Papers.
    Scolly (La Junta) Grant Papers.
    Secretary of the Territory. Old Land Titles.
    Seventh Census, 1850, New Mexico (partial).
    Sheriff and Collector's Record, Collections of Revenues—Licenses, 1847–1867.
    United States District Court, County of Taos, Book A, 1851–1857.
San Miguel County, Office of the County Clerk, Las Vegas, New Mexico.
    Deed Book No. 1.

Santa Fe County Court House, Santa Fe, New Mexico.
   Deed Record Books, Santa Fe County.
State Planning Office, Santa Fe, New Mexico.
   Lecompte. Janet. "Ceran St. Vrain's Stone Mill at Mora." Cultural Prop-
   erties Review Committee.

Government Publications

Abel, Annie Heloise, ed. *The Official Correspondence of James S. Calhoun: While
   Indian Agent at Santa Fe and Superintendent of Indian Affairs in New Mexico.*
   Washington, D.C., 1915.
Coolidge, Richard H., comp. *Statistical Report on the Sickness and Mortality in
   the Army of the United States, 1839–1855.* Washington, D.C., 1856. 34th
   Cong., 1st Sess., Sen. Exec. Doc. 96.
———. *Statistical Report on the Sickness and Mortality in the United States Army,
   1855–1860.* Washington, D.C., 1860. 36th Cong., 1st Sess., Sen. Exec.
   Doc. 52.
El Diario de la Cámara de Representantes de la Asamblea del Nuevo Méjico (1861).
   Santa Fe, 1862.
Haydon, Ferdinand V., *Preliminary Field Report of the United States Geological
   Survey of Colorado and New Mexico.* Washington, D.C., 1869.
Heitman, Francis B. *Historical Register and Dictionary of the United States Army.*
   2 vols. Washington, D.C., 1903.
Rencher, Abraham. *The Annual Message of Governor Rencher Delivered before the
   Legislative Assembly, Territory of New Mexico, December 8th 1858.* Santa Fe,
   1858.
*Reports of Exploration and Surveys to Ascertain the Most Practicable and Economical
   Route for a Railroad from the Mississippi River to the Pacific Ocean, Made under
   the Direction of the Secretary of War in 1853–6.* 12 vols. Washington, D.C.,
   1856–61.
*Revised United States Army Regulations, of 1861, with an Appendix Containing the
   Changes and Laws Affecting Army Regulations and Articles of War to June 25,
   1863.* Washington, D.C., 1863.
Romero, Matías. *Memoria de Hacienda y Crédito Público, Correspondiente al Cuad-
   ragésimoquinto Año Económico.* Mexico, D.F., 1870.
Springer, Frank. [Territorial Statutes and Land Claim Reports,] 2 vols. History
   Library of the Museum of New Mexico, Santa Fe. Collection of government
   documents and some other materials specially bound together for Frank
   Springer. In some cases only parts of documents are included, and titles
   have not always been preserved.
Thian, Raphael P. *Notes Illustrating the Military Geography of the United States.*
   Washington, D.C., 1881.

United States Army. *General Regulations for the Army of the United States.* Washington, D.C., 1847.

———. *Revised Regulations for the Army of the United States.* Philadelphia, 1861.

United States Congress. House of Representatives.

    30th Cong., 1st Sess., Exec. Doc. 41, Reports of explorations.

    32d Cong., 1st Sess., Exec. Doc. 2. Report of the Secretary of War, 1851.

    32d Cong., 2d Sess., Exec. Doc. 1, II. Report of the Secretary of War, 1852.

    35th Cong., 1st Sess., Report 457. Private land claims in the Territory of New Mexico, 1852.

    36th Cong., 1st Sess., Exec. Doc. 14. Private land grants in New Mexico, 1860.

    42d Cong., 1st Sess., Report 320. To confirm certain land claims in New Mexico, 1860.

    42d Cong., 2d Sess., Exec. Doc. 181. Private land grants in New Mexico.

United States Congress. Senate.

    31st Cong., 1st Sess., Exec. Doc. 12. Marcy and Simpson reports, 1850.

    31st Cong., 1st Sess., Exec. Doc. 64. Reports on routes from San Antonio to El Paso, 1850.

    31st Cong., 2d Sess., Exec. Doc. 1, II. Report of the Secretary of War, 1850.

    32d Cong., 1st Sess., Exec. Doc. 1. Report of the Secretary of War, 1851.

    37th Cong., 2d Sess., Exec. Doc. 1, II. Report of the Secretary of War, 1861.

Weightman, Richard H. *Speech of the Hon. Richard H. Weightman of New Mexico, Delivered in the House of Representatives, March 15, 1852.* Washington, D.C., 1852.

White, L. C., Koch, Sumner S., Kelley, William B., and McCarthy, J. F., Jr. *Land Title Study.* Santa Fe, 1971.

Books

Abert, James W. *Abert's New Mexico Report, 1846–'47.* Albuquerque, 1962. First published as 30th Cong., 1st Sess., Sen. Exec. Doc. 23, 1848.

———. *Western America in 1846–1847.* San Francisco, 1866.

Aldrich, Lorenzo D. *A Journal of the Overland Route to California & the Gold Mines.* Los Angeles, 1950. First published in 1851.

Altshuler, Constance Wynn, ed. *Latest from Arizona.* Tucson, 1969.

Barnes, Will. *Arizona Place Names.* Tucson, 1960.

Barry, Louise. *The Beginning of the West.* Topeka, Kans., 1972.

Bartlett, John Russell. *Personal Narrative of Exploration and Incidents in Texas, New Mexico, California, Sonora, and Chihuahua.* 2 vols. New York, 1856.

Bieber, Ralph P., ed. *Marching with the Army of the West.* Glendale, Calif., 1936. Contains the journals of Abraham R. Johnston and Marcellus Ball Edwards and the diary of Philip Gooch Ferguson.

Brevoort, Elias. *New Mexico, Her Natural Resources and Attractions.* Santa Fe, 1874.

Brewerton, George D. *Incidents of Travel in New Mexico.* Ashland, Calif., 1969.

Callon, Milton W. *Las Vegas, New Mexico, the Town That Wouldn't Gamble.* Las Vegas, N.M., 1962.

Carroll, H. Bailey, and J. Villasana Haggard, eds. and trans. *Three New Mexico Chronicles.* Albuquerque, 1942.

Conkling, Roscoe P., and Margaret B. Conkling. *The Butterfield Overland Mail, 1857–1869.* 3 vols. Glendale, Calif., 1947.

Cooke, Philip St. George. *The Conquest of New Mexico and California in 1846–1848.* New York, 1878.

Cullum, George Washington. *Biographical Register of the Officers and Graduates of the U.S. Military Academy, at West Point, N. Y., from Its Establishment, March 16, 1802, to the Army Re-Organization of 1866–67.* 2 vols. New York, 1868.

Davis, William W. H. *El Gringo; or New Mexico and Her People.* New York, 1857.

Eccleston, Robert. *Overland to California on the Southwestern Trail, 1849.* Edited by George P. Hammond and Edward H. Howes. Berkeley and Los Angeles, 1950.

Edwards, Frank S. *A Campaign in New Mexico with Colonel Doniphan.* New York, 1966.

Emory, William H. *Lieutenant Emory Reports.* Edited by Ross Calvin. Albuquerque, 1951. First pubilshed in 1848.

Foreman, Grant. *Marcy & the Gold Seekers.* Norman, 1939.

Frazer, Robert W. *Forts of the West.* Norman, 1965.

———, ed. *Mansfield on the Condition of the Western Forts, 1853–54.* Norman, 1963.

———, ed. *New Mexico in 1850: A Military View.* Norman, 1968.

Furniss, Norman F. *The Mormon Conflict, 1850–1859.* New Haven, Conn., 1966.

Gibson, George R. *Journal of a Soldier under Kearny and Doniphan, 1846–1847.* Edited by Ralph P. Bieber. Glendale, Calif., 1935.

———. *Over the Chihuahua and Santa Fe Trails, 1847–1848.* Edited by Robert W. Frazer. Albuquerque, 1981.

Goetzmann, William H. *Army Exploration in the American West, 1803–1863.* New Haven, Conn., 1959.

Gregg, Josiah. *Commerce of the Prairies.* Edited by Max L. Moorhead. Norman, 1954.

Hafen, LeRoy R., ed. *Ruxton of the Rockies.* Norman, 1850.

Hall, Thomas B. *Medicine on the Santa Fe Trail.* Dayton, Ohio, 1971.

Hamlin, Percy Gatling, ed. *The Making of a Soldier: Letters of General R. S. Ewell.* Richmond, Virginia, 1935.

Hammond, George P. *The Adventures of Alexander Barclay, Mountain Man.* Denver, 1976.

Hammond, John Fox. *A Surgeon's Report on Socorro, New Mexico, 1852.* Santa Fe, 1966.

Horn, Calvin. *New Mexico's Troubled Years.* Albuquerque, 1963.

Hughes, John T. *Doniphan's Expedition.* Chicago, 1962. First published in 1848.

Huning, Franz. *Trader on the Santa Fe Trail.* Albuquerque, 1973.

Jackson, W. Turrentine. *Wagon Roads West.* New Haven, Conn., 1965.

Keleher, William A. *Turmoil in New Mexico, 1846–1868.* Santa Fe, 1952.

Kennerly, William C. *Persimmon Hill, A Narrative of Old St. Louis and the Far West.* Norman, 1949.

La Farge, Oliver. *Santa Fe, the Autobiography of a Southwestern Town.* Norman, 1959.

McNitt, Frank. *The Navajo Wars.* Albuquerque, 1972.

Magoffin, Susan Shelby. *Down the Santa Fe Trail and Into Mexico.* Edited by Stella M. Drumm. New Haven, Conn., 1962.

Meriwether, David. *My Life in the Mountains and on the Plains.* Edited by Robert A. Griffen. Norman, 1965.

Möllhausen, Baldwin. *Diary of a Journey from the Mississippi to the Coast of the Pacific with a United States Government Expedition.* 2 vols. London, 1858.

Moorhead, Max L. *New Mexico's Royal Road: Trade and Travel on the Chihuahua Trail.* Norman, 1958.

The Mora Grant of New Mexico. Washington, D.C., n.d.

Pancoast, Charles Edward. *A Quaker Forty-Niner.* Edited by Anna Paschall Hannum. Philadelphia, 1930.

Robinson, Jacob S. *A Journal of the Santa Fe Expedition under Colonel Doniphan.* Edited by Carl L. Cannon. Princeton, N.J., 1932. First published in 1848.

Sacks, B. *Be It Enacted: the Creation of the Territory of Arizona.* Phoenix, 1964.

Settle, Raymond W., and Mary Lund Settle. *War Drums and Wagon Wheels, the Story of Russell, Majors and Waddell.* Lincoln, Nebr., 1966.

Sonnichsen, C. L. *Pass of the North.* El Paso, 1968.

Stratton, Porter A. *The Territorial Press of New Mexico, 1834–1912.* Albuquerque, 1969.

Sunder, John E., ed. *Matt Field on the Santa Fe Trail.* Norman, 1960.

Taylor, Benjamin F. *Short Ravelings from a Long Yarn, or Camp March Sketches on the Santa Fe Trail.* Santa Ana, Calif., 1936. First published in 1847.

Taylor, Morris F. *First Mail West, Stagecoach Lines on the Santa Fe Trail.* Albuquerque, 1971.

Tevis, James H. *Arizona in the '50's.* Albuquerque, 1954.

Turner, Henry Smith. *The Original Journals of Henry Smith Turner with Stephen*

Watts Kearny to New Mexico and California, 1846. Edited by Dwight L. Clarke. Norman, 1966.

Twitchell, Ralph E. *The Leading Facts of New Mexican History.* 5 vols. Cedar Rapids, Iowa, 1911–17.

———. *The Story of New Mexico's Ancient Capital, Old Santa Fe.* Chicago, 1963.

Udell, John. *Journal Kept During a Trip Across the Plains.* Los Angeles, 1946. First published in 1868.

Walker, Henry Pickering. *The Wagonmasters.* Norman, 1966.

Watts, John S. *Indian Depredations in New Mexico and Arizona.* Tucson, 1964. Originally pubished in 1858.

Webb, James Josiah. *Adventures in the Santa Fé Trade, 1844–1847.* Edited by Ralph P. Bieber. Glendale, Calif., 1931.

Westphall, Victor. *The Public Domain in New Mexico, 1854–1891.* Albuquerque, 1965.

Wislizenus, Adolph. *Memoir of a Tour to Northern Mexico, 1846–1847.* Albuquerque, 1969. Originally published in 1848 as 30th Cong., 1st Sess., Sen. Misc. Doc. 26.

Articles and Pamphlets

Allison, W. H. H. "Santa Fe as It Appeared during the Winter of the Years 1837 and 1838." *Old Santa Fe,* II (October 1914): 170–83. Reminiscences of Colonel Francisco Perea.

———. "Santa Fe in 1846." *Old Santa Fe,* II (April 1915): 392–406. Further Perea reminiscences.

Bieber, Ralph P. "The Papers of James J. Webb, Santa Fé Merchant, 1844–1861." *Washington University Studies,* XI, Humanistic Series, No. 2 (1924): 255–305.

Bloom, John P. "New Mexico Viewed by Anglo Americans, 1846–1849." *New Mexico Historical Review,* XXXIV (July 1959): 165–98.

———. "Notes on the Population of New Mexico, 1846–1849." *New Mexico Historical Review,* XXXIV (July 1959): 200–202.

Bloom, Lansing B., ed. "Bourke on the Southwest." *New Mexico Historical Review,* X (October 1935): 271–322. Part seven of the Bourke journal.

———, ed. "From Lewisburg (Pa.) to California in 1849. (Notes from the Diary of William H. Chamberlin." *New Mexico Historical Review,* XX (January 1945): 14–57; (April 1945): 144–80; (July 1945): 336–57.

Carson, William G. B., ed. "William Carr Lane, Diary." *New Mexico Historical Review,* XXXIX (October 1964): 274–332. Second of two parts.

Chávez, Angélico. "New Names in New Mexico, 1820–1850." *El Palacio,* LXIV (September–October 1957): 291–318.

Fierman, Floyd S. "Peddlers and Merchants—the Jewish Businessman on the Southwest Frontier, 1850–1880." *Password*, VIII (Summer 1963): 43–55.

Frazer, Robert W. "Army Agriculture in New Mexico, 1852–53." *New Mexico Historical Review*, L (October 1975): 313–34.

———. "Fort Butler: the Fort That Almost Was." *New Mexico Historical Review*, XLIII (October 1968): 253–70.

———. "Purveyors of Flour to the Army: Department of New Mexico, 1849–1861." *New Mexico Historical Review*, XLVII (July 1972): 213–38.

Galloway, Tod B., ed. "Private Letters of a Government Official in the Southwest." *Journal of American History*, III (No. 4, 1909): 541–54. Letters of John Greiner.

Goodrich, James W. "Revolt at Mora, 1847." *New Mexico Historical Review*, XLVI (January 1972): 49–60.

Green, Richard R. "Origins of the Foreign-Born Population of New Mexico During the Territorial Period." *New Mexico Historical Review*, XVII (October 1942): 281–87.

Hardeman, Nicholas P. "Charles A. Warfield." In *The Mountain Men and the Fur Trade of the Far West*, edited by LeRoy R. Hafen, VII, 353–69. Glendale, Calif., 1969.

Lazelle, Henry M. "Puritan and Apache: A Diary," edited by Frank D. Reeve. *New Mexico Historical Review*, XXIII (October 1948): 269–301; XXIV (January 1949): 12–53.

Lecompte, Janet. "Charles Town." In *The Mountain Men and the Fur Trade of the Far West*, edited by LeRoy R. Hafen, I, 391–97. Glendale, Calif., 1965.

Lee, John D. "Diary of the Mormon Battalion Mission," edited by Juanita Brooks. *New Mexico Historical Review*, XLII (July 1967): 165–99; (October 1967): 281–332.

McGrorty, William B., ed. "William H. Richardson's Journal of Doniphan's Expedition." *Missouri Historical Review*, XXII (January 1928): 193–236.

McLarty, Vivian K., ed. "Letters of William H. H. Gist, a Volunteer from Weston, Missouri, in the War with Mexico." *Missouri Historical Review*, XLVIII (April 1954): 237–48.

Martin, Mabelle Eppard, ed. "From Texas to California in 1849." *Southwestern Historical Quarterly*, XXIX (October 1925): 128–42. Part two of three parts.

Miller, Darlis A. "Carleton's California Column: A Chapter in New Mexico's Mining History." *New Mexico Historical Review*, LIII (January 1978): 5–38.

Moore, John Hammond, ed. "Letters from a Santa Fe Army Clerk, 1855–1856." *New Mexico Historical Review*, XL (April 1965): 141–64. Charles H. Whilden letters.

Myers, Lee. "Military Establishments in Southwestern New Mexico: Stepping Stones to Settlement." *New Mexico Historical Review*, XLIII (January 1968): 5–48.

Parish, William J. "The German Jew and the Commercial Revolution in Territorial New Mexico, 1850–1900." *New Mexico Historical Review,* XXXV (January 1960): 1–29. The first of two parts.

Pedersen, Gilbert J. "A Yankee in Arizona: the Misfortunes of William S. Grant, 1860–1861." *Journal of Arizona History,* XVI (Summer 1975): 127–44.

Sacks, Benjamin. "The Origins of Fort Buchanan, Myth and Fact." *Arizona and the West,* VII (Autumn 1965): 207–26.

Strickland, Rex W. "Six Who Came to El Paso, Pioneers of the 1840's." *Southwestern Studies,* I (Fall 1963).

Taylor, Morris F. "Campaigns Against the Jicarilla Apaches, 1854." *New Mexico Historical Review,* XLIV (October 1969): 269–91.

Twitchell, Ralph E. "Historical Sketch of Governor William Carr Lane, Together with Diary of His Journey from St. Louis, Mo., to Santa Fe, N. M., July 31st, to September 9th, 1852." *Historical Society of New Mexico, Papers,* No. 20 (November 1, 1917).

Wyman, Walker D. "Freighting: A Big Business on the Santa Fe Trail." *Kansas Historical Quarterly,* I (November 1931): 17–27.

———. "The Military Phase of Santa Fe Freighting, 1846–1865." *Kansas Historical Quarterly,* I (November 1932): 415–28.

Newspapers

Daily Alta California (San Francisco). January 5, 1861.

Los Angeles Star. February 2, 1861.

Missouri Republican (St. Louis). 1849–50.

New Mexican (Santa Fe). November 28, 1849; December 8, 1849.

San Francisco Herald. February 7, 1861; August 16, 1861.

Santa Fe New Mexican. Scattered issues.

Santa Fe Republican. 1847–49.

Santa Fe Weekly Gazette. 1851–61.

Maps

Reconnaisance of Santa Fe and Its Environs made by order of Brig. Genl. Kearny by Lt. W. H. Emory, Corps Topl. Engrs. & Lt. J. F. Gilmer, Corps of Engineers. Aug. 19h 1846. Manuscript, History Library, Museum of New Mexico, Santa Fe.

Territory and Military Department of New Mexico Compiled in the Bureau of Topl. Engrs. of the War Dept. chiefly for military purposes under the authority of Hon. J. B. Floyd, Sec. of War, 1859. Manuscript, History Library, Museum of New Mexico, Santa Fe.

Index

Abell, John N., 21, 198n
Abiquiu, New Mexico, 16, 114, 153
Abiquiu, Post of: facilities rented for, 55;
 mentioned, 5, 40, 50, 58, 62
Ácoma Pueblo, 48
Adobes: as building material, 39;
 purchased from individuals, 91, 128;
 contracts for, 140, 162, 224n;
 mentioned, 222n
Agents: employed by army, 43, 48, 49,
 83, 84; duties of, 56
Agriculture: vegetable production, 29,
 231n; civilian farmers hired for, 62;
 attracted by posts, 126, 139, 161, 165,
 182, 186; army impact on, 186;
 production of, 186; decline in number
 of farmers, 232n
Aguilar, José de, 137, 223n
Albuquerque, New Mexico: facilities
 occupied in, 16, 29; general depot
 transferred to, 89; general depot
 removed from, 182; mentioned, 16,
 29, 33, 43, 69 passim, 99, 102, 103,
 107, 113, 114, 118, 141, 145,146,
 149, 157, 159, 160, 171, 172, 178,
 181, 190
Albuquerque, Post of: facilities rented
 for, 54–55; reestablished, 68;
 agriculture at, 68, 72; expense of
 maintenance, 94; public objection to
 abandonment of, 159; mentioned, 40,
 50, 62, 90, 148, 151, 176, 177, 204n
Alexander, Edmund B., 95
Algodones, New Mexico, 56, 83, 218n
Alvarez, Manuel, 11, 70, 196, 210n
Amos, W. W., 21, 198n
Anglo Americans: increase in number of,
 19; attitude of, 24; resident in
 department, 185–86; mentioned, 17,
 22, 27, 55, 188

Antiscorbutics: issued to troops, 4, 5, 38,
 54; wild plants as, 220n
Anton Chico, New Mexico, 76, 119,
 153, 171
Apache Indians, 65, 76, 91, 111, 120,
 121,127, 128, 140, 142, 150, 158,
 163, 179, 182, 185, 205n, 221n, 232n
Apache Springs: Fort McLane established
 at, 162
Aravaipa, Fort. See Fort Breckinridge
Ardinger, William O, 199n
Arivaca Ranch, 159, 161, 227n
Arizona County: created, 221n
Arizona Mining and Trading Company,
 120–21
Arizona Territory: created, 183; plans for,
 227–28n
Armendáriz, Josefa Ortiz de, 92
Armendáriz, Pedro Ascue de, 92, 209n
Armijo, Manuel, 16, 29, 103, 196n,
 210n
Armijo, Rafael: acquires corn by lien,
 103
Army of the West: composition of, 2;
 shortage of supplies for, 5; mentioned,
 1, 10, 14
Arroba: described, 206n
Arroyo Hondo, New Mexico, 78

Baca, Domingo: grass and fodder contract
 with, 50
Backus, Electus, 64, 70, 71, 100
Bacon: wastage during shipment, 4–5;
 mentioned, 8, 35, 51, 112, 138, 156,
 223n
Barceló, Gertrudis (La Tules), 24, 55,
 199n
Barclay, Alexander: erects trading post,
 63; sues government, 63, 88–89; leases
 Fort Union reserve to army, 63, 89